**A Resource Guide
for Human Service
Professionals**

WORKING WITH PREGNANT AND PARENTING TEENAGE CLIENTS

**Neil Cervera and
Lynn Videka-Sherman,
Editors**

Thomas J. Kinney,
Series Editor

Robert Richardson,
Managing Editor

Family Service America
11700 West Lake Park Drive
Milwaukee, WI 53224

and

Rockefeller College Press
University at Albany, State University of New York
135 Western Avenue
Albany, NY 12222

This document was produced under a contractual agreement between the New York State Department of Social Services and the Social Welfare Continuing Education Program of the Professional Development Program in conjunction with the School of Social Welfare, University at Albany, State University of New York, through the Research Foundation of State University of New York.

. . . . .

Nelson A. Rockefeller College of Public Affairs and Policy

University at Albany

State University of New York

. . . . .

Professional Development Program
Social Welfare Continuing Education Program

Thomas J. Kinney,
Director

Eugene Monaco,
Deputy Director

. . . . .

Services/Management/AIDS Training Unit

Alan M. Parsons,
Associate Director for
Continuing Professional Education

. . . . .

Publications and Media Resources Unit

Sally Berdan,
Unit Director

ISBN 0-87304-248-4

Acknowledgments

. . . . .

We would like to thank Commissioner Cesar Perales of the New York State Department of Social Services, Robert Donahue of the New York State Department of Social Services, and Thomas Kinney, Eugene Monaco, and Alan Parsons of the Professional Development Program of Rockefeller College for inviting us to contribute our thoughts to this useful series. Our thanks are also due to all the authors who permitted us to use their articles. We also want to thank Sally Berdan and the staff of the Publications and Media Resources Unit of Rockefeller College's Professional Development Program for their input, patience, and attention to detail, especially Lisa Hoenig, who entered the data, and Sue Gutbezahl, who designed the book. We also wish to thank Diane Tesiny for our graduate students and the students for their tireless work and efforts.

85948

Contents

. . . . .

Foreword

. . . . .

Working with Pregnant and Parenting Teenage Clients, edited by Professors Neil Cervera and Lynn Videka-Sherman, is the seventh in a series of ten resource guides for human service professionals. The resource guide series is an integral part of the collaborative efforts of the School of Social Welfare and the Professional Development Program of Rockefeller College, University at Albany, and the New York State Department of Social Services to produce quality instructional materials to support professional development and in-service training for personnel employed in public social services agencies and allied human service settings.

Each resource guide has a specific focus and addresses identified needs of human service workers, supervisors, and administrators. The resource guides are designed for use in academic coursework as well as as in agency training programs. They are intended for those currently employed in human service settings and those preparing to enter the profession.

Recognition for this series should go to Robert Donahue of the New York State Department of Social Services for the guidance and input of his staff in the instructional development process. They have made consistent efforts to encourage higher education institutions and agency trainers to implement instructional programs to provide competent staff for human service programs. I wish to recognize Richard Nathan for his commitment to continuing professional development and a vision of the university of the future. Overall, I wish to recognize the very special efforts of the editors of the resource guide, whose vision, ability to translate need into academically sound, yet practical materials, and perseverance made this volume possible.

This work integrates theoretical literature and research findings on the interrelationships between the sociocultural issues involved in working with pregnant and parenting teenage clients and effective service or treatment programs. I wish to extend special thanks to Professors Cervera and Videka-Sherman for the format, substance, and overall conceptualization of the guide. This effort represents an extension of their research, practice experience, and commitment to improving the quality and effectiveness of services provided for pregnant and parenting teenage clients. It is our hope that this guide will foster new instructional programs as well as support existing courses.

Thomas J. Kinney
Director, Professional Development Program and
Resource Guide Series Editor

Introduction

. . . . .

Neil Cervera

Nationally, there is significant concern about teenage pregnancy. Each year, approximately one million adolescents become pregnant (Hofferth and Hayes, 1987). About one-half million teens carry their babies to term, and the other half million abort or miscarry the fetuses. Those young women who give birth account for 20% of all births in the United States (U.S. Bureau of Census, 1984). The majority of these births are to unmarried mothers, and nearly half of the unmarried mothers are 18 years old and under (Hofferth and Hayes, 1987). Alarmingly, children 14 years old and younger deliver about 10,000 babies a year; this startlingly high number has remained constant for more than a decade (U.S. Bureau of Census, 1984). The United States leads all other developed western nations in its high rate of adolescent pregnancy and childbirth (Hofferth and Hayes, 1987).

From the mid-fifties onward, the birth rate to single white teenage mothers between 15 and 19 years old increased from 4.15 to 14.9 per thousand, while the rate of births to black nonmarried adolescent mothers in the same age cohort doubled, rising from 46 to about 92 per thousand (U.S. Bureau of Census, 1983). However, a disproportionate number of minority teens give birth. Currently, white adolescents, ages 15 to 19 years old, have the highest increase in unwed births (U.S. Bureau of Census, 1983). Additionally, scholars estimate that between 85% and 90% of all teenagers decide to keep their children rather than place them for adoption (DeAnda and Becerra, 1984).

The increasing number of teens keeping and raising their babies has led to an awareness of teenage pregnancy's psychosocial and medical consequences. In 1985, for example, one estimate of public monies spent on teenage childbearing was 15 billion dollars (Hofferth & Hayes, 1985). Zelnick, Kanter, and Ford's (1981) findings indicate that early pregnancy leads to low birth weight babies and infant mortality. Using data from 1982, Hofferth and Hayes (1987) also found that twice as many infants of 10- to 14-year-old mothers were of low birth weight as compared to infants born to 20- to

1

24-year-olds. Low birth weight babies are at a higher risk for death, mental retardation, and other health problems. In addition, teens choosing to raise their babies are at great risk of not completing their educational or vocational training. As a result, these adolescents become dependent upon public welfare and family assistance (Furstenberg, 1976, 1987). Age alone, however, cannot account for these astonishing medical and social problems.

Over the last twenty-five years, family structure has changed considerably. From the early sixties to the mid-eighties, the number of households headed by females has doubled (U.S. Bureau of the Census, 1984). In contrast, two-parent households declined by about five percent. Ninety percent of all single-parent households are headed by women, and minorities have a higher percentage of single-parent households than whites (U.S. Bureau of Census, 1984). Single-parent households have been linked to poverty. In turn, poverty has been cited as increasing the likelihood of a teen engaging in premarital sex and becoming pregnant (Zelnick et al., 1980). Adolescent girls and boys from single-parent homes are more likely to be sexually active at an earlier age than teenagers from intact families (Zelnick et al., 1980).

Several reasons have been cited for single parenthood and poverty contributing to early teenage sexuality and pregnancy. Being a single parent can be stressful. As a result, there may be a decreased ability to supervise adolescents adequately (Hofferth & Hayes, 1987). Moreover, teens may perceive a lack of affection and attention within single-parent homes; the parental separation can create an emotional atmosphere of rejection and neglect. Studies indicate that adolescent girls who have premarital intercourse tend to have a hostile parent who offers little affection (Hofferth & Hayes, 1987). However, these studies have not articulated the reasons for the hostility. Another cause of early intercourse, pregnancy, and childbearing may be dating parents who provide modeling behavior which leads to tacit approval of a teen's sexual activity (Hofferth & Hayes, 1987). But mothers (and fathers) who are comfortable with their sexuality may be better able to communicate to their offspring about responsible sexual behavior (Hofferth & Hayes, 1987). Teens who have a good rapport with their parents about human sexuality issues are more likely to practice setting limits for themselves or use contraception (Hofferth & Hayes, 1987). But many teens have neither ready access to contraception nor clear understanding of human sexuality.

The social, health, and psychological risks to pregnant or parenting teens and their offspring are clear. Adolescents who are raising children or are pregnant need a number of supportive services, for example, day care, vocational training, education, and adequate health care. These concrete services, in addition to family help, can prevent serious difficulties from arising and reduce the likelihood of a life of poverty.

Perspectives on Teenage Pregnancy

Over the last few decades, adolescent pregnancy has been viewed as an individual personality defect, a family difficulty, and as an adolescent crisis. Each viewpoint has some merits and limitations. The following section is intended to introduce the reader to major questions raised in the literature. A discussion of a case management model follows this review.

A number of investigators have examined teenage pregnancy from an individual personality perspective. This viewpoint dominated the literature in the forties, fifties, and early sixties. Basically, the pregnancy was viewed as a means of expiating guilt and making amends for defects in the young woman's psyche. Young (1954), for example, interpreted the pregnancy as an indication that the teen had poor self esteem, self doubts, and a poor relationship with her mother. Some authors also concluded that the teen had difficulty separating from her mother; the pregnancy allowed the teen to become independent while maintaining dependence on her family (Bonan, 1963; Clothier, 1960). The common theme in these reports is that an unconscious intrapsychic difficulty creates the conditions necessary to become pregnant. Some authors, however, traced the intrapsychic problems to family pathology.

For many teens, being pregnant was not a conscious choice. Interpreting teenage pregnancy from a purely psychological perspective loses an important social dimension. Thirty to forty years ago, a woman's options were limited by two very important considerations: there were no legal means of obtaining abortions, and there were few effective means of contraception. As a result, many young women chose to surrender their offspring. For that time period, females and males had few alternatives to choose from, namely marrying, surrendering the baby, or raising a child alone. Single parenthood was an unlikely solution before the 1960s.

In the 1960s, experts in adolescent pregnancy began to view teenage pregnancy as a symptom of inadequate family functioning. A number of studies (for example, Ulvedad and Feeg, 1983; Coddington, 1979; Malmquist, Kresulz, and Spano, 1966; Smith, 1975, Festinger, 1971) found that pregnant teenagers were exposed to incest, drugs, and domestic violence. Other studies found marital difficulties, mother-daughter or father-daughter hostility, or single-parent homes as the underlying difficulty leading to teenage pregnancy (Abernathy and Abernathy, 1974; Miller, 1974). Often, the families being described were in a crisis state. Being in crisis, however, might explain the disruption in the family and limit the caseworker's accuracy in describing or interpreting pathology and family difficulties.

Another family viewpoint on teenage pregnancy has been that it stabilizes a family in crisis (Furstenberg and Crawford, 1978). The pregnancy is seen as transforming negative relationships in the family to positive ones. The teen's mother has the opportunity to advise and assist her pregnant daughter, and siblings can aid in child rearing. Additionally, the teen's (or baby's) father can serve as a role model for the baby. This particular view of the family shifts the emphasis from what is wrong with the teenager and her family towards a family model which emphasizes competency, support, care, mastery, and adaptation.

For the most part, the out-of-wedlock literature has perceived teenage pregnancy from a pathological perspective. As a counterpoint, there may be

3

a number of other reasons for nonmarried childbirth. For example, teens may lack knowledge about human sexuality or be misinformed about birth control. Among certain ethnic, racial, or socioeconomic groups, being pregnant at an early age may be acceptable (Bucholz and Gol, 1987). Teens, too, are not future-oriented and are less likely to understand early childbearing's consequences and challenges.

Teenage pregnancy can also be perceived as a significant developmental change. Under the best circumstances, pregnancy is a crisis. It leads to a dramatic change in the adolescent's life. It requires significant readjustments. Adolescent pregnancy may be disruptive or create the opportunity for positive changes. In order to assist the adolescent in adapting to the pregnancy and parenthood, the human service professional must assess the teenager's health, educational/vocational, housing, financial, parenting, and psychological needs.

Case Management for Pregnant and Parenting Teens

It is important for the helping person to determine not only the types of support needed, but also who in the environment can be counted on to provide the support. Mother, father, sisters, brothers, baby's father, and significant others may perceive the pregnancy differently; some relatives may be more helpful than others. Relatives, friends, and significant others may offer different types of services. Various helping agents (nurses, social workers, babysitters, physicians, etc.) and supportive services (schools, day care centers, well-baby clinics, parent education information, etc.) may be needed to help the young mother and her child.

Ideally, an admixture of family and community services, along with the teen's coping strategies, may prove to be the best means of providing a comprehensive intervention plan. Being able to sort out the multiple needs and being flexible in the case management process can be beneficial to the mother and baby. A teen may need help in finding adequate housing. Her mother may need to be counseled in order to adjust to the pregnancy, but an aunt may be able to baby-sit while the teen is attending school. Another teen may need to have day care while attending school, but have adequate health and housing services.

Appropriate case management is an effective tool in helping pregnant or parenting teens to cope with their own and their babies' needs. Case management means planning and designing services that are coordinated among all service providers with effective client involvement and input. Accurate psychological, social, health, and educational information is needed to evaluate a client's needs, which must be documented in a case record (DeGennaro, 1987; Brindis et al., 1987). The case management model combines the best concepts from social casework and community organization. A case management system means that the caseworker assumes responsibility for the client's well-being (DeGennaro, 1987). But, the case manager avoids doing for the client that which the client is capable of doing for him/herself. The following functions must be included in a case management approach:

1. A network of formal community service resources must be developed to assist unwed teens. This can be best accomplished through a coordinated community task force led by a council of human services, a mental health board, or a youth bureau. Input from case managers, human services personnel, and teenage consumers must also be obtained. Services should include, for example, day care centers, school districts, health and nursing services, public transportation services, family and child guidance centers, etc. Written agreements and linkages between the agencies, spelling out each agency's function, methods for referral, client entry points, and coordinated case planning must be in place prior to the beginning stages for client service. There is the potential for haphazard service provision if the community does not have an agreed-upon plan.

2. Each agency must have clear goals and objectives in assisting pregnant and parenting teens. The case management agency must help teens obtain services. The agency's intervention model must emphasize strengthening the client's coping and adaptive capacities.

3. Client evaluation must emphasize client strengths rather than client difficulties. Case managers must be able to assess client difficulties, but not allow the problems to overshadow client strengths, inner resources, or family or community resources. One-to-one counseling in order to identify teens' concerns, finding alternative courses of action, and choosing among their options are also important. Group work activities with pregnant and parenting teens can provide modeling, support, education, and interpersonal problem solving. Task-focused groups can center upon parenting skills, La Maze classes, relationship to the baby's father, life skills management for parent teens, etc. Workers providing group and individual counseling must work together to evaluate client progress and future needs. The primary case manager must actively coordinate the intra- and interagency services for effective help (Brindis et al., 1987).

4. Client case planning must be goal-directed with a client contract. Other community resources must be called upon if the agency does not have the appropriate resources. Function #1 above is extremely important; formal linkages between agencies help to complement existing services, lessen the likelihood of overlapping services, and insure that agencies act in the client's best interests rather than competitively with one another.

5. Case management plans must include the aid of natural support systems (family, friends, community centers, etc.). *An evaluation of the possible impediments in the natural support system must be understood by the case manager.* Being able to work with the resistances from significant others or community programs is important to a successful client plan. Family participation in helping the teen has proven to be important in improving the chances of a teen's success at parenting. Family involvement in the case management plan may enhance a teen's ability to cope. Parents may provide useful information to the social worker about the teen's and baby's adjust-

ment. Parents may be another checkpoint in case monitoring (Brindis et al., 1987).

6. Monitoring in the case management plan will help to evaluate client progress towards mutual agency-client objectives. Evaluating services also insures that other agencies are supporting the plan. From this perspective, case managers can modify or add to an existing plan.

7. The client must participate in evaluating the treatment plan through written and oral feedback. In terminating with the client, the case manager must instruct the client about how to obtain services in the future, if necessary.

8. After a reasonable time period (perhaps six to eight weeks), the case manager should follow up on the case to ensure that client progress is continuing. Agencies must have the systems available to allow clients to seek help again, and caseworkers must have the time to motivate clients to re-enter treatment again, if necessary.

Within a case management approach, the case manager must be able to do the following tasks: network and make plans with a variety of agencies, mediate and broker with a number of community and natural support systems, have clinical skills (assessment, interviewing skills, values, follow-up skills, client-centered educational techniques, etc.), in order to identify and resolve concrete problems in a client's everyday life. This model assumes that the case manager has a deep understanding of the ecological needs of a pregnant or parenting youngster and can be flexible in coordinating services on a variety of levels. This model also assumes that the case manager understands that pregnant adolescents have multiple needs. The client must be understood as the agent of change who interacts with a number of people and services.

Changing a client's environment may produce positive changes within the pregnant teen and her social reality. Helping to shape and mold a supportive environment can enhance a client's ability to cope and provide life-building mastery skills. In order to be effective, the worker must frequently contact the client and other service providers. For this reason the client and case manager must select small, accomplishable tasks leading to an achievable goal. The case objectives are best spelled out in concrete behavioral terms. It is easier for clients and workers to evaluate the progress made when contracts are spelled out clearly. If there is a lack of progress, this can then be evaluated and acted upon in a helpful, problem-solving manner.

Articles Included in the Reader

Within the case management framework outlined above, a number of articles have been chosen for this resource guide. Each article was chosen for a specific purpose in order to assist the helping professional in understanding the different facets of teenage pregnancy and intervention. A word or two on each article will help the reader to understand how each article can enhance a case manager's objectives.

The resource guide begins with Rose Bernstein's (1965) classic article on teenage pregnancy. This article addresses the family's and teenager's strengths and worries during a nonmarried pregnancy. Bernstein, too, argues that the case worker must understand the family dynamics. Edith Freeman's (1987) article addresses adolescent developmental issues. Freeman compares normal adolescent development with development of a teen who is pregnant. Lucille Grow's (1979) article cites the changes that occur during a teenage pregnancy; she contrasts the differences between teens who surrender their babies and those who choose to keep their children.

After the above discussions, the resource guide unfolds a case management approach to social services delivery. Maria Roberts-DeGennaro's (1987) article provides a model for social casework. Brindis, Barth, and Loomis (1987) discuss a particular approach to case management with parenting teens. Their article draws attention to the psychological and concrete services needed for parenting teens. Schinke's (1978) article argues that a single-casework approach to helping teenagers leads to inadequate service delivery. Schinke describes a multiple casework intervention process that can lessen the problems teens can encounter.

Because teenage pregnancy may create social and psychological tensions, the resource guide has three articles on child abuse and neglect. This particular area has been greatly debated within the field. Bolton, Laner, and Kane (1980) suggest that adolescent parents, because they are young, are at greater risk of mistreating their children. Kinard and Klerman (1980) also draw upon a similar theme, yet they are cautious in drawing their conclusions. Zuravin's article points out that social support is a mediating variable that can lessen the likelihood of abuse.

The resource guide next focuses its attention on the family and cultural perspective. Furstenberg and Crawford (1978) discuss family support as a powerful factor in reducing teenage pregnancy's harmful effects on adolescents, such as reducing poverty and school drop-out. De Anda and Becerra (1984) contrast Hispanic and white pregnant teens. For whites and English-speaking Mexican mothers, siblings and putative fathers provided the most support. De Anda and Becerra point out that, unfortunately, Mexican Spanish-speaking teens had the least support, since their relatives lived elsewhere. Butts (1981) and Martinez (1981) address black and Hispanic cultural issues that are important factors in the delivery of services to pregnant teenagers.

The teenage father's experience is also reflected in Robinson's (1988) article. The father's perspective (and his family's) suggests that teenage fathers can meet their parenting obligations and have a supportive relationship with the baby and the baby's mother. In a related article, Barret and Robinson (1982) tease out other critical points from the father's perspective, such as the male's viewpoint on the pregnancy and birthing process, male guilt, precocious sexuality, and the conflict between the young man's developmental and parenting needs.

For the last section, school-based programs have been selected for the resource guide. Meares' (1979) article describes an interdisciplinary approach to help teen parents to cope with pregnancy, parenting, and schooling. Her article supports the service delivery concept that a school district can provide educational and social support to the teen. The Doty and King (1985) article provides the reader with a model of interagency collaboration as a way to provide teens with information on human sexuality and family planning. Doty and King also address the collaboration between the City of New York Education Department, a private agency, and a school of social work that provided pupils with human sexuality counseling. Schinke, Gilchrist, and Small (1979) provide a cognitive behavior intervention approach to help youngsters think through their choices about contraception, consequences, and sexual behavior.

Bibliography

Abernathy, V., & Abernathy, G. (1974). Risk for unwanted pregnancy among mentally ill adolescent girls. *American Journal of Orthopsychiatry, 44*, 442–449.

Bernstein, R. (1966). Unmarried parents and their families. *Child Welfare, 45*, 185–193.

Bonan, A.F. (1963). Psychoanalytic implications in treating unmarried mothers with narcissistic character structures. *Social Casework, 44*, 323–329.

Brindis, C., Barth, R.P., & Loomis, A.B. (1987). Continuous counseling: Case management with teenage parents. *Social Casework, 69*, 164–172.

Bucholz, E.S., & Gol, B. (1986). More than playing house: A developmental perspective on the strength in teenage motherhood. *American Journal of Orthopsychiatry, 56*, 347–359.

Clothier, F. (1943). Psychological implications of unmarried parenthood. *American Journal of Orthopsychiatry, 13*, 531– 549.

Coddington, R.D. (1979). Life events associated with adolescent pregnancies. *Journal of Clinical Psychiatry, 40*, 180–185.

Coddington, R.D. (1979). The significance of life events as etiologic factors in the diseases of children: II - A study of a normal population. *Journal of Psychosomatic Research, 40*, 205–213.

De Anda, D., & Becerra, R.M. (1984). Support networks for adolescent mothers. *Social Casework, 65*, 172–181.

De Gennaro-Roberts, M. (1987). Developing case management as a practice model. *Social Casework, 8*, 466–470.

Festinger, T.B. (1971). Unwed mothers and their decisions to keep or surrender children. *Child Welfare, 50*, 253–263.

Furstenberg, F.F. (1976). The social consequences of teenage parenthood. *Family Planning Perspectives, 8*, 148–164.

Furstenberg, F.F. (1976). *Unplanned parenthood.* New York: Free Press.

Furstenberg, F.F., & Crawford, A. (1978). Family support: Helping teenage mothers to cope. *Family Planning Perspectives, 10*, 322–333.

Hofferth, S., & Hayes, C. (1987). *Risking the future* (Vol. II). Washington, D.C.: National Academy Press.

Malmquist, C.P., Kiresak, T., & Spano, R. (1966). Personality characteristics of women with repeated illegitimacies: Descriptive aspects. *American Journal of Orthopsychiatry, 36,* 476–484.

Smith, E.W. (1975). The role of the grandmother in adolescent pregnancy and parenting. *Journal of School Health, 45,* 278–283.

Ulvedad, S.K., & Feeg, V.D. (1983). Profile: Pregnant teens who choose childbirth. *Journal of School Health, 53,* 229–233.

U.S. Bureau of the Census. (1984). *Statistical abstracts of the United States: 1985* (105th Edition). Washington, D.C.

Zelnik, M., & Kantner, J.F. (1980). Sexual activity, contraceptive use, and pregnancy among metropolitan area teenagers. *Family Planning Perspectives, 12,* 230–7.

Are We Still Stereotyping the Unmarried Mother?

. . . . .

Rose Bernstein

The theory of out-of-wedlock pregnancy currently accepted among social workers and members of other helping disciplines is that it is symptomatic and purposeful, an attempt by the personality to ease an unresolved conflict. The extent to which we are committed to this point of view can be seen in some typical excerpts from the literature:

> The caseworker should recognize that pregnancy for the unmarried woman is a symptom of underlying emotional difficulty. [She] is a person who solves her emotional problems through acting out, as exemplified by the pregnancy.[1]

> We recognize unmarried motherhood as a symptom of a more pervading personality difficulty.[2]

> Her illegitimate pregnancy is the result of an attempt to solve certain emotional conflict [sic]...[3]

> [The unmarried mother]...has failed to attain a mature pattern of adaptation to the demands of her social reality.[4]

> ...everything points to the purposeful nature of the act. Although a girl would...not plan consciously...to bear an out-of-wedlock child, she does act in such a way that this becomes the almost inevitable result.[5]

The popular magazine articles have been echoing this point of view. In many situations it may be a useful approach. The results of treatment are often dramatic and gratifying when a girl is able to make use of help in understanding and dealing with some of the underlying problems related to her out-of-wedlock pregnancy. However, in contacts with residents in a maternity home, one becomes concerned about the limited applicability of this theory in a number of cases. One has the impression that in some situations factors other than, or in addition to, underlying emotional pathology have been of greater significance; that emphasis on a single point of view has prevented us from seeing other essential aspects of the experience and, correspondingly, has resulted in a limited treatment offering. This has seemed a good time, therefore, to re-examine the theory and look at other hypotheses which might be applicable in our work with unmarried mothers.

Social Mores

By and large, unmarried motherhood in our society is looked on as the violation of a cultural norm. It should therefore be possible to isolate and identify the norm in question. But this is not easy. For one thing, it is not clear whether the offended norm is the taboo against extramarital relations or against bearing a child out of wedlock. We point to the symptomatic nature of the pregnancy ("there are no accidental conceptions"), but in speaking of prevention we are unable to clarify what we are trying to prevent—unsanctioned sex experience or out-of-wedlock pregnancy.

> Some communities are more or less resigned to widespread sexual experimentation (among teen-agers), yet indignantly aroused and condemning when such experimentations result in out-of-wedlock pregnancy.[6]
>
> If one observes public reactions today, one can hardly escape the conclusion that it is not so much the sexual relationship to which we object as the fact of the baby.[7]

Actually we are not dealing with a single norm, but with a multiplicity of norms which will vary according to cultural and ethnic groups, social or educational sophistication, peer practices, and so forth. These norms will vary not only from one girl to another but also for the same girl, according to the group she is most strongly related to at a given period in her life. The girl whose group or family loyalties at the age of seventeen preclude sexual experience may be safer from out-of-wedlock pregnancy at that time than she is at the age of twenty-two, when her major satisfactions may reside in a group whose climate sanctions or invites such activity.

Our society has been undergoing a change in its sexual behavior. The relaxation of taboos which usually accompanies the upheavals of war has been accelerated in the last two generations by the development of a widely publicized psychology. Permissiveness, self-expression, sexual adjustment, and freedom from inhibition have become in some quarters the marks of the well-adjusted American. The idea of extramarital sex experience is accepted among many college students; among some groups its practice is almost a social *sine qua non*.

However, the professed code of behavior has not kept pace with the changing practices, and the ideal of chastity and marriage continues to be cherished along with other cultural fictions.[8] As long as the violation of the professed value is conducted with a decent regard for secrecy or is not otherwise detected, society is content to accept the implied and overt contradictions resulting from the gap between our professed and operational codes.

Most adults sooner or later arrive at some sort of equilibrium in this cultural tightrope-walking act within which their satisfactions and their consciences manage a reasonably peaceful coexistence. For the young person searching for standards such a balance is not so easily achieved. When those from whom her standards are to be derived—the guardians of our social mores—are operating on more than one set of values, it is not surprising that she herself should question the validity of the professed code. The realism in the seemingly cynical "It's just that I was unlucky enough to get caught" cannot be lightly dismissed.

The uncertainty in our point of view as professional people may well be a reflection of the confusion in the society in which we participate and the role to which the community assigns us as social workers. As members of contemporary society we tolerate the original sexual activity. In deriving our social attitudes from the society that fosters the agencies we represent, we are expected to deplore the activity when confronted with its outcome. Identified with the unmarried pregnant girl who must hide from a censuring community, we reach out to comfort and counsel her. In addition we have our own private views to deal with. To say that a girl is in some respects an inevitable casualty of social change would almost make it appear that we approved of her sexual activity. We are uncertain as to what stand we should take toward extramarital sex experience, or whether we wish to take a stand at all. Yet a noticeable increase in the incidence of illegitimate births compels our attention. We are indeed on the horns of a dilemma.

The extension of unmarried motherhood into our upper and educated classes in sizable numbers further confounds us by rendering our former stereotypes less tenable. Immigration, low mentality, and hypersexuality can no longer be comfortably applied when the phenomenon has invaded our own social class—when the unwed mother must be classified to include the nice girl next door, the college graduate, the physician's or pastor's daughter. In casting about for an appropriate explanation for her predicament we find it more comfortable to see the out-of-wedlock mother as a girl whose difficulty stems from underlying, preexisting personality problems. We are forced into the position of interpreting the situation primarily in terms of individual pathology, failing to recognize the full extent to which the symptom may be culture-bound. We do, when pressed, acknowledge the possible influence of cultural factors, but in the main we do not tend to incorporate these elements significantly into our thinking.

There are no ready answers to this perplexing question, but as social workers we cannot deal adequately with the problem of the unmarried mother unless we see it within the framework of our conflicting mores. We must make room in our thinking for factors in the social scene—not only as they contribute to unwed motherhood, but also as they color the girl's reaction to her out-of-wedlock status in pregnancy.

It is understandable that we should incline toward a theory of underlying pathology as the cause of unmarried motherhood. Frequently, when we see the illegitimately pregnant girl, she presents a picture of severe disturbance. Guilt, panic, suspicion, and denial are not uncommon reactions. More often than not she will give a history of deprivation in primary relationships. However, if we are to assess correctly the sources and appropriateness of these reactions, we must take into consideration the circumstances under which we are seeing them. Two compelling factors in these circumstances are the crisis itself and the specifics of pregnancy and maternity. They are important not only for their diagnostic meaning but also because of their implications for practice in our work with unmarried mothers.

Crisis

We know that in a crisis situation current functioning may be disrupted, past vulnerabilities exposed, and hitherto manageable conflicts stirred up. Earlier feelings of guilt, deprivation, and the like may be reactivated. The unmarried pregnant woman, seen at a point of crisis, may exhibit a whole range of disturbed reactions. To be sure, each girl will experience her unwed motherhood in accordance with her basic personality make-up and will integrate it into her own patterns of reaction and behavior. However, crisis can produce distortions of one's customary patterns, and we cannot assume that her reactions in a crisis situation represent her characteristic mode of adaptation to reality any more than we can say that an acute pneumonia is characteristic of a person's physiological endowment, even though he may have some pulmonary susceptibility. A girl may become an unmarried mother because she has had pre-existing problems, or she may be having problems because she is an unmarried mother. Her behavior may be a true reflection of underlying emotional pathology, or it may be an appropriate response in an anxiety-producing situation. She may be manifesting primarily a resurgence of the latent guilt and unresolved conflicts which are ingredients in all human adjustment and which have been stirred up under acute stress.

Unmarried mothers as seen in a maternity home appear to experience these crises in stages, with periods of relative calm between, rather than in an unbroken line. Each girl seems to have her own pattern of stress alternating with well-being. For each the crisis-precipitating factor seems to be different at different times. It may be related to elements in the pregnancy. ("The emotional crises of pregnancy are produced mainly through stimulation by biological processes within the mother..."[11]) or it may result from news of the baby's father, her own parents, or some other external source. Our knowledge and experience are rather limited in this area. Perhaps we should be directing some of our efforts toward learning to recognize the signs of these crises, in order to anticipate and prepare for them if possible—to know when intervention is indicated and when the potentials for self-healing inherent in crisis situations had best be left to do their own work; to try to understand so that we may learn to deal with the rhythms of crisis in the unmarried mother.

A recognition of the crisis factor in unmarried motherhood should give us pause in our routine use of psychological testing of the resident in a maternity home, and in the requirement for prescribed casework interviews. One may hope that it will prompt us to interpret with great caution the results of projective tests and questionnaires, devices which appear to be taking on increasing importance in the diagnosis of unmarried mothers. Personality traits registered at a time of crisis, though applicable to the time and circumstances under which the tests are administered, can be interpreted in only a limited way as ongoing characteristics of the unmarried mother, individually or as a group. (The provocative nature of some of the test questions might also be considered.) Otherwise we are likely to emerge with a personality picture that does not fit the observations of many of us who are seeing unmarried mothers in their day-to-day living.

Note some conclusions from a recent study:

> ...acting out anti-socially is a primary characteristic of the unwed mother... There does not appear to be much difference between the unwed mother and other delinquent females.

> The unmarried mother is bitterly hostile...more so than all patient groups.

> They are unfitted for psychotherapy because they deny problems and in their defensiveness appear aloof and independent, thus rejecting help and their basic dependency needs.[10]

Pregnancy and Motherhood

It is generally accepted that the experience of pregnancy can contain elements of crisis even for the married woman. "So-called 'normal pregnant women' might be highly abnormal, and even if they are not, they are anxious to a degree beyond that of the so-called 'normal non-pregnant female.'"[11] "Particularly during the first pregnancy women are apt to suffer terrifying dreams and phantasies of giving birth to a dead or misshapen child."[12] With the additional pressures to which the unmarried pregnant woman is subjected, we should not be surprised to see an intensification of the reactions which in her married counterpart we are prone to accept with tolerant indulgence. In themselves they are not necessarily signs of severe pathology. By the same token, the "normal deviations" of adolescence should figure prominently in our assessment of the meaning of out-of-wedlock pregnancy in the teen-ager.

Pregnancy and parturition constitute a continuing experience in physiological and emotional change. Each period seems to have its biological characteristics and typical emotional concomitants. There is still much uncharted territory in our knowledge of this psychobiological phenomenon, but obstetricians, psychiatrists, and others working with married pregnant women are becoming increasingly interested in the importance of these factors. As members of a helping discipline we have an obligation to incorporate into our work with the unmarried mother whatever relevant information is available. We may not be able to apply it very specifically as yet, but recognition of the significance of such factors can influence the ways in which we respond to a girl's reactions, the areas in which we offer help, and the manner in which we offer it.

It can affect our decision whether to reassure or to explore for deeper meaning at a given point. It may influence our interpretation of a girl's dependent leaning toward her mother or a mother-person. It will have a bearing on our reaction to her apprehensiveness about her growing attachment to a baby which she must relinquish—the ease with which we can help her to accept herself as a prospective mother and experience pregnancy and motherhood in as constructive a way as possible. It will have much to do with the strength we can lend her in the face of a separation from her baby, so that she can liberate and experience her feelings of motherliness toward her child. The "some day if I marry and have a baby *of my own....*," inadvertently voiced by many girls who will be surrendering their babies, should give us pause as to its implications regarding their efforts to prepare for the interruption of a biological process which does not readily lend itself to alteration by social stricture.

For most unmarried mothers this is a first experience in motherhood and as such it may be an important influence in the image a girl establishes of herself as a mother-person. Part of our goal should be to help her emerge from it with as positive an image of herself as a mother as her personality and circumstances will permit. To do this we need to be ready, at appropriate points, to de-emphasize the unmarried, socially deviant aspect of her experience and accentuate its normal motherhood components. In fact we may well ask ourselves whether, in failing to exploit the full possibilities of motherhood for the unmarried mother, we may not be encouraging the blocking out of large areas of affect in her experience in maternity, whether she is surrendering her baby or keeping it.

In general, it might be well to examine our uncritical assumption that for the mother who must relinquish her child early separation is invariably indicated. Perhaps we need to consider the possibility that there are differences in the rates at which biological ties between mothers and babies are loosened, just as there are differences in the strength of these ties; that variations in the timing of the separation may therefore be indicated; that a premature separation may be as injurious as indefinite temporizing; and that perhaps the community has a responsibility to furnish the resources whereby such individual differences can be provided for.

If we see illegitimate pregnancy primarily as a symptom of underlying emotional pathology, we are likely to interpret much of an unmarried mother's behavior in similar terms. We shall be on the alert for signs of pathology and shall undoubtedly find them; one wonders whether we may not sometimes even be guilty of promoting the "self-fulfilling prophecy."[13] In trying to assess the nature and degree of disturbance, no matter how skillfully we proceed we may turn valid exploration into inappropriate probing, and find ourselves contributing to the very disturbance we are trying to diagnose.

The extent to which pathology orientation can skew our thinking can be illustrated in two fairly typical experiences we are likely to meet in our work with unmarried mothers—"denial" and planning for the baby.

Denial

The unmarried mother's use of "denial" is a source of some concern to social workers. We tend to see it in her efforts to delay her admission to the maternity home, in her remaining in ordinary clothing beyond the appropriate time, in her reluctance to discuss plans for the baby just yet, in her unwillingness to talk. This may well be a denial of sorts, but is it bad?

Unless a girl is seriously disturbed, it is a fairly safe guess that she is not denying to herself the fact of her pregnancy. The question then is, what is she denying and to whom? Is she expressing the feeble hope that there may have been an error in diagnosis after all (a not uncommon reaction in married women), or could she be trying to minimize the implications of her abandonment by the baby's father? She may be struggling with the problem of maternal affect, seeking to protect herself psychologically from a growing interest in a baby she may have to give up.

In assessing the meaning of denial, we may do well to take cognizance of our own role in fostering it. As agents of the community, we offer the unmarried pregnant girl anonymity in a protected shelter; we provide out-of-town mailing addresses; we encourage her to deny her maternity by plans for the early placement of her baby, so that she can resume her place in the community as though nothing had happened. What we interpret as pathology may be the girl's valid use of a healthy mechanism to protect herself in crisis from a threatening reality. She is behaving the way society requires, in order to avoid permanent impairment of her social functioning. There are times when the girl who does not deny should perhaps be of greater concern to us than the one who does.

Planning for the Baby

Our assumption that illegitimate pregnancy is invariably rooted in personality pathology has led us to accept uncritically certain further assumptions deriving from the basic ones:

1. That the same neurotic conflict which resulted in the out-of-wedlock pregnancy will motivate the girl in planning for her baby.

> Her decision about the baby is based not upon her feeling for him as a separate individual but upon the purpose for which she bore him.[14]

2. That adoption is the preferred plan for the babies of unmarried mothers.

> It is not an unwarranted interference with the unmarried mother to presume that in most cases it will be in the child's best interests for her to release her child for adoption....The concept that the unmarried mother and her child constitute a family is to me unsupportable.[15]

3. That the girl who relinquishes her baby is healthier than the one who keeps hers.

No doubt many girls who should be relinquishing their babies are keeping them. Conversely, it may well be that some girls who are relinquishing their babies should keep them. One mother may be giving up her baby for reasons as neurotic as another's who keeps hers. However, if we are committed uncritically to the assumptions outlined here, we are less likely to give the adoption plan the thorough-going exploration that we devote to the plan to keep the baby, nor are we likely to examine the extent to which factors in the girl *and* in society are responsible for making one plan more desirable than another.

Actually we do not have enough verified data regarding the long-range outcomes of their plan to substantiate one assumption over the other. In the meantime we are subscribing to a point of view that states in effect that the presence of neurotic conflict automatically cancels out the validity of an impulse which is biologically determined. A mother, married or unmarried, may be severely neurotic in her motivation toward motherhood and still be substantially maternal. If we fail to take cognizance of this, we are taking only a partial view of the problem and are likely to give the unwed mother an incomplete or distorted service in the various aspects of her problem.

Technically we may claim that our underlying point of view does not influence us and that each girl is allowed to make her own decision regarding her baby. And technically this is probably correct in most cases. But the subtle communication of our essential attitude cannot be denied—as observed by one girl who felt she was being pressured into surrendering her baby: "It's not what Mrs. K says exactly, it's just that her face lights up when I talk about adoption the way it doesn't when I talk about keeping Beth."

Summary

In our emphasis on a single theory of causation with regard to unmarried motherhood we are overlooking other important aspects of this phenomenon. As a result we may be depriving ourselves of meaningful diagnostic perceptions and failing to make full use of the rich treatment possibilities inherent in the experience for the girl. The additional factors of social mores, crisis, and the specifics of pregnancy and motherhood are offered for consideration here. They are presented not as substitutes for the currently accepted theory of underlying emotional conflict as causative in out-of-wedlock pregnancy, but rather as added dimensions which can extend our horizons and increase the effectiveness of our work in this area. Nor are these factors thought of as relevant for all unmarried mothers. It is hoped that they may be evaluated and applied with the same diagnostic discrimination, and on as individual a basis, as any theory.

If we are to help the unmarried pregnant woman to weather her experience with a minimum of damage, and if possible exploit it as a point of departure for her maturing as a woman, we must help her understand what is happening to her in terms of her personal psychological make-up, her biological experience, and the social world of which she is a part. To do this we must be ready to accept multiple theories of causation; we need to explore without bias as many of the relevant ingredients as we can identify, and bring them all to bear in our effort to understand and help her. We must be ready to divest ourselves of some of the stereotyped images of the unmarried mother to which we have uncritically committed ourselves, and to recognize the conflicts in our own roles as social workers in relation to this problem.

We need to search for ways of broadening our knowledge and applying it more meaningfully in diagnosis and treatment of the unmarried mother. We need to think in terms of hypotheses to be truly tested rather than closed systems of explanation for which we are impelled to find substantiating evidence.

References

1. Margaret W. Millar, "Casework Services for the Unmarried Mother," *Casework Papers 1955*, Family Service Association of America, New York, 1955, p. 93.

2. Louise K. Trout, "Services to Unmarried Mothers," *Child Welfare*, Vol. 35, No. 2 (1956), p. 21.

3. Jane K. Goldsmith, "The Unmarried Mother's Search for Standards," *Social Casework*, Vol. XXXVIII, No. 2 (1957), p. 69.

4. Irene M. Josselyn, M.D., "What We Know About the Unmarried Mother." Paper read at National Conference of Social Work, June 1953.

5. Leontine Young, *Out of Wedlock*, McGraw-Hill Book Co., New York, 1954, p. 22.

6. Lola A. Bowman, "The Unmarried Mother Who is a Minor," *Child Welfare*, Vol. 37, No. 8 (1958), p. 13.

7. Leontine Young, *op. cit.*, p. 6.

8. For an extended discussion of this problem see Max Lerner, *America As a Civilization*, Simon & Schuster, New York 1957, pp. 657–688.

9. Gerald Caplan, *An Approach to Community Mental Health*, Grune and Stratton, New York, 1961, p. 165.

10. Edmund Pollock, "An Investigation into Certain Personality Characteristics of Unmarried Mothers." Unpublished doctoral dissertation, New York University, 1957, pp. 103, 110, 141.

11. J.C. Hirst and F. Strousse, "The Origin of Emotional Factors in Normal Pregnant Women," *American Journal of the Medical Sciences*, Vol. 196, No. 1 (1938), p. 98.

12. Florence Clothier, M.D., "Psychological Implications of Unmarried Parenthood," *American Journal of Orthopsychiatry*, Vol. 13, No. 3 (1943), p. 541.

13. Robert K. Merton, *Social Theory and Social Structure*, Free Press of Glencoe, 1957, pp. 421–426.

14. Leontine Young, *op. cit.*, p. 199.

15. Joseph H. Reid, "Principles, Values, and Assumptions Underlying Adoption Practice," *Social Work*, Vol. 2, No. 1 (1957), p. 27.

Interaction of Pregnancy, Loss, and Developmental Issues in Adolescents

. . . . .

Edith M. Freeman

Losses are associated with normal developmental changes that occur during adolescence. Pregnancy may affect an adolescent's experience of these losses or may cause additional losses. In addition, the complex changes brought on by pregnancy may increase an adolescent's stress and problems in coping with life situations. Social workers and other professionals may focus on adjustment to pregnancy as the first priority, while ignoring opportunities to help these clients address losses. Such an approach diminishes the opportunity to enhance clients' management of current as well as future developmental changes.

The literature does not address loss as experienced by adolescent mothers. Although the literature on losses experienced by young people is growing, much of it focuses only on losses due to divorce or separation of parents or to the death of significant others.[1] The literature on practice with adolescents generally emphasizes pregnancy prevention without also exploring the losses involved when developmental changes and pregnancy occur simultaneously.[2] The present article explores some of the common losses that may accrue during adolescence, as well as special losses that confront young mothers, and describes practice principles for helping young mothers to resolve their losses. Case examples are used to illustrate how these principles can be applied in practice situations.

Freeman, E.M. (1987). Interaction of Pregnancy, Loss, and Developmental Issues in Adolescents. *Social Casework: The Journal of Contemporary Social Work,* 68, 38–46. Reprinted by permission of Family Service America, publisher.

Developmental Issues and Losses That Confront Adolescents In General

General adolescent development has been explored extensively elsewhere.[3] However, many authors have de-emphasized some of the issues involved in the adolescent phase.[4] The following discussion briefly summarizes these issues and explores interrelationships among them. It also addresses circumstances in which the handling of these issues can result in losses for the adolescents.

DEVELOPMENTAL ISSUES AND TASKS

Common developmental issues for adolescents include *1)* identity, *2)* separation from the family of origin, *3)* friendship, *4)* courtship, and *5)* career planning.[5] (See Table 1 for a description of these issues and tasks.) Although each of these issues may be confronted to some degree during other developmental phases, the tasks and the intensity of focus pertain uniquely to adolescence. For example, individuation, or acknowledgment of each child as a separate being in the family, is an important issue throughout the life cycle. However, the actual emotional, functional, and financial separation and the accompanying stress generally occur during adolescence. Table 1 illustrates how parents and adolescents may respond to separation and other important issues of this phase. Each individual experiences these issues in a unique way, but the manner in which young people effect separation and the issues that are emphasized as evidence that this process is proceeding vary.

Developmental issues are interrelated. Consequently, adolescents work on them in combination rather than in an isolated or sequential manner. Responses to some of these issues can have positive or negative effects on how other issues are handled. For example, the issue of friendship can have a positive impact on separation from parents. The latter can be enhanced when adolescents have satisfying peer relationships that allow them to shift their point of reference for values and behavioral norms from the family to peers and finally to the self.

On the other hand, some developmental issues can have negative effects on others, depending on how adolescents respond to them. For example, courtship and identity issues can impact negatively on each other. A teenage girl may date an individual who reinforces her sexual identity but she may experience a decrease in self-esteem and a negative self-concept if pregnancy and losses in other relationships result from the courtship experience. In addition, the effects of these losses may affect future functioning of the adolescent in these same areas. Therefore, one must be aware of how inadequate responses to developmental issues can result in these types of losses for some adolescents.

POTENTIAL LOSSES

Elizabeth Kubler-Ross and others have described a series of predictable stages of grief associated with the loss of a loved one due to death. These stages are *1)* denial, *2)* shock and anger, *3)* acceptance, *4)* bargaining, and *5)* true acceptance.[6] Empirical research has documented the occurrence of these stages and the crisis reactions involved.[7] Although these stages are somewhat predictable, it is assumed that individuals can experience them in a manner based on their past experiences with losses and their current resources for coping. Often, they move back and forth between stages or stay in a particular stage of grief, such as anger, for a prolonged period, because they need more time to accept the loss. In addition, they may lack sufficient resources, such as adequate support systems or knowledge, for coping with those losses.[8]

These stages of grief have been generalized recently to a broader range of losses in the elderly, such as changes in physical and mental functioning, status and roles, significant relationships, and possessions and familiar surroundings.[9] Although the needs of elderly and young people are different, these stages can be generalized to similar changes experienced by adolescents (see Table 1).

Whether adolescents experience such changes as a loss depends on several factors, one of which is the quality of relationships between adolescents and important people in their environments. For example, loss can occur when adolescents behave in ways that encourage parents to set external controls and to limit independence or when parents delay developmental milestones by not allowing the adolescent to drive, handle money, or set his or her own curfew. The responses of the adolescent and the parents may be due to mutual ambivalence about separation and may result in a loss of trust and loss of opportunity for the adolescent (see Table 1).

Loss can also occur due to lack of opportunity or knowledge. Having the opportunity to anticipate and plan for changes, having knowledge about how to handle these changes, and having opportunities to practice or try out skills related to new developmental tasks can affect the extent of loss.

Finally, the adolescent's perspective about developmental changes may determine whether loss occurs. For example, if adolescents perceive situations as crises from which they do not expect to recover, they may indeed experience loss. Resources for coping may be ignored or used inappropriately. If adolescents perceive that some valuable aspect of their lives has been irretrievably taken away, they may experience this kind of change as a loss. As an example, separation from a peer is more likely to be experienced as a loss if the individual feels unable to initiate new friendships without undue stress. Understanding the social, emotional, and physical changes required of adolescents in general provides the foundation necessary for exploring how some of these developmental issues are intensified by the adjustments that pregnant adolescents are required to make.

Impact of Pregnancy on Developmental Issues

Pregnancy affects the needs/resource balance in the lives of young women; that is, their needs may become more complex due to adjustments

	TABLE 1.

Developmental issues that confront adolescents.

Developmental Issues	Tasks
1. Identity: self-concept, body image, racial identity, and sexual identity.	Gradually develop clear and consistent perspective about self and related needs.
	Use image of self as a framework for interacting with significant others and for meeting identity needs such as autonomy and relatedness.
2. Separation from the family of origin (in emotional, functional, and financial areas) takes place throughout adolescence and into the young-adult phase.	Gradually become independent from parents by developing ability to make decisions independently, to complete own role responsibilities independently, and to develop a means for earning own income and for supporting a separate household in the near future.
3. Friendship: appropriate and satisfying peer relationships.	Develop an adequate peer network for meeting evolving needs such as companionship and relatedness.
	Establish a balance between the need for peer support and acceptance and standards for self-acceptance.
4. Courtship: relationships with the opposite sex.	Develop standards and norms for relationships with the opposite sex.
	Make informed choices based on these standards on when to start dating (within parental limits), whom to date, the extent of intimacy to engage in and whether to use some form of birth control if intimacy includes sexual intercourse.
5. Career planning and career choice.	Select a career or trade that reflects interests, aptitudes, and identity.
	Complete the steps necessary for meeting the requirements for this career or trade and for obtaining financial independence.

Potential Responses	Potential Losses
Adolescents may select peer models to observe and emulate (some may be undesirable from the adult perspective). Adolescents may test new values, attitudes, and behaviors that conflict with those of the parents as a natural growth process.	If parents renegotiate rules, clarify and consistently enforce existing rules, and do not overreact to testing, losses may not occur. If parents are inconsistent, inflexible, and devalue or restrict access to peer models, distance between them and the adolescent may lead to a loss in relationship and a loss of identity.
Ambivalence about separation in adolescents can lead to unreasonable demands for independent functioning, coupled with destructive behavior that encourages parents' efforts to provide external controls and to limit independence. Parents may take the demands for independence by the adolescent at face value and accede to them. Adolescents may be aware of their own or their parents' ambivalence about separation and therefore pace or slow down separation process.	Delaying or putting off developmental milestones related to separation may be experienced as a loss of opportunity or loss of trust by some adolescents. Allowing developmental milestones to occur too rapidly can result in a loss of security and premature loss of childhood. Anticipating and pacing of milestones related to separation can prevent or lessen potential losses.
Peers may be used as "sound-boards" for testing out ideas. Peer acceptance may be equated with sameness, security, and belonging. Strict rules for loyalty and conformity among peers may be supportive and restrictive.	Failure to conform to peer standards may result in loss of relationships, status, and self-esteem. Violation of standards for self-acceptance to gain peer support may lead to a loss of identity and self-respect.
Choices may be made by default because of a lack of awareness about alternatives to physical and social pressures for greater sexual intimacy (new situations with which they do not have resources for coping). Parents may ignore the risk situation or may provide (or allow) birth control without teaching the adolescent how to process the issue of alternatives and consequences.	Violation of parental standards about intimacy can result in loss of parental relationships. Violation of their own standards over time or in a significant area related to courtship can result in loss of control and loss of self-esteem. Failure to develop standards for courtship can result in loss of identity.
Career choice based on interests, aptitudes, and identity. Overidentification with family or peers can lead to a career choice based on others' influence. Career choice can become a sign of rebellion against parental control.	Failure to develop (or a denial of) own interests and aptitudes regarding career choice can result in loss of control over life, which may also delay separation from parents.

required by pregnancy, while their access to resources for meeting these needs may become more limited. This situation can result in an exaggerated emphasis on common developmental issues and a configuration of issues as follows: 1) social relationships (courtship, peer, and family-separation issues), 2) physical appearance (identity issues), and 3) educational opportunities (career-planning issues). These issues are discussed in terms of the additional tasks that pregnancy requires, typical responses by adolescents and significant others to these tasks, and the potential losses that are involved.

SOCIAL RELATIONSHIPS

Social relationships for adolescent expectant mothers may involve immediate and extended family members; peers; professionals in social agencies, schools, and medical facilities; and the father of the child. Pregnancy may cause modification of old roles and initiation of new roles, which in turn may alter relationships with these significant others. For example, expectant mothers continue in the role of daughter to their parents; however, this role is modified when they become parents themselves. In making decisions about their own child, they may begin to make decisions about themselves that their parents previously made.

These young women may also be expected to develop a new role in regard to courtship issues. As a parent, they may be expected to confer with the father of their child in planning for the child's current and future needs. However, this may occur at a time when the courtship relationship with the father is conflictual or may no longer exist. Thus their need for acceptance, support, and autonomy may be heightened when they have few resources.[10]

In regard to social relationships, the adolescent mother must build a support system that addresses the impact of pregnancy on common developmental issues such as courtship, peer relationships, and family separation—a support system that will meet the social relationship needs that exist due to pregnancy. Such a support system also helps with decisions related to pregnancy and development, that is, decisions about pregnancy outcomes, day-care arrangements, financial resources, and how to handle courtship and sexuality issues in the future. Without a support system, the mother is unable to make the necessary modifications to social roles and relationships.

Some young mothers may require assistance to avert loss of relationships or to compensate if relationships are, in fact, lost. Sometimes the parents' angry rejection of the pregnant adolescent may extend for a long period, which may in turn create distance in the parent-child relationship and result in a loss of acceptance and support. Parents may become more strict with their younger daughters, because they are fearful about the negative effects that the older daughter's pregnancy might have on siblings. This response may disrupt or lead to a loss in sibling relationships if younger siblings withdraw from the pregnant adolescent as a result. If parents, through fear about the effect of the pregnancy on future social relationships, send the adolescent to live with relatives or friends, additional losses may occur. Pressure by school officials to change from a home school to a special program for teenage parents may also lead to loss experiences. Despite the advantages of such programs, their positive effects may be diminished if the mother is not involved in decisions about which school she will attend.

Maintaining current peer relationships is critical; however, peers often withdraw, or the expectant mother may become the focus of curiosity. Both responses may result in a loss of relationships and in a failure to deal effectively with the issues of friendship and loyalty. A similar result may occur if the father of the child is unable or unwilling to accept the pregnancy. Such a response from the father may prolong the young woman's denial of the pregnancy or may destroy their relationship if the mother moves toward true acceptance and the father does not.

PHYSICAL APPEARANCE

Physical changes due to pregnancy may add to existing stress caused by physical changes due to development. They may negatively modify the individual's body image and self-concept, thus affecting identity issues and how the adolescent feels about herself. These changes also emphasize differences between the adolescent mother and her peers at a time when not being different and having peer acceptance are developmentally important.

The expectant mother must respond to these physical changes by adjusting to new requirements in diet, sleeping patterns, exercise, and health care. This adjustment or compliance may be hindered by the individual's acceptance or denial of the pregnancy. If the expectant mother is still angry, denying the pregnancy, or bargaining, adequate coping with changes in physical appearance and the tasks that must be completed may be delayed. In these situations, young women may experience a loss of body image and a loss of control over their lives at a period when autonomy is very important developmentally.

Significant others and health-care providers may increase loss of control by blaming the young woman if health problems develop. They may assume that pregnancy should naturally lead to adult-like responses to health requirements without realizing that such responses are not typical of adolescents. It should be remembered that the adolescent expectant mother has had no transition period to practice control over her life.

EDUCATIONAL OPPORTUNITIES

Education may be affected by the life changes introduced by pregnancy; this in turn impacts on the related task of career choice. If the expectant mother drops out of school, she may no longer have access to the resources in the school district that are designed for students who need special help. Pregnancy may also introduce new barriers to educational goals. For example, fatigue or physical complications may interfere with study. These barriers may seem insurmountable to young women who are already overwhelmed by developmental and pregnancy-related issues. If they are not interested in school or have a history of underachievement or failure, they may be less likely to overcome these obstacles.

The education-related task is to identify barriers and develop problem-solving skills necessary for addressing them. The expectant mother must also anticipate barriers that may occur after delivery of the child, including the need for adequate day-care services, transportation to and from the day-care facility and the school, and financial resources for increased living expenses. The amount of support that adolescent mothers receive from important others will determine whether they remain in school before and after the delivery and whether they attend regularly.

Parents, peers, and well-meaning school staff sometimes respond to the requirements of this task by encouraging these students to curtail their educational goals and do not attempt to provide help in handling some of the real barriers to achieving these goals. For adolescents who have begun to make a career choice or who want to complete school, lack of support and of adequate resources may result in a loss of educational opportunity. This is a loss for which they may grieve both in the present and the future as its effects on life-style become apparent. Knowledge of the manner in which pregnancy impacts on developmental issues for adolescents is important if social workers are to address real and potential losses.

Practice Principles

Loss of relationships with parents and others may cause some adolescent mothers to be distrustful of any new adults in their lives, including helping professionals. They may expect negative judgments from social workers about their pregnancy. Some social workers' personal values about adolescent sexuality may make them ineffective in their work with such clients. Both clients and workers may contribute to ineffective work on clients' problems.

Four principles are particularly important for improving practice with pregnant adolescents. The first principle involves the use of an explicit contract that is negotiated with the client during the initial stages of treatment. Anthony Maluccio and Wilma Marlow reported on the effectiveness of clear, written contracts with clients who are difficult to engage.[11] The written contract helps facilitate engagement with this client group because it clearly indicates the time limits of the contract and clarifies the work to be done. Joining in the helping process may be easier to accomplish because the bases and timing for it have been made clear. The client's involvement in negotiating an explicit written contract helps decrease feelings of powerlessness and eases feelings of loss of control and status that may be experienced during pregnancy.

The second principle involves the use of visual or concrete means for identifying current and past losses as well as the effects of pregnancy on social relationships, identity, and other developmental issues. Such tools help identify whether losses have been resolved satisfactorily and how relationships and separations have been handled in the past. They also facilitate effective termination between worker and client and help resolve old losses.

Procedures such as the time line, the ecomap, the life-history grid, and the writing of an autobiography are useful in identifying potential losses and significant events that led to past losses and as tools for contracting the work to be done in regard to unresolved losses.[12] They can also be used to anticipate future losses and to lessen their impact through planning. For example, it is possible to plan how a young woman being transferred from her home school to a school for teenage parents can initiate contacts in the new school before the move and continue old social relationships from the home school after the move. They illustrate in a concrete manner the progress that the client has made in these areas and are useful for discussion and evaluation during termination.

The third principle involves the focus for helping, which should be on all aspects of the pregnant adolescent's life, not just on the pregnancy. A broad-based assessment not only insures that the intervention is appropriate, but also allows the client to see that the worker is not "stuck" on the pregnancy. It enhances engagement as well, because it helps identify many of the client's concerns, which may include common developmental issues that confront all adolescents. The worker is able to analyze the client's progress in handling these issues and other problems and the impact that pregnancy may have on the client's progress. Moreover, the worker may be able to explore with clients how pregnancy may or may not be part of their efforts to work on developmental issues such as separation from parents.

If losses have occurred because of developmental issues or pregnancy, the worker can help clients assess the stage of grief they are experiencing. The worker can help the client find ways to resolve the grief by suggesting activities and discussion topics that will lead through all stages of grief. Effective resolution of old losses helps make the client-worker relationship more meaningful.

The fourth principle involves using broad-based assessment procedures to identify barriers to educational opportunities and significant others—issues that must be considered if the intervention is to be effective. Significant others can include parents or guardians, the father of the expected child, peers, siblings, or adults in other systems (for example, the school). For example, a widowed mother was unable to resolve her disappointment about her daughter's pregnancy, because the mother felt she had not fulfilled her deceased husband's expectations of her as a parent. She was unable to provide the emotional support her daughter needed until several months after the child was born. The social worker helped the mother and daughter focus on how the mother experienced her daughter's pregnancy as a loss of support from the daughter and how the mother's reaction interfered with the daughter's need to become an effective parent.

In other situations, the father of the expected child may pressure the mother to make a decision about abortion, relinquishment, or keeping her child. Working only with the client may be ineffective and may increase the adolescent mother's fear about losing her relationship with the father—a fear that may hinder her in making an informed decision. Involving significant others periodically or on a regular basis may be useful. Also, teaching these clients how to use significant others as resources facilitates the transition period after termination.

CASE EXAMPLES

The following case examples illustrate how these four principles work in actual practice.

> K, a seventeen-year old pregnant adolescent, was referred by her school counselor to a mental health consultant who provided services to her school. She lived with her younger sister and recently divorced mother. The initial assessment indicated that her school achievement was above average, her mother was supportive and had a very positive relationship with her, and that K had plans for attending junior college in a few months. She seemed to be coping well with the pregnancy. The teenage father of her child worked and had plans for providing some financial support. The counselor identified the pregnancy as K's only problem.

> The social worker from the mental health center used an ecomap as part of her assessment of K. As a result, the worker discovered a major imbalance in the amount of support that K provided to others compared with the amount she received. K indicated that her peers, the father of her child, and even her mother to some extent saw her as someone who was very responsible and on whom they could depend. Some peers who had previously consulted with K on personal problems now avoided her. K dealt with these losses in relationships and status by denying their importance or by bargaining, that is, by saying that they would become her friends again when they saw that she "put her life back together." K was planning for her future alone (for example, career choice, child care, transportation arrangements, and so forth), while her mother and the father of her child unknowingly held back the input that K desired because they saw her as being independent.

The ecomap helped identify K's ambivalence about her growing independence and her new pregnancy-related responsibilities. It also illustrated her feelings of being emotionally severed from her own father. These past and present losses, developmental and pregnancy-related issues, and conflicts with her boyfriend about how his goals for the future fit with hers became the focus for intervention.

Some interviews included K's mother and others included the father of the child. Their input was achieved, and K's independence was maintained. Individual interviews focused on how K could develop new relationships, resolve her pain from the loss of some peers, and reestablish a relationship with one of these peers. Because K's father did not wish to be included in the sessions, it was not possible to involve him directly. However, K worked on their relationship through tasks and activities outside of the sessions (for example, K talked with him about her feelings about the divorce and her sense of loss and involved him as part of her support network in exploring resources for current medical and future educational expenses).

This case illustrates three practice principles: *1)* the social worker used a visual procedure to facilitate assessment; *2)* the assessment included focus on important areas of concern in addition to the pregnancy; and *3)* significant others who were important to the problem situation and its resolution were involved in the intervention process. Although an ecomap was periodically used to focus the work, a formal contract to identify time limits and the focus of work was not used. As a consequence, termination was not planned; however, termination occurred after six months, when the client suggested that the sessions end because her time was limited due to enrollment in junior college. K worked through some of her concerns about separation and independence; career choice; and her relationships with her boyfriend, mother, and peers. She moved toward true acceptance of losses that she had previously denied and reestablished lost ties with her father.

As a postscript to this case, later analysis of an audiotape of what turned out to be K's final session indicated that the worker missed an opportunity to terminate effectively. The client had talked about her future plans, but no discussion was initiated about the work that had taken place (the many productive changes in the client's life space) or what the experience had meant to the worker and the client. The ecomap could have been used for this review. K had included the worker as a source of support on the ecomap, thus illustrating the worker's importance to the client. The worker overlooked K's vulnerability to loss at termination, because she viewed her as more mature and less dependent than most teenagers.

> Fifteen-year-old S was referred to a hospital social worker when she went to a clinic for a pregnancy examination. S indicated that her parents and other relatives were extremely angry with her, because she had concealed her pregnancy beyond the time when an abortion would have been safe. When the social worker met with her, S talked very little except in response to the worker's questions about her pregnancy. When a second interview began the same way, the social worker turned to an exploration of other areas of S's life. The worker discovered that S had an interest in writing and that she felt that she was able to express herself much more freely in written form. They contracted for S to write her autobiography as a way of helping the social worker to get to know her and as a tool for helping S to achieve distance from her situation.
>
> When S returned with her autobiography on a follow-up visit, the worker was able to review important events and relationships in S's life. They decided to use each session to focus on a different part of the autobiography. Grammatical and spelling errors in the writing led the social worker to make a mental note to explore at a more convenient time S's school adjustment and the potential for her dropping out of school. Meanwhile, they focused on the content of the autobiography, which showed S's fears about her parents' anger and the pain involved in the loss of their support. It also indicated that she had unexpressed anger about her pregnancy and her parents' response and toward her boyfriend whom she felt had completely abandoned her. Discussion of these losses helped her to admit her uncertainty about how to handle questions from peers about her pregnancy and her concerns about her sexuality and self-image, which had changed due to the pregnancy. She was also unclear about the importance of diet and exercise.
>
> Although identifying and working on these developmental issues and those related to pregnancy was helpful to S, she had a persistent concern that her parents were going to send her out of town to live with her grandparents because of the embarrassment her pregnancy caused them with members of their church. S saw this as a greater threat than the other losses that she had

already experienced. The social worker helped S identify her feelings about a possible move, the adjustments that she might be required to make if the move occurred, and the social relationships and familiar surroundings she might be leaving behind. She also helped her identify some positive aspects of the move, such as an opportunity for her to develop a closer relationship with her grandparents. When S failed to keep her next appointment at the clinic, a call to her home indicated that she had been sent to stay with her grandparents. The mother provided the social worker with S's new address. The mother did not want help in exploring any of her concerns or options related to the pregnancy, such as adoption. The worker wrote a letter to S. She used S's autobiography to review her progress in working through a difficult period in her life and to let S know how much the relationship and experience had meant to her. The worker assumed that their discussion on the changes that S could anticipate as a result of the move (including social relationships she would leave behind) was the beginning of their termination process.

In this example, the worker applied three practice principles. First, the worker used a concrete procedure that reinforced the client's talent in writing in order to explore potential losses and other developmental issues. However, no effort was made to involve the parents or other significant individuals in S's environment in the sessions; consequently, the worker missed an opportunity to help the parents look at alternatives for handling their anger and disappointment about the pregnancy and to help them become a support network for S—an intervention that might have prevented the move or some of the other losses in social relationships and familiar surroundings that S may have experienced during the move. Second, the assessment focused on areas other than the pregnancy (courtship and sexuality in general, educational opportunity or school adjustment, and identity). Third, it involved the use of an explicit verbal contract. Over a period of three months, S progressed from being angry about her losses in terms of the stages of grief to a recognition that she could grow from the experience. A letter was used to complete the termination process since their work was disrupted by the move. Although this method of termination did not allow S to express her feelings directly about the progress made on her problems and her relationship with the worker, she did respond to the worker's letter. She indicated that it meant a lot to know that the worker was still concerned about her and that their discussions had been helpful during a period when she felt that she was completely alone.

These two case examples illustrate four important practice principles for effective work with pregnant adolescents. The principles can help social workers recognize the impact that natural development issues and issues related to pregnancy have on losses in these clients' lives. They also help identify the kinds of interventions that lessen the possibility that the helping relationship will add to the losses experienced by this client group.

Notes

1. Edith M. Freeman, "Loss and Grief in Children: Implications for School Social Workers," *Social Work in Education,* 6 (Summer 1984):241–258; and

Susan Cho, Edith M. Freeman, and Shirley Patterson, "Adolescents' Experience with Death: Practice Implications," *Social Casework*, 63 (February 1982):88–94.

2. Mary B. Doty and Myramae King, "Pregnancy Prevention: A Private Agency's Program in Public Schools," *Social Work in Education*, 7 (Winter 1984):90–99; and Steven P. Schinke, "School-Based Model for Preventing Teenage Pregnancy," *Social Work in Education*, 4 (January 1982):128–139.

3. Erik A. Erikson, "Life Cycle," in *Life Span Development*, ed. Martin Bloom (New York: Macmillan, 1980), p. 19; and George Kaluger and Meriem F. Kaluger, *Human Development: The Span of Life* (St. Louis: Times Mirror/Mosby, 1984), p. 121.

4. Pauline McCullough, "Launching Children and Moving On," in *The Family Life Cycle: A Framework for Family Therapy*, ed. Elizabeth Carter and Monica McGoldrick (New York: Gardner Press, 1980), p. 171.

5. Erikson, "Life Cycle," p. 29; and Kaluger and Kaluger, *Human Development*, p. 419.

6. Elizabeth Kubler-Ross, *On Death and Dying* (New York: Macmillan, 1968); and Bertha Simos, *A Time to Grieve: Loss as a Universal Human Experience* (New York: Macmillan, 1979).

7. Eric Lindemann, "Symptomatology and Management of Acute Grief," *American Journal of Psychiatry*, 101 (September 1944):141–148; E. Furman, *A Child's Parent Dies—Studies in Childhood Bereavement* (New Haven, Conn.: Yale University Press, 1974); and R. Seligman et al., "Effect of Earlier Parental Loss in Adolescence," *Archives of General Psychiatry*, 31 (August 1974):141–148.

8. Kubler-Ross, *On Death and Dying*; and Simos, *A Time to Grieve*.

9. Edith M. Freeman, "Multiple Losses in the Elderly: An Ecological Approach," *Social Casework*, 65 (May 1984):287–296.

10. Josefina J. Card and Lawress L. Wise, "Teenage Mothers and Teenage Fathers: The Impact of Early Childbearing on the Parents' Personal and Professional Lives," *Family Planning Perspectives*, 10 (June–July 1978):199–205; and Lloyd Bacon, "Early Motherhood, Accelerated Role Transition and Pathologies," *Social Forces*, 57 (March 1974):333–341.

11. Anthony Maluccio and Wilma Marlow, "The Case for the Contract," *Social Work*, 19 (January 1974):28–37.

12. Nancy J. Court, "The 'Time Line': A Treatment Tool for Children," *Social Work*, 25 (May 1980):235–236; Carel Germain and Alex Gitterman, *The Life Model of Social Work Practice* (New York: Columbia University Press, 1980), p. 20; and James E. Anderson and Ralph A. Brown, "Life History Grid for Adolescents," *Social Work*, 25 (July 1980):321–322.

Today's Unmarried Mothers: The Choices Have Changed

· · · · ·

Lucille J. Grow

eginning in the 1950s and continuing through the early 1970s, a number of studies attempted to distinguish between characteristics of unwed mothers who kept their children and those who surrendered them for adoption. The study populations were clients of social agencies, including residents of maternity homes. In many of the studies, the populations were totally white; in those involving other races, findings by race were usually reported separately.

Explanations during this period as to why some unwed women surrendered their babies and why others kept them were both psychological and sociological. Psychologically, the mothers who kept their children were considered less stable and more emotionally needy than those who decided upon adoption. The sociological viewpoint regarded unwed mothers who opted to keep as social deviants or as members of a subculture whose mores were at variance with those of society at large.

During the last decade or so, Americans have witnessed more relaxed attitudes with regard to sex, a questioning of the need for marriage, and a rejection of the inviolability of the traditional two-parent family. Concomitantly, there has been a shift away from adoption as the inevitable solution for the child born out of wedlock. Today the white unwed mother who keeps

Reprinted by permission from Child Welfare 58 (6), 363-371. Copyright 1979 The Child Welfare League of America, Inc.
This study was supported by Grant OCD-CB-456 from the Children's Bureau, Office of Child Development, U.S. Department of Health, Education and Welfare.

her child is more like than different from many female heads of other one-parent families in her community. Do the characteristics formerly observed in women who kept as opposed to those who surrendered their children still apply? In line with the questions raised by Festinger [3:253–263], do personal inadequacy and/or social deviancy or alienation explain why some unwed mothers surrender and others keep and rear their children now?

The Mothers In the Study

The findings reported here come from a study the author has directed since 1973 concerning young married and unmarried women who kept their babies, together with a small number of mothers who planned to surrender their children. All of the women were white, primaparous and between 14 and 24 years old when they gave birth. They had delivered during an 8 month period, beginning Nov. 1, 1973. Deliveries were in hospitals in Milwaukee and in a hospital adjacent to Milwaukee County, and it was through the cooperation of these hospitals, a maternity home just outside Milwaukee and the Wisconsin State Department of Social Services that we gained access to these young mothers. Since Wisconsin state law requires that every unwed mother be offered the services of a social agency, about three-fourths of the women had had at least one contact with a social worker.

Of the 210 white unmarried mothers, 182 kept their children. Twenty-three mothers had opted for adoption prior to their baby's birth or immediately thereafter, and five made this decision a few months later. Their median age was 18.9. Almost all the mothers were interviewed in their own homes, usually within a month after the baby's birth. (Followup interviews were held 3 years later with more than 90% of these mothers, all of whom retained legal custody of their children.)

Comparisons between mothers who surrendered and those who kept their children were made on over 100 variables that might be relevant to distinguishing between the groups. These included social characteristics of the mothers and their families, their parents' socioeconomic status, the women's educational attainment and employment history, their experiences prior to and during pregnancy and childbirth, their attitudes about pregnancy and marriage, their emotional well-being, and information about the putative fathers of their babies. Differences were considered significant if on the chi-square test they achieved the .05 level or beyond.

Variables that distinguished between mothers who kept and mothers who surrendered included age and education of the mothers, the marital stability of their parents, the mothers' living arrangements during pregnancy, their student status, the timing of their request for help, and aspects of their relationship with the putative father. Some of the earlier studies had found these variables, as well as others, significant in distinguishing between the groups of mothers. This paper compares findings in the earlier studies with the present study's findings on unwed women who made the decisions in late 1973 and 1974.

Variables Characteristically
Reported To Be Associated with
Mother's Decision

Several studies concerned with differences between unwed mothers who surrendered and those who kept their children were conducted on women who were pregnant during the 1950s and early 1960s. In those years, resolution of an out-of-wedlock pregnancy for a white woman was most usually marriage or adoption [4:132]. A white unmarried woman who kept her child was deviating from the mainstream of social norms, although not necessarily from norms within her own subculture.

The most recent available data come from the late 1960s. During this period the impression grew that white unwed mothers were less likely to place their babies for adoption than they had been in the past.[1] Unlike those in the 1950s and early 1960s, unwed women during this later period may have been subject to less social pressure, and the differentiating characteristics of those keeping as opposed to those surrendering their babies may have begun to change.

Five variables associated with the mother's decision were identified by two or more of the four major studies conducted in the United States of unwed mothers who surrendered their babies during the 1950s and early 1960s. Using the California Personality Inventory to compare characteristics of mothers keeping and mothers surrendering, Vincent found that mothers who kept had less positive personality profiles than those who surrendered their children for adoption [9:185–201]; Jones and his colleagues, who administered the Make a Sentence Test and the Cattell 16 Personality Factor Test to the unwed women in their study, reported similar findings [5:224–230; 7:1–6; 8:103–109]. In addition to less positive personality profiles, mothers who kept their children were more likely to be Catholic; came from lower socioeconomic backgrounds; were older; and had less education than the mothers who surrendered.

Only two studies deal with decisions of unwed mothers pregnant during the late 1960s—a study by the author [1:115–125] and Festinger's.[3] Although neither study reported on the parental socioeconomic status (SES), my study found that mothers who kept their children came from lower income families than those who surrendered. Similar to Vincent's earlier study, the two later studies found that a significantly larger proportion of women who kept as compared with those who surrendered their children came from broken homes. My study during the late 1960s found that religion was not associated with the mother's decision.

Although Festinger found older age to be significant in the mother's decision, my early study found no such association. On the other hand, I found that white mothers who kept their babies had less education than those who surrendered, whereas Festinger found no association between the mothers' education and the decision to keep or surrender. Neither study reported on personality factors associated with the mother's decision.

By the late 1960s, being a member of a particular religion no longer was found to distinguish between mothers who kept and mothers who surrendered. The association between keeping and education (lower) and age (older) was no longer so clear. On the other hand, no data had been presented to rule out the possibility that unwed mothers who kept their children were more likely to have more personality problems, to come from lower SES homes, and to be the products of broken homes than mothers who surrendered.

The lack of association between religion and the mother's decision was sustained in the current study. Unlike the results of some earlier studies, there was no difference in parental SES between the groups as measured by a two-item index of occupation and educational attainment of the fathers of the unmarried women. Similarly, no difference was found in the emotional health of the two groups of mothers as measured by Langner's Psychiatric Impairment Index [6:10–21]. Although this test and tests used by earlier researchers are not comparable, these results, in addition to other data obtained from the women, indicate that the women who kept their children were no more or no less disturbed than those who decided to surrender.

Consistent with some of the earlier findings, although no differences were found other than an index of childhood stress, more of the women who decided to keep their children had come from parental homes broken by separation or divorce. Among those who never entered college (high school dropouts as well as those who completed high school), similar proportions of mothers kept and surrendered. However, of those who attended or completed college, a larger proportion surrendered their children than kept them. The findings of lower education among keeping mothers is consistent with the findings of some of the earlier studies.

The current study's finding on the age variable differed from those of earlier studies. Although the proportions of women under 18 years old opting for adoption or keeping were similar in the studies, in the current study a much smaller proportion of women who kept their children were 21 years of age or older as compared with those who surrendered—18% versus 36%. In contrast to earlier findings, it was found that younger women—that is, those under 21—were more likely to keep than surrender their children.

Additional Findings

Festinger reported on differences concerning several other characteristics that earlier studies either did not explore or else did not find to discriminate between the two groups of mothers. She found that fewer of the keeping than surrendering mothers were living with either their parents or relatives at the time they came to the agency for service, as well as after the birth of their child. Mothers keeping their children were more often nonstudents, had sought help earlier, had known the putative father longer and were more likely to maintain contact with him than was the case among mothers who were surrendering. Also, when the mother and the putative father were not of the same race, the mother was more likely to keep than surrender.

35

In my study similar associations were found between the mother's decision and her student status, the timing of her request for help,* the length of time she had known the putative father, and the currency of her contact with him. However, no difference was found with regard to the mother's decision and the race of the putative father. On the other hand, it was found that among unwed women pregnant more recently, proportionately twice as many mothers who kept their children than those who surrendered lived with either parents or relatives during their pregnancy—64% versus 32%.** After the baby's birth, no differences in living arrangements were found between mothers who kept and those who surrendered.

Other Distinguishing Characteristics Found in the Current Study Population

Nine other variables or measures were found significant in distinguishing between mothers keeping and mothers surrendering. Mothers who kept were more likely to have spent their childhood years in cities with populations of 500,000 or more. Fewer of them reported attending church regularly—14% versus 46% of the surrendering mothers. The women who kept their children were far more likely than the surrendering mothers to have first confided in the baby's father when they became aware of their pregnancy. They also were more likely to report that the baby's father was supportive of them during pregnancy.

An index of informal helps received by these mothers during pregnancy, including help from their family, the baby's father and from their best friend, revealed that the keeping mothers received help from these three sources to a far greater degree than did the mothers who surrendered. A third of the mothers who kept their children reported receiving help from all three sources, in contrast to only 7% of the surrendering mothers. Conversely, whereas only 13% of the keeping women said they had had no help or else help from only one of these three sources, 36% of the surrendering women reported this to be the case.

Four other differences were found between the two groups of women. Fewer keeping than surrendering mothers reported current feelings of rest-lessness—20% versus 46%. Proportionately more of the women who have decided on keeping their children, as opposed to their counterparts, had considered terminating their pregnancy—78% versus 54%. A nine-item attitudinal index that included a variety of possible reactions to the pregnancy

---

* In Festinger's study, seeking early help was defined as initiating agency contact by the beginning of the fourth month of pregnancy or earlier; the current study defined it as obtaining prenatal care within the first trimester.

**This difference was largely due to the higher proportion of the surrendering mothers who utilized maternity residences during pregnancy. When these users were excluded from the analysis, the difference, while still substantial, was not significant.

revealed that whereas 30% of the keeping women had relatively positive attitudes, this was true of only 7% of the surrendering women. Conversely, slightly more than a third (36%) of the keeping women could be classified as having negative attitudes, in contrast to about two-thirds (64%) of the women who surrendered their children.

The one other difference that distinguished between these groups of women related to their feelings about motherhood and marriage. When the mothers were asked whether they thought it was better to be married or not to be married when having a baby, less than two-thirds (62%) of the keeping mothers but almost all of the surrendering mothers (96%) thought it better to be married.

Summary and Conclusions

Comparisons of the characteristics of recently pregnant unmarried mothers keeping and surrendering their children were made on those items that were found to distinguish between the two groups in earlier reported studies. Consistent with earlier findings, more of the keeping than surrendering mothers were from parental homes broken by divorce or separation, were more often nonstudents, had less education, had sought help earlier, had known the putative father longer and were more likely to have lived with parents or relatives during pregnancy. Additional distinguishing characteristics found among these more recently pregnant women included demographics, behavioral and attitudinal differences as well as differences in the degree of informal support that keeping and surrendering mothers received during their pregnancy.

Women who opt for adoption are now in the minority and indeed, these women may be reflecting the traditional values of previous decades. They were more likely to have grown up in smaller cites and towns, were less likely to have considered the possibility of abortion and were more likely to believe that children should be reared in two-parent homes. Although no differences were found in the religious affiliation of the two groups, women who surrendered their babies were far more likely to be regular churchgoers. This fits with their more conventional views on abortion and the family.

The women who kept their children were more likely to have received support from family and friends during pregnancy. They were also more likely to have maintained contact with the putative father, suggesting that some entertained the prospect of eventual marriage to him or, at least, some financial assistance from him. That the keeping mothers were younger than their counterparts may reflect less cautiousness than would be true for older women, as well as less awareness of the responsibilities entailed in childrearing. Since fewer of them were attending school, they were less likely to have career plans and perhaps viewed the prospect of childrearing as less of a change in life style than it would be considered by the women who chose adoption. In addition, since more of the keeping than surrendering mothers had lived in one-parent homes themselves, they may have been less likely to see a continuation of this one-parent pattern as a handicap for themselves and their child.

Neither social deviancy nor the psychological explanations of previous years adequately explain why some of the pregnant unwed women of this decade decide to keep and others decide to surrender. In today's society a social milieu has evolved that has adapted to changes in points of view regarding marriage and the family. A pregnant unwed woman coming from such a milieu will most likely keep her child. For her it is not psychologically or socially deviant. A pregnant unwed woman exposed to the traditional social milieu that adheres to older conventions is more likely to surrender her child. Similarly, she is a product of her environment, and cannot be regarded as either psychologically or socially deviant.

References

1. Grow, Lucille J. *A New Look at Supply and Demand in Adoption*. New York: Child Welfare League of America, 1970.

2. "The Unwed Mother Who Keeps Her Child," in *The Double Jeopardy— The Triple Crisis: Illegitimacy Today*. New York: National Council of Illegitimacy, 1969.

3. Festinger, Trudy Bradley. "Unwed Mothers and Their Decisions to Keep or Surrender," *Child Welfare*, L,5 (July 1971).

4. Herzog, Elizabeth. "The Chronic Revolution: Births Out of Wedlock," *Clinical Pediatrics*, 5 (1966).

5. Jones, Wyatt C., Meyer, Henry J., and Borgatta, Edgar F. "Social and Psychological Factors in Status Decision of Unmarried Mothers," *Journal of Marriage and the Family*, XXIV (August 1962).

6. Langner, Thomas S., et al. "Psychiatric Impairment in Welfare and Non-Welfare Children," *Welfare in Review*, VII, 2 (March–April 1969).

7. Meyer, Henry J., Borgatta, Edgar F., and Fanshel, David. "Unwed Mothers' Decisions About Their Babies: An Interim Replication Study." *Child Welfare*, XXXVIII, 2 (1959).

8. Meyer, Henry J., Jones, Wyatt, and Borgatta, Edgar F. "The Decision by Unmarried Mothers to Keep or Surrender Their Babies," *Social Work*, 1, 2 (1956).

9. Vincent, Clark. *Unmarried Mothers*. New York: Free Press of Glencoe, 1961.

Developing Case Management as a Practice Model

. . . . .

Maria Roberts-DeGennaro

ithin the past several years, a new concept in social work—case management—has transformed traditional practice into a new and more useful model.[1]

> Good case management implies continuity of services, planfulness (i.e., rational decision-making) in designing and executing a treatment package, coordination among all providers of services, effective involvement of the clients, timeliness in moving clients through the process, and maintenance of an informative and useful case record.[2]

The concept of case management combines the best ideas of direct-service practice with the best ideas of community practice on behalf of a particular at-risk population. Most models of social work practice usually address only one of the traditional intervention methods, that is, casework, group work, or community organization. Case management integrates some aspects of all three traditional methods of social work practice.

Case Management Functions

The functions of case management appear to vary with different programs for particular at-risk populations. For example, Charles Rapp and John Poertner suggest that case management replaces the traditional casework model and emphasizes the role of case managers as professional decision makers in public child welfare.[3] They suggest that the role of the case

Roberts-DeGennaro, M. (1987). Developing case management as a practice model. *Social Casework: The Journal of Contemporary Social Work*, 68, 466–470. Reprinted by permission of Family Service America, publisher.

manager in public child welfare consists of four major functions: *1)* assessment, *2)* service planning, *3)* brokerage, and *4)* community intervention. The balanced service system model of case management for community mental-health centers delineates five case-management functions: *1)* assessment, *2)* planning, *3)* linking, *4)* monitoring, and *5)* advocacy.[4] The Senior Care Action Network's Case Management Model Project developed a model that emphasizes five general functions: *1)* entry (including case finding, prescreening, and intake), *2)* assessment, *3)* case goal setting and service planning, *4)* case-plan implementation, and *5)* review and evaluation of client and program status.[5]

The author and Jack Stumpf developed a case management model that was used in training child-welfare workers in two states.[6] The author has since revised the case-management functions of this model to include the following:

1. A network of formal resources and services, including a network of contracted services that could assist the targeted at-risk population in problem solving and in decision making.

2. Target population access to the goals and resources of the agency in which the case manager works.

3. Assessment of the client's strengths and needs, with an emphasis on strengths rather than on problems.

4. Development of a case plan by using the basic steps in goal planning for and with the client.[7]

5. Client-agency contract and, if appropriate, secondary collateral contract.[8]

6. Design for and with the client an individualized service network and a natural helping network.

7. Implementation of the case plan and mobilization of the client's networks.

8. Monitoring of delivery of services under the case plan and modification of the plan, if necessary.

9. Evaluation with the client whether the agreed-upon activities were effective.

10. Termination of the case, which includes informing the client of the reentry requirements into the system, discussing progress, and making explicit what case closing means to the client.

11. Follow up after termination in order to ensure that no new problems have emerged that require further intervention.

The functions emphasized in this model do not constitute, in and of themselves, a case-management system. A case-management system means that a case manager of a case-management team assumes total responsibility and is accountable for the well-being of the client while avoiding doing for the client that which the client is capable of.[9]

Psychotherapy as a Case-Management Task

The major question in defining case management has been whether psychotherapy should be considered a case-management task. Should the case manager be restricted to coordinating and expediting care delivered by others? Or should he or she also perform therapeutic functions? Some contend that paraprofessionals should perform case-management functions.[10]

In contrast, H. Richard Lamb suggests that case-management functions are part of the normal duties of a conscientious therapist.[11] Only through therapeutic involvement can a case manager acquire the in-depth knowledge of the patient to adequately assess needs and facilitate the processes for meeting them. Lamb believes that persons who perform case-management functions should be referred to as therapist-case managers. He states that the therapist needs to perform case-management functions in order to avoid adding another layer to our bureaucratic service delivery systems. For example, in making and coordinating a referral between treatment and rehabilitation agencies, questions arise in regard to the client's social history and case plan. The therapist-case manager is in a better position to address such issues directly than is a case manager who must refer questions to the therapist and broker the communication between the two agencies. Kermit Wiltse and Linda Remy suggest that it is a misconception to think that the case manager's role is limited to only brokering services or that direct practice is not a feature of case management.[12] Direct practice under a case-management practice model changes substantially. Rather than providing long-term therapy or treatment, short-term, task-centered work is emphasized. Case management, therefore, focuses on helping clients identify and resolve concrete problems in their everyday lives.

Regardless whether case managers should provide long-term therapy or short-term, task centered work, research indicates that, in practice, case managers often perform therapeutic functions. A nationwide survey of 211 case managers in fifteen community-support projects found that 60 percent of the case managers had been trained as therapists.[13] A survey of directors of mental-health centers in Georgia found that 75 percent of the directors expected their case managers to perform psychotherapy.[14]

Systems Approach

Even if the case manager performs therapeutic functions, the emphasis in therapy is on the outer rather than the inner aspects of social problems. In other words, the case manager focuses on the system within which the individual must function, rather than on the individual's inner thought processes. With therapeutic emphasis on changing the social system, clients are viewed as agents of change, not as victims.[15]

Systems theory, that is, the person-in-situation gestalt or configuration, is the conceptual foundation of case-management practice. The case manager must understand the client in the context of his or her interactions or transactions with the external world.[16]

The case manager links the client to the complex service-delivery system and is responsible for ensuring that the client receives appropriate services in a timely fashion.[17] Case management provides a conceptual unity to problem solving, regardless of the nature of the target system, and is a way of thinking about how to proceed, regardless of the level in the system at which one works or the role that one happens to fill.[18]

The typology of systemic problems developed by Ronald Lippitt and colleagues helps one understand the systems approach to case management.[19] In order to maintain viability, a system copes with problems, some of which are internal to the system and others of which are external. Internal problems include distribution of energy, mobilization of energy, and communication within the system. External problems include achieving correspondence between internal and external reality, setting goals and values for action, and developing skills and strategies for action.[20]

The case manager's role is to assist clients by helping them deal with any or all of these system problems. Case managers provide continuity, assist in the coordination of agency contacts, and aid the client in problem solving. The case manager works with the client by linking, coordinating, negotiating, and mediating services. Consequently, the case manager is in touch frequently with service providers in order to ensure that all service linkages are in place and sufficiently secured. As a result, case managers may spend a great deal of their time processing paperwork or communicating with other service providers. They converse endlessly with other service providers in order to ensure that all service linkages are in place and sufficiently secured. They span the boundaries, thereby facilitating delivery of services to the client.[21] Nevertheless, the boundary work that is performed by case managers is crucial and is where social work is, or should be, centered.[22]

Boundary work probably strengthens the case manager's ability to move freely within and across the system. Incorporating the social-system approach into practice, case managers learn how simultaneously to comprehend the system from the micro to the macro levels and to move freely within and across the system in all its complexities.[23] The negotiations and coordination efforts in which the case manager is involved help maintain a check on the degree of correspondence between the needs of the client system and the environmental resources available to meet those needs.

Probably the most complex form of boundary work is performed by case managers in the juvenile justice system. In this system, the case manager must interact with the representatives of other institutions in collecting evidence, preparing court reports, and testifying in court. At the same time, the case manager must have the clinical competency to provide short-term, task-centered treatment.

Case managers must also engage all involved parties in the development of the case plan. Therefore, the formal network of contract agencies, other community resources, and the informal helping network are all involved in the client's case plan. If the client's informal helping network (that is, family, friends, and neighbors) is mobilized, the client will continue to have a source of support after the case is closed. A successful case manager enables clients to control their lives to the fullest extent possible.

A major task in short-term, task-centered treatment is to train the client in techniques that will help him or her modify the environment in order to prevent the future development of maladaptive behavior.[24] Emphasis is on learning and on restructuring the client system, rather than on understanding historical events in the client's life.[25] The client's "ability to gain ego mastery spurs motivation toward greater maturity, as the ego strives toward attainment of enhanced self-reliance and self-approval."[26]

Client Participation

The client's fullest participation is promoted in case-management practice, as is evident in the basic steps that the case manager uses in goal planning.[27] First, the case manager involves the client from the beginning by initiating with the client an assessment of the client's strengths, needs, and situation. No assessment is complete if it does not highlight the strengths that have enabled the client to manage his or her affairs thus far.

The assessment process consists of critical scrutiny of the client's situation in order to understand the nature of the difficulty with increasing detail and accuracy.[28] Successful case-management practice depends, in part, upon the case manager's ability to make an accurate assessment and, in turn, to make appropriate referrals and recommendations.

Second, the case manager and the client select a reasonable, specific, and measurable goal that can be achieved within a short period. Case management should always operate within time limits. Research demonstrates that clients who receive time-limited services show at least as much improvement as clients who receive open-ended services. In addition, most improvement occurs relatively soon after services begin and most courses of service turn out to be relatively brief, regardless of the original plan.[29]

Third, the case manager and the client review the client's strengths, then identify those that might be helpful in achieving the goal.

Fourth, the case manager spells out the tasks necessary to achieve each goal. The case manager and client should select small tasks that will lead to the achievement of the goal.

Finally, the case manager must document, usually in the form of a contract, who will do what and when they will do it. The contract should specify the following: 1) goals based upon the assessment of the client's situation or problem, 2) time limits of the contract terms, 3) actions that the client, case manager, and others will take to realize the stated goal, 4) the individuals who are responsible for carrying out the action, and 5) costs for failing to carry out the actions.[30]

Client participation under a case-management practice model is aimed at improving the quality of social service delivery system decisions. During each step in the decision-making process, questions must be addressed and decisions must be made. For example, when making an assessment, questions are asked in order to make decisions rather than to diagnose the pathology of the individual. Under a case-management model, one must think of decision making as a movement toward achievable goals rather than in terms of pathology and individual treatment. Teaching case managers to organize and document the most pertinent information at the appropriate decision point is an important part of their professional training.[31]

Case Management Training

Social work educators and practitioners need to take a leadership role in preparing social workers to think in case-management terms. Research indicates that social work is the profession most frequently represented in several fields of practice that emphasize case management, including community mental health, public child welfare, and long-term health care.[32]

Linda Kurtz and co-workers concluded from their survey of more than 400 case managers in mental-health and mental-retardation centers in Georgia that social workers and other professionals who have graduate and baccalaureate degrees are expected to occupy case-management positions within mental-health settings.[33] Case management was also found to be the most commonly assigned and most highly emphasized function in mental-health practicums, according to a survey of twenty-nine undergraduate social work programs. More than one-third of the students studying for undergraduate degrees in social work were placed in mental-health settings.[34] Also, public child-welfare workers are becoming case managers. Tools are needed in order to assist them in defining their new case-management role.[35]

To meet case-management responsibilities, the case manager must have extensive training and continuing education in various areas, for example, assessment, clinical skills, management, planning, advocacy, networking, human relations, and so forth. In addition, social workers who assume management positions must supervise and teach case managers. The case-management duties of a supervisor include planning of assignments, delegating work assignments, helping the case manager deal with work-related problems, reviewing the case manager's work, and modifying the specifications of existing or future tasks.[36] However, supervisors generally receive little training in performing these supervisory functions.

The case manager must also have the complete support and backing of his or her agency. The case manager must develop or have access to an existing network of available resources to use on behalf of a client. However, resources are often inadequately supplied, insufficiently comprehensive, or of poor quality. As resources continue to diminish, case managers are faced with serious problems in their attempts to mobilize the client's service network.[37]

Professional responsibility for implementing the case-management practice model requires top-level administrative support in an agency and the involvement of workers who use this model. Substantial commitment from administrators and social workers at all organizational levels is required if a successful case-management model is to be implemented.

Notes

1. Kermit Wiltse and Linda Remy, "Conceptual Statement on Case Management for Family and Children's Services" (Child Welfare Services Grant 426, Arizona State University School of Social Work, Tempe, Ariz., June 1982), p. 1.

2. Anne Cohn and Beverly DeGraaf, "Assessing Case Management in the Child Abuse Field," *Journal of Social Service Research*, 5 (1/2, 1982):29–43.

3. Charles Rapp and John Poertner, "Public Child Welfare in the 1980s: The Role of Case Management," *Perspectives for the Future: Social Work Practice in the 80's,* ed. Kay Dea (Silver Spring, Md.: National Association of Social Workers, 1980), pp. 70–81.

4. Joint Commission on Accreditation of Hospitals, "Principles for Accreditation of Community Mental Health Service Programs" (Chicago: Joint Commission on Accreditation of Hospitals, 1979), p. 19.

5. Jack Stumpf, "Case Management with the Frail Elderly: A Training Manual," vol. 1 and 2 (Long Beach, Calif., Case Management Model, Senior Care Action Network, December 1981).

6. Maria Roberts and Jack Stumpf, "Training Manual on Case Management and Case Monitoring for Child Welfare Workers" (Child Welfare Teaching Grant, 09-CT-68, School of Social Work, San Diego State University, San Diego, Calif., June 1983).

7. Martha Jones and John Biesecker, "Goal Planning in Children and Youth Services" (Child Welfare Grant, 90-C-1444, Millersville State College, Millersville, Pa., 1980).

8. Ibid.; and Theodore Stein, Eileen Gambrill, and Kermit Wiltse, *Children in Foster Homes: Achieving Continuity of Care* (New York: Praeger Special Studies, 1978).

9. Gary Miller, "Case Management: The Essential Service," *Case Management in Mental Health Services,* ed. Charlotte Sanborn (New York: Haworth Press, 1983), pp. 3–16.

10. Murray Levine, "Case Management: Lessons from Earlier Efforts," *Evaluation and Program Planning,* 2 (Summer 1979):235– 243.

11. H. Richard Lamb, "Therapist-Case Managers: More than Brokers of Services," *Hospital and Community Psychiatry,* 31 (November 1980):762–764.

12. Wiltse and Remy, "Conceptual Statement on Case Management," p. 8.

13. Alice Gail Bernstein, "Case Managers: Who Are They and Are They Making Any Difference in Mental Health Service Delivery?" (Ph.D. diss., University of Georgia, Athens, Georgia, 1981).

14. Dennis Bagarozzi and Linda Farris Kurtz, "Administrator's Perspectives on Case Management," *Arete,* 8 (Spring 1983):13–21.

15. Wiltse and Remy, "Conceptual Statement on Case Management," p. 3.

16. Florence Hollis, "The Psychosocial Approach to the Practice of Casework," *Theories of Social Casework,* ed. Robert Roberts and Robert Nee (Chicago: University of Chicago Press, 1970), pp. 35–75.

17. Peter Johnson and Allen Rubin, "Case Management in Mental Health: A Social Work Domain?" *Social Work,* 28 (January-February 1983):49–55.

18. Wiltse and Remy, "Conceptual Statement on Case Management," p. 6.

19. Ronald Lippitt, Jeanne Watson, and Bruce Westley, *Dynamics of Planned Change* (New York: Harcourt Brace, 1958).

20. Gordon Hearn, "General Systems Theory and Social Work," in *Social Work Treatment*, 2nd ed., ed. Francis Turner (New York: Free Press, 1979), p. 346.

21. Walter Deitchman, "How Many Case Managers Does It Take to Screw in a Light Bulb?" *Hospital and Community Psychiatry*, 31 (September–December 1980):788–789.

22. Hearn, "General Systems Theory and Social Work," pp. 350–353.

23. Ralph Anderson and Irl Carner, *Human Behavior in the Social Environment* (Chicago: Aldine, 1978).

24. Wiltse and Remy, "Conceptual Statement on Case Management," p. 9.

25. William Reid, *The Task-Centered System* (New York: Columbia University Press, 1978).

26. Sidney Wasserman, "Ego Psychology," in *Social Work Treatment*, p. 39.

27. Jones and Biesecker, "Goal Planning in Children and Youth Services."

28. Hollis, "The Psychosocial Approach to the Practice of Social Work," p. 51.

29. Reid, *The Task-Centered System*.

30. Jones and Biesecker, "Goal Planning in Children and Youth Services;" and Stein, Gambrill, and Wiltse, *Children in Foster Homes*.

31. Wiltse and Remy, "Conceptual Statement on Case Management," p. 12.

32. Case Management Research Project, "A Comparative Analysis of Twenty-Two Settings Using Case Management Components" (Center for Social Work Research, University of Texas at Austin, Austin, Texas, 1980).

33. Linda Farris Kurtz, Dennis Bagarozzi, and Leonard Pollane, "Case Management in Mental Health," *Health and Social Work*, 9 (Summer 1984):201–211.

34. Allen Rubin and Kathleen Powell, "Mental Health Service Priorities and the BSW: An Exploratory Study of Labor Force Implications" (New York: Council on Social Work Education, 1980).

35. Rapp and Poertner, "Public Child Welfare in the 1980s," pp. 70–71.

36. Michael Austin, *Supervisory Management for the Human Services* (Englewood Cliffs, N.J.: Prentice-Hall, 1981), p. 102; and Ralph Rowbottom, Anthea Hey, and Daniel Billis, *Social Service Departments: Developing Patterns of Work and Organization* (London: Heineman, 1974).

37. Stuart Schwartz, Howard Goldman, and Soshanna Churgin, "Case Management for the Chronic Mentally Ill: Models and Dimensions," *Hospital and Community Psychiatry*, 33 (December 1982):1006–1009.

Continuous Counseling: Case Management with Teenage Parents

. . . . .

Claire Brindis, Richard P. Barth, and Amy B. Loomis

Although a variety of adolescent pregnancy programs have been developed in the United States during the past fifteen years,[1] few have provided the comprehensive services envisioned in the 1978 Adolescent Pregnancy Act (PL 95-626), which created the Office of Adolescent Pregnancy Programs. Most programs provide categorical services for teenage parents, such as school programs and health clinics for pregnant teens, and although these programs are often better than previous services, they fall short of the mandate. The structure of categorical programs makes them less likely to provide the range of services that teenage parents need. Illustrative of these shortcomings are programs that help teenage parents who are already enrolled in school but miss those who dropped out before the pregnancy and programs that endeavor to return new mothers to mainstream schools within a few months after birth but fail to support long-lasting involvement in educational programs.[2]

Comprehensive programs appear more promising but often suffer from service gaps and problems in coordinating services.[3] Effectively marshaling existing resources is the key to provision of services. The importance of case coordination to provision of comprehensive services is recognized in Title XX—the Adolescent Family Life Act (AFLA)—of the Public Health Services Act. The act identifies ten core services that every project must make available to its pregnant and parenting clients, either directly or by referral to a cooperating agency. Most of the forty-six AFLA agencies use case managers to orchestrate services and to demonstrate problem-solving and interpersonal skills that are needed by teenage parents to enlist community resources—especially in the areas of child care, health, housing, education, and employment.

Case-management activities have been described in various social-work settings. In mental health, case management includes activities during all phases of service delivery (from intake through diagnosis), developing treatment plans, managing service delivery and referral, and following up and terminating services with clients who are ready to leave the system.[4] In public child welfare, a good case manager improves the continuity of services, designs and executes a planned treatment package, coordinates diverse providers of services, effectively involves the client, directs clients through the process in a timely way, and maintains an informative and useful case record.[5] Case management in health care involves a sequence of activities including case funding, assessment, case planning, service authorization, monitoring, and reassessment.[6] Case management in teenage parent programs has not previously been described in the professional literature.

Teenage Pregnancy and Parenting Project

The Teenage Pregnancy and Parenting Project (TAPP) has provided services since 1981. Coordinated by the Family Service Agency of San Francisco and the San Francisco Unified School District, TAPP is an interagency comprehensive service-delivery system that employs case managers who are called continuous counselors. The Project offers youth a range of programs; however, all programs include a relationship with a continuous counselor that lasts for up to three years or until the client is nineteen years old. Continuous counselors—a term coined by TAPP because it describes the social worker-client relationship and its longevity better than does the term "case manager"—help clients plan and, as needed, enroll and participate in community-service systems and programs. Continuous counselors are not tied to any particular system of service delivery (for example, the public health system, a hospital, a maternity home, or a school). Rather, the continuous counselor helps clients obtain critical services that he or she needs from existing systems. Programs that serve TAPP clients include schools; social, nutritional, employment, and obstetrical services; public health nursing care; appropriate community services for clients and their families; food supplement programs; a Teen Well Baby Clinic; and infant day care. Continuous counselors follow their clients across programs, systems, and geographic areas. No matter what program or programs clients enroll in, the continuous counselor continues to assist them.

The TAPP program is effective. Compared with national and local norms, TAPP clients have fewer repeat pregnancies (2 percent and 10 percent at one and two years postpartum, respectively, compared with the national average of between 40 percent and 67 percent at two years), stay in school for a longer period after delivery (67 percent enrolled one year after birth compared with 20 percent nationally), and fewer low-birth-weight infants (10.8 percent compared with 14.1 percent for San Francisco teenagers).[7] Two factors were significantly correlated with higher birth- weight rates: school enrollment and contact with case managers. Teenagers who were enrolled in special high schools for pregnant teenagers had dramatically fewer low-birth-weight infants (4.9 percent) than did school dropouts (16.7 percent), even though these clients, who were enrolled in the special Pregnant Minors School, had more risk factors associated with low-birth-weight rates (for example, inadequate prenatal care, younger than eighteen years old, black, and unmarried). The TAPP clients who attended school had more contact with continuous counselors, more group and individual counseling sessions, more nutrition counseling and childbirth education, and more health and parenting classes than did the TAPP clients who did not attend school. (Available data do not attest to the strength and direction of the association among continuous counseling, TAPP direct services, school participation, and low-birth-weight rates.)

The effectiveness of TAPP has prompted California to pass its own version of the Family Life Act to promote the development of comprehensive teenage pregnancy and parenting services on a statewide basis. The Project's apparent success, the new California legislation, and the congruence between the TAPP model and the national legislative mandates suggest the importance of understanding the activities of continuous counselors in comprehensive services to adolescent parents. The present article describes the activities and tasks of continuous counselors, considers contributions and barriers to successful case management, and discusses the continuous counselor's role in implementation of comprehensive teenage-parent programs. Discussion of these issues is informed by the authors' experience with TAPP and questionnaires and interviews that were completed by thirteen continuous counselors. Two staff members who work closely with case managers (an employment counselor and the director of the infant nursery) and three case-management supervisors were also queried about case management; their responses are not included in the statistics reported below, but their ideas contribute to the description of continuous counseling.

Characteristics and Activities of
Continuous Counselors

Most continuous counselors at TAPP are female (62 percent) and nonwhite (77 percent). Staff members typically hold a master's degree; one staff member holds masters' degrees in counseling and rehabilitation. Most staff members (70 percent) had not worked as case managers before their employment at TAPP. On the average, case managers have been employed for twelve months by TAPP (range six months to longer than two years). The modal (77 percent) case-manager contact with clients was one to three hours per client per month, and the length of meeting times ranged from ten minutes to twelve hours per client per month. At the time of the present study, the number of case loads per case manager ranged from thirty-five to forty cases, with intake responsibilities (case loads are now at thirty to thirty-five, with reduced responsibility for intake). Case managers described their major activities as counseling and brokering.

COUNSELING

In addition to one-to-one counseling, case managers engage in group work and family mediation.

One-to-one counseling. One-to-one counseling is used by continuous counselors to help achieve all of their role functions. Meetings with adolescent mothers and fathers often focus on decision making and developing strategies for initiating change. These one-to-one counseling activities are directed at helping clients define their concerns, identify alternative courses of action, choose among their options, plan for ways to achieve chosen outcomes, and maintain their motivation during the inevitable difficulties and detours. These problem-solving activities help build the relationship between the client and the counselor. To maintain their counseling opportunities, continuous counselors also engage teenage clients in less task-oriented conversations and activities, which also contribute to the relationship.

Group counseling. The majority of continuous counselors hold group sessions. These sessions include family group meetings as well as support, education, and problem-solving groups for pregnant teenagers and teenage fathers. Counselors indicate that these groups effectively (1) incorporate support and information, (2) decrease isolation and the clients' sense that only they are experiencing this problem, and (3) enable group members to see a range of available problems, opinions, and options. Groups are not without drawbacks in that they require extensive work to establish and maintain and do not involve all clients equally. Groups are often unsuccessful at addressing difficult client decisions and problems and do not, therefore, significantly reduce the need for one-to-one counseling by continuous counselors.

Family mediation. Research indicates that family participation is important for improving the outcomes of adolescent parenthood.[8] Because the period of pregnancy is tumultuous for the teenager and his or her family, continuous counselors established contact with members of the client's family in 83 percent of cases (range 45 percent to 100 percent). The mother is contacted in 92 percent of the cases and grandmothers, brothers, sisters, and guardians are contacted in approximately 25 percent of the cases. The client's father, stepparent, and aunts may also be included. Case managers reported that family involvement helps the parent come to terms with the pregnancy and helps cement the relationship between the client and continuous counselors by demonstrating the counselor's interest in the total life of the teenager. In cases in which the mother-daughter relationship is unalterably chaotic (approximately 15 percent of cases), continuous counselors help the client establish alternative sources of support and cope with the home situation.

The parents and the case manager often work as a team on mutual goals. Continuous counselors rely, at times, on the parent's help to assure that the client follows through with the referrals and other program components. Parents call on counselors when they feel they need help or are concerned about specific issues regarding their daughter's pregnancy or use of services. Parent involvement also contributes to the monitoring of services. Continuous counselors viewed most parents as attentive to their responsibilities and as effective partners in their efforts to ensure that clients follow through on referrals and continue to use services.

BROKERING

Continuous counselors reported that brokering is their second most significant enterprise. Specific activities include identification of services, case consultation, assisting clients in their efforts to receive concrete services, acting as a liaison with the broader community of social services, outreach to special populations (for example, monolingual Hispanic males and females and school dropouts), ensuring that clients attain services, and following up on service providers to make sure that clients receive appropriate services. Continuous counselors described a variety of other brokering activities, including conducting case conferences that involve various agencies; participating in planning groups; and conducting home, school, and social-agency visits with their clients.

The TAPP staff were asked to estimate the percentages of time they spent providing counseling and brokering services. Their answers ranged from 100 percent to 30 percent, with an average of 63 percent for counseling and 37 percent for brokering. No comparable data are available from other service sectors, but we suspect that case management with teenage parents requires high levels of counseling because of the urgent decisions faced by clients and their limited problem-solving experience and skill.

Counseling and Brokering Interactions

Case managers are challenged daily in their efforts to identify, obtain, and enroll clients in services.[9] When asked to identify services that are difficult to obtain, case managers most often cited child care (77 percent), housing (46 percent), and employment (31 percent). When asked how they responded to these difficulties, 62 percent indicated that they actively pursued services for their clients until they located one. As one case manager stated, "I make lots of calls to people or places who might have information or knowledge of other resources available that I don't know about. That's exactly what makes a good case manager. I search and persist until I find something for my client." Thirty-eight percent of the case managers indicated that they did not involve themselves in locating new service providers, primarily because they felt that they did not have enough time to explore alternatives, particularly when doing so would take time away from other commitments. Counselors reported that case-load size hindered their performance. This complaint echoes the findings of studies of case management in mental-health services and in child-abuse treatment programs that high work loads interfere with the success of case managers and their clients.[10]

The staff were also asked to name the services that their clients are reluctant to accept. Most often mentioned were public health nurses (31 percent), followed by birth-control services (15 percent) and school continuation (15 percent). Family visits, adoption, day care, group counseling, mental-health counseling, and unpaid training programs were also mentioned. Case managers reported that male clients were particularly unlikely to accept one-to-one counseling, medical assistance, and counseling referrals to other agencies.

Without support, assistance, and follow-up, clients often do not pursue beneficial services. Continuous counseling with adolescent parents requires that the counselor be skillful in responding to the client's hesitation and ambivalence; 77 percent of the counselors indicated that they respond to client hesitation about using services by presenting service options as being attractive and obtainable while allowing the client to make the final choice. To achieve this end, 30 percent of the counselors played an assertive role by arranging for the teenager actually to meet the service provider so that services could be explained, assisting in setting up initial appointments so that the client could try out the service, and following up with the client to see whether he or she had tried the service. Several case managers explained that they acted as a mediator between the client and potential service provider. For example, the case manager may have the client meet the public-health nurse in a neutral location, rather than in the person's home. Another strategy that was mentioned was involving parents and partners in exploring the pros and cons of a service option. Patience in the decision-making process was also mentioned as an important factor; many clients accepted the suggested services after much time had elapsed. Overall, respondents reported that helping clients obtain the various services that they need requires persistence and patience.

Many clients' lives are quite transient and challenge case managers to stay informed about the status and whereabouts of their clients. When asked to identify the strategies that they use to achieve this end, the majority said that they rely on a close relationship with clients and effective networking with agencies that provide services to their clients. Case managers maintain either phone or home-visit contact at least twice a month; very high-risk clients are contacted weekly. The case manager also communicates with those service providers who are directly involved with their clients (for example, child-care staff, school personnel, medical staff). When all else fails, home visits and stopping by favorite haunts are common strategies.

The survey asked continuous counselors to list the types of service strategies that they use and how frequently they use them. Table 1 summarizes their responses. The two most commonly used strategies (calling to set up appointments with the client in the office and having the client call to set up an appointment while the continuous counselor is present) reflect case manager efforts to help clients become self-sufficient, thus empowering them to "navigate" the social- and health-service maze. Case managers recognize that although a certain amount of positive modeling or "hand-holding" is necessary (particularly with younger and non-English-speaking clients), the client needs to take some initiative. Thus case managers help clients practice "system-survival" skills so that eventually they are able to transfer these skills to other situations in their lives. The delicate balance that is necessary for achieving an appropriate facilitator role is very much dependent on the interaction between the client and case manager. Thus it is imperative that

TABLE 1.
Case management activities and their occurrence.*

Activity	How frequently used (%)		
	Used with most clients	Used with a few clients	Almost never used
Call to set up appointment with the client in the office	69	31	
Have client call to set up appointment while case manager is present	62	31	7
Home visit or telephoning clients	46		
Visit the service agency with client to ensure that a client attends	39	61	
Check with client's partner or parent to see if task has been completed	39	8	
Have client attend the service with a friend	7	54	39
Follow up with agency to see if client showed up	15		
Case conference at neutral site	15		
Meet client at other community site	15		
Role playing before client performs task	8		
Have client write notes and diaries on paper	8		
Have client notify the case manager after completing the task	8		

* Responses do not add up to 100 percent because respondents only rated activities that they nominated

case managers have a repertoire of strategies that promote their clients' self-reliance.

The use of strategies to help clients follow through on services is common; many clients do not become engaged in the services provided directly or by referral through TAPP and thus need this kind of help. Case managers reported that clients need help to follow through with their plans so that they do not lose their childcare slot or so they return to school. According to case managers, it was particularly difficult to get clients to attend appointments if they had a history of not being "connected."

Case Manager Tasks and Training

Case managers were given a list of twelve tasks and asked to rate how often they had the opportunity to perform the task, how often this occurred as part of their jobs, and whether they were trained to perform this task. Table 2 summarizes their responses. Curiously, many counselors rated "outreach to potential clients" and "providing health education" in the "rare" category. When asked about these responses, case managers indicated that they had too little time and training to perform these tasks. Whereas health education may occur in medical settings, the need and natural opportunity for providing health education to TAPP clients suggest that continuous counselors should engage in this activity more often. Evidence that teenagers' compliance with medical and health regimens (for example, the use of oral contraceptives) is

TABLE 2.

Occurrence and preparation for case managers' major tasks.

Task	Occurrence (%)				Were you trained to perform this task?	
	Rarely	Some-times	Often	Very often	Yes (%)	No (%)
Record keeping			23	77	69	31
Case planning		15	23	62	54	46
Counseling clients individually			62	38	54	46
Information and referral activities		23	38	38	69	31
Follow-up	8	8	46	38	69	31
Attending case conferences	15	31	31	23	54	46
Outreach to service providers		54	23	23	38	62
Counseling clients' families and partners		62	31	7	46	54
Counseling clients in groups	8	38	54		69	31
Attending other meetings		38	54	8	69	31
Outreach to potential clients		54	23	23	38	62
Providing health education	23	38	31	8	31	69

inadequate and that they need substantial coaching underscores the importance of health education.[11]

Case Management with Teenage Fathers

The teenage father is included in the program when feasible. Although staff encourage the father's involvement, many clients do not want their child to be involved with the father even, in some cases, when a current relationship exists between the child's mother and father. On the average, continuous counselors attempted to involve two of every three teenage fathers in the treatment. They reported that their success rate for establishing contact was

35 percent. Individual case managers report a strikingly varied success rate in contacting fathers (range 2 percent to 95 percent). Counselors who did involve fathers generally agreed that "the increased interest on the part of the father enhanced his ability to support and nurture the client." Other staff did not report deleterious results from male involvement but implied that the father's participation is not very important since the female client is engaged in the TAPP system whether or not a relationship has been established with the father.

Staff opinion was split on whether differences exist in case planning for male and female clients: 54 percent indicated that a difference did exist and 46 percent indicated that no difference existed. The staff generally agreed, however, that the initial engagement of fathers must be special. Males were perceived as requiring more 1) outreach because many refuse or do not know how to ask for help; 2) concrete, tangible services specific to their needs (especially employment counseling); and 3) specific information about and ways to become involved in the pregnancy, delivery, and parenting. In spite of these role differences, the majority of male and female case managers reported that they were committed to extending all services to fathers and father figures.

Contributors to Successful
Case Management

A positive relationship facilitates the case manager's collaboration with adolescent parents. Case managers reported that they were able to establish a good relationship with 75 percent of their clients. A good relationship was defined as one with good rapport between client and counselor, empathy, honesty, and mutual trust. Among the factors identified as most important in developing good relationships with clients were 1) formal and informal time spent together over an extended period, 2) the counselor's physical availability to the client so that he or she could join the client when seeking social services or provide the client with concrete services, 3) the client's ability to follow through in obtaining the assistance arranged through TAPP case managers, and 4) the psychological availability of the case manager as evidenced by advocacy and support.

Time availability was reported as the major barrier to establishing good relationships. Spending adequate time with each client was particularly crucial for overcoming clients' suspicion of "helpers." Because many clients can only be reached after work hours, the agency encouraged the use of "comp time" so that work hours were more flexible. Finally, case managers' personal styles also blocked relationships—particularly insufficient perseverance in follow-up with clients who had broken appointments, who could not be reached because they did not have a telephone, or who moved without informing the case manager.

The types of knowledge and skills that were most often mentioned as being important to successful case management can be categorized in the following manner: *1)* counseling and communication skills (69 percent), *2)* knowledge about adolescents and how to deal with them effectively (54 percent), *3)* knowledge about community resources (38 percent), *4)* knowledge about pregnancy, labor, delivery, and birth control (32 percent), and 5) inter- and intraorganizational skills (23 percent). (These figures equal more than 100 percent, because multiple skills were mentioned by staff members.) Other factors that were considered essential for effective case management include *1)* good relationships with other service providers (30 percent), *2)* adequate time to perform all case management tasks (23 percent), and *3)* effective organizational management and positive interpersonal support among co-workers (23 percent). Less frequently mentioned skills include the ability to motivate clients, the ability to teach clients personal financial planning, and the ability to communicate effectively. In addition, adequacy of available services (for example, housing and day care) was a factor in developing good relationships with clients.

PROBLEMS IN CASE MANAGEMENT

The most important problem experienced by the staff was the inadequate amount of time available for completing each of their case-management activities. (Respondents were, however, evenly divided as to whether their case load did or did not permit adequate time for each client.) Counselors expressed a desire to provide more counseling in addition to the multiple services they coordinate. Thus the extensive demands on the counselor to coordinate a myriad of social services often limit the time available for one-to-one counseling. This conflict appears to be greatest for two groups of case managers: *1)* those who have had limited experience as a case manager and thus may rely more on counseling and *2)* those who have more than thirty-five cases. As such, 31 percent of the staff indicated that they had difficulties with time management and that they needed to learn how to balance the amount of time spent on each case and in each activity. An additional 23 percent noted that some of their clients were unable or unwilling to work with them in an appropriate manner.

They saw these clients only during times of crisis and evidently these individuals were not interested in receiving the comprehensive package of services required by the program.

When the staff were asked to identify potential solutions to these problems, the majority (54 percent) expressed interest in reducing the caseload size by adding additional case managers to the staff. Another suggestion was to categorize cases as beginning, ongoing active, and inactive so that counselors could achieve balance in their case load. Although this method was apparently successful in some child-welfare agencies, TAPP tried this approach early in its history and abandoned it. The status of TAPP clients is so mercurial that valid and lasting predictions of the extent of service that a case will require cannot be determined. Another suggestion was to assign staff to work in their areas of interest or expertise. Although effort is made to assign cases by factors such as cultural appropriateness, case assignments are made primarily to balance the current number of clients on staff members' case loads and not to match, for example, counselors who desire to provide more clinical counseling with those clients in great need of counseling. Although matching counselors with clients might make continuous counselors' activities more satisfying and more effective, such an arrangement fails to recognize the developmental changes in the continuous counselor-client relationship. Clients need continuous counselors who have both counseling and brokerage skills, because their problems and the activities needed to resolve these problems vary across time. For example, a client who is thrown out of her house and is suicidal at the beginning of her pregnancy needs crisis counseling and family therapy. As the situation stabilizes, the continuous counselor may act predominantly as the client's broker while arranging for prenatal care and the client's return to an educational program. If the baby's father breaks off their relationship, counseling may again be needed. The client who has a continuous counselor who is capable of and willing to switch between counseling and brokering roles receives optimum service.

Conclusion

The role of case managers in assuring the delivery of comprehensive services to teenage parents has received little attention. The case manager's impact clearly goes beyond an effective, ongoing relationship with a client and family to meet particular needs. In addition to counseling and brokerage, continuous counselors serve as a cost-efficient resource for their communities, ensure that available resources are used effectively, identify service gaps, encourage the development of new services, and avoid service misuse and duplication.

Ensuring that teenage parents receive high-quality and continuous services requires organization, qualified staff, proper information, and a manageable work load. For the case manager to be effective, he or she must have an appropriate case load. Maintaining a balance between counseling and brokering role functions is important to most, but not all, case managers. (Future evaluations should query clients about the relative importance of the counseling and brokering roles.)

Many case managers stated that they felt their academic training had not prepared them for the many roles that they play as case managers. Few respondents, for example, indicated that they were prepared for family meetings or reported the use of role-rehearsal procedures for promoting clients' accomplishment of tasks.[12] In some cases, staff were disquieted by the discrepancy between their image of themselves as clinicians and their case-management roles. Although schools of social work could certainly do more to train case managers in case-management skills, training must compete with graduate students' overwhelming interest in clinical training.[13]

Health education is another skill in which case managers need training. Although social workers are not trained to be health professionals, those who work in maternal and child health settings must become familiar with common health problems of pregnant women and infants, understand their nutritional needs, and be able to suggest strategies for promoting personal health-management skills that contribute to a successful pregnancy outcome. Although most case managers appear familiar with these issues, their confidence, knowledge, and limited time with clients do not allow them to reinforce health-education information. Agencies should recognize that health management is an important skill; additional training in this area may be necessary for counselors.

The uneven response of case managers about their success in contacting fathers is striking. Some continuous counselors contacted almost every father. They were clearly influenced by the existence, ethics, and logic of TAPP's model Fatherhood Project, which enables TAPP to provide services to fathers. Although almost all staff reported that the participation of female clients and their relationships with clients improved as a result of outreach to the male partner, they did not all act on this observation. Continuous counselors who rarely involved fathers may lack skill in outreach or may believe that involving fathers is not an efficient use of their time. A recent evaluation of services to adolescent fathers suggests that father involvement is associated with higher birth weights.[14] Moreover, fathers have a right to be involved with their children, and children have a right to enjoy the benefits of interacting with their fathers.[15] Whatever the reasons, failure to inform fathers of their opportunities and rights means that those rights are not protected. Teenage-parent programs must attempt to involve more fathers in the treatment process.

Many agencies have noted the success of TAPP and are attempting to develop comprehensive service networks. The present study does not isolate the ways in which the roles of continuous counselors contribute to TAPP's success. Comparing the success of case managers who emphasize counseling with those who emphasize brokering would be helpful. Future studies should also measure the activities of case managers with regard to the appropriateness of the resources that are identified to address the adolescent mother's needs.

Notes

1. Lorraine V. Klerman, James F. Jekel, and Catherine S. Chilman, "The Service Needs of Pregnant and Parenting Adolescents," in *Adolescent Sexuality in a Changing American Society: Social and Psychological Perspectives for Human Services Professions*, 2nd ed., ed. Catherine S. Chilman (New York: Wiley-Interscience, 1976).

2. Gail L. Zellman, *The Response of the Schools to Teenage Pregnancy and Parenthood* (Santa Monica, Calif.: Rand Corporation, 1981).

3. Richard A. Weatherley et al., *Patchwork Programs: Comprehensive Services for Pregnant and Parenting Adolescents* (Seattle, Wash.: Center for Social Welfare Research, 1985).

4. Jane Mueller and Michael Hopp, "A Demonstration of the Cost Benefits of Case Management Services for Discharged Mental Patients," *Psychiatric Quar-*

terly, 55 (January 1983):17–24; and Charles A. Rapp and John Poertner, "Public Child Welfare in the 1980s: The Role of Case Management," in *Perspectives for the Future: Social Work Practice in the '80s,* ed. Katherine Dea (Washington, D.C.: National Association of Social Workers, 1983).

5. Anne V. Bertsche and Charles R. Horejsi, "Coordination of Client Services," *Social Work,* 25 (March 1980):94–98; and Marlin Blizinsky and William J. Reid, "Problem Focus and Outcome in Brief Treatment," *Social Work,* 25 (March 1980):89-98.

6. Rosalie A. Kane, "Case Management in Health Care Settings," in *Case Management in Human Service Practice,* ed. Marie Weil and James M. Karls (San Francisco: Jossey-Bass, 1985).

7. Claire Brindis and Carol Korenbrot, "Evaluating the Teenage Pregnancy and Parenting Project" (Unpublished report prepared for the Office of Adolescent Pregnancy Programs, Department of Health and Human Services, San Francisco, Calif., University of California at San Francisco, Institute for Health Policy Studies, 1985).

8. Frank F. Furstenberg, Jr., and Albert G. Crawford, "Family Support," *Family Planning Perspectives,* 10 (November-December 1978):322-336; and William A. Hargreaves et al., "Measuring Case Management Activity," *Journal of Nervous and Mental Disease,* 176 (October 1984):296–300.

9. Andrew Weissman, "Industrial Social Services: Linkage Technology," *Social Casework,* 57 (January 1976):50–54.

10. Joseph Intagliata and Frank Baker, "Factors Affecting the Delivery of Case Management Services to the Chronically Mentally Ill," *Administration in Mental Health,* 11 (Winter 1983):75–91; Peter J. Johnson and D. J. Fried, "Implementing Dilemmas in North Carolina's Willie M. Program," *Child Welfare,* 63 (September– October 1984):419-430; Peter J. Johnson and Allen Rubin, "Case Management in Mental Health: A Social Work Domain?" *Social Work,* 28 (January-February 1983):49–55; and Anne H. Cohn and Beverly DeGraaf, "Assessing Case Management in the Child Abuse-Field," *Journal of Social Service Research,* 5 (Fall–Winter 1982):29–43.

11. Christine A. Bachrach, "Contraceptive Practice Among American Women, 1973-1982," *Family Perspectives,* 16 (November–December 1984):253–259.

12. Ronald H. Rooney and Marsha Wanless, "A Model for Caseload Management Based on Task-Centered Practice," in *Task-Centered Practice with Families and Groups,* ed. Anne E. Fortune (New York: Springer, 1985).

13. Albert Rubin and Peter J. Johnson, "Direct Practice Interests of Entering MSW Students," *Journal of Education for Social Work,* 20 (Spring 1984): 5–16.

14. Richard P. Barth, Mark Claycomb, and Amy Williams, "Services to Adolescent Fathers: Effects on Birthweights of Infants of Adolescent Mothers" (Unpublished paper, School of Social Welfare, University of California at Berkeley, 1985).

15. Michael E. Lamb, "The Role of the Father: An Overview," in *The Role of the Father in Child Development,* ed. Michael E. Lamb (New York: John Wiley, 1976).

Teenage Pregnancy: The Need for Multiple Casework Services

. . . . .

Steven P. Schinke

Teenage pregnancy is a subject of increasing concern in the United States. The news media, federal legislators, and the White House[1] all have expressed alarm over the apparent epidemic of adolescent pregnancy and childbearing. This article recaps the scope of the phenomenon, highlights associated problems, and summarizes past interventive efforts. More important, the article describes a multiple casework services approach to understanding and preventing the serious consequences of this social problem.[2]

Incidence and Prevalence

In contrast to the generally declining United States fertility rates, the number of teenage pregnancies has steadily increased.[3] In 1974, for instance, more than one million teenagers became pregnant.[4] Of these pregnancies, 59 percent resulted in live births, representing one out of every five babies born in this country.[5] Over 27 percent of these pregnancies were terminated by induced abortion;[6] the final 14 percent were reported as miscarriages.[7] Because the prevalence of intercourse among never-married teenagers increases each year,[8] the number of teenage pregnancies will probably continue to grow.

Reprinted by permission from Steven P. Schinke, Teenage pregnancy: The need for multiple casework services, *Social Casework: The Journal of Contemporary Social Work* 59(7), 406-410. Copyright 1978 Family Service America, publishers.

Preparation of this article was supported in part by Grants HD-11095 and HD-02274 from the National Institute of Child Health and Human Development, and by Maternal and Child Health Project No. 913 from the Bureau of Community Health Services, United States Public Health Service, Department of Health, Education, and Welfare.

Associated Problems

Research studies confirm a number of medical risks to teenage mothers and their babies. When compared to mothers aged twenty or older, teenage mothers show increased incidences of severe anemia, pregnancy toxemia, labor complications, and later development of cervical cancer. Their babies show higher mortality rates than those born to older mothers.[9] In addition, children of teenage mothers have a higher risk of congenital defects and mental and physical handicaps, including epilepsy, cerebral palsy, retardation, blindness, and deafness.[10]

Teenage pregnancy is also associated with social and psychological problems. By interrupting or ending formal education, such pregnancies can mean reduced earning power for young parents.[11] One frequent result is dependence on public assistance and the social welfare system.[12] Teenage pregnancy incurs other societal expenses as well; for example, the significantly greater number of neurologically and physically impaired children born to teenagers requires costly professional and institutional services.[13] Further, the stresses of hastily negotiated marriages create psychological problems for young parents, increasing the likelihood of subsequent marital problems and eventual divorce.[14] Finally, children in many adolescent marriages appear to be especially at risk for neglect and abuse.[15]

Past Interventive Efforts

Past interventive efforts with problems of teenage pregnancy have assumed one single underlying cause—the lack of access to health information and family planning services. For this reason, social and health programs over the last ten years have offered sex education and low-cost contraceptives to sexually active teenagers, along with offering comprehensive medical care to pregnant teenagers.[16] Several hospital-based programs using this approach have reported modest successes in reducing some medical risks to teenage mothers and their children; but most of these programs have reported disappointing results.[17] Few teenagers were reached before their first pregnancy, and subsequent pregnancy rates were not reduced significantly. In short, past interventive programs have failed to change the contraceptive behavior of young people and have only slightly improved the prenatal care of participating teenagers already pregnant.

Multiple Casework Services

Creating access to health information and family planning services has not been enough. A multiple casework services approach can better address the social problems raised by teenage pregnancy, childbearing, and parenthood. Such an approach puts attention on three opportunities for social casework; primary prevention, early intervention, and postpartum services.

PRIMARY PREVENTION

Primary prevention is the single most important opportunity for casework services with teenagers at risk for pregnancy. Clearly, the only time social workers or other professionals can help prevent an unwanted teenage pregnancy is before conception. Primary prevention opportunities expand when practitioners move from the single-cause approach to a broad developmental conceptualization of the problem.

Not relying solely on sex education and contraception availability, the developmental approach identifies many factors—situational, social, interpersonal, and maturational—that interact to lead adolescents into unprotected sexual activity. Findings from a recent survey support this approach by suggesting that adolescents risk pregnancy "not by any form of pathology, moral or otherwise, but by a unique convergence of factors which are 'normal' to the lives of many."[18] Adolescence is a period of physical growth demanding mastery of critical developmental tasks, not the least of which is learning responsible sexual behavior. Adolescent-sexuality theorist Nathaniel N. Wagner points out:

> The teenager must adjust to changes in the size and shape of the body with possibilities for different and more mature behavior. The concept of self undergoes rapid change as people begin to respond differently to the individual because of his or her changing physical appearance.[19]

Clearly, adolescents of both sexes must learn the skills for coping with these sometimes bewildering changes.

Casework services in primary prevention should help adolescents learn a repertoire of interpersonal skills necessary for responsible adult roles, including appropriate sexual behavior. One training model, for example, uses small groups to facilitate sharing situations and behaviors group members find difficult or frustrating.[20] Group members acquire new, more adaptive behavioral responses, receiving feedback, coaching, and positive reinforcement from leaders and other members. Typical training includes learning to refuse unreasonable requests, making requests of others, and initiating a variety of interactions with peers, parents, and coworkers. Practice in the groups and actual use of these learned responses give group members alternate ways of dealing with difficult situations and frustrating demands. Empirical findings from research suggest that interpersonal skill training combined with accurate contraception information has great potential in the prevention of unwanted teenage pregnancy.[21]

INTERVENTION

The needs of already pregnant teenagers provide another opportunity for social casework. Unfortunately, one important source of support for these teenagers has been victim to a political and bureaucratic anomaly: Many states do not consider low-income pregnant women eligible for public assistance until after their babies are born.[22] Therefore, Medicaid support for prenatal care and cash payments for maintaining nutritional needs are denied many pregnant teenagers. As a result of such constraints, 60 percent of the mothers under age fifteen receive no prenatal care during the crucial first trimester of pregnancy. In general, teenage mothers are twice as likely as mothers in their early twenties to give birth without prenatal care.[23]

Casework with the pregnant adolescent should begin as soon as a positive result for the pregnancy test is established. Such early action depends on extensive program publicity and on good referral networks. The successes of Zero Population Growth and Planned Parenthood publicity efforts suggest that up-to-date and confidential referral networks can be effective. Professionals, including physicians, family planning counselors, teachers, school nurses, and others likely to encounter adolescents early in pregnancy must have current resource lists of community social services. Parents should also have access to materials describing appropriate community resources, and the adolescents themselves need frequent reminders of social work resources for young parents. Naturally, one key link in the dissemination of such information is the public schools.

Once social work contact is initiated, either through referral or outreach, the pregnant adolescent and her partner should both explore alternatives to carrying the pregnancy to term. The decision to interrupt a pregnancy is a difficult one, usually made after much deliberation. Other options for the couple should also be systematically evaluated. Decisions regarding continued education, marriage, changes in career plans, and custody of the child can benefit from non-judgmental, professional guidance. As suggested by Betty Russell and Sylvia Schild, making such major life decisions may represent an initial exposure to the independence and responsibilities of adulthood.[24] Casework services facilitate this decision-making process when the worker acts concurrently as advocate for the needs of mother, father, and unborn child.

POSTPARTUM SERVICES

Too often casework services for teenage parents end when mother and child leave the delivery hospital. Over 350 programs for pregnant adolescents and school-age parents notwithstanding, an estimated two out of every three teenage mothers are not reached by the educational or maternal-infant programs designed for them.[25] Moreover, teenage parents' needs to continue education, to seek employment, or to enroll in vocational training are frequently thwarted by the expense or lack of adequate daycare facilities for children under the age of two.[26]

Focused outreach activities to teenage parents can ameliorate some of the untoward consequences of early childbearing. One referral procedure for contacting postpartum mothers is self-evident: All teenage mothers should receive at least one social work visit before hospital discharge. As Judith Bemis, Evelyn Diers, and Ruth Sharpe suggest, social workers should then offer concrete services, including making daycare arrangements, finding housing, and seeking vocational training resources.[27] Also, the temporary support of homemaker services should not be overlooked. Another important social work role is serving as the young parents' advocate in dealing with public assistance departments, schools, hospitals, and other bureaucracies.

In addition to mustering community resources, social workers can give direct clinical services to teenage parents. For example, research on training school-age parents in job interviewing documents the positive impact of brief, intense instruction on specific skills and on "hireability" ratings assigned by professional personnel specialists.[28] Given the availability of appropriate instructional materials, social workers and allied professionals can also provide formal and informal training in the fundamentals of child development.[29] Because data show high subsequent pregnancy rates for adolescent mothers,[30] frequent offers of family planning services are imperative. Finally, because marital dysfunction statistics give teenage marriages a poor prognosis, workers must be alert for opportunities to extend individual and dyadic counseling services.

Summary

The scope and associated problems of teenage pregnancy clearly warrant the widespread attention given this social phenomenon. Unfortunately, most past programs dealing with adolescent pregnancy have yielded disappointing results. These failures stem from the inadequacy of a single-cause perspective. Instead, social service needs of this population can best be met along a multiple casework services continuum. This approach finds three opportunities for profitable delivery of casework services: primary prevention, early intervention, and postpartum services. The author's recent experience has shown the success of focused, direct intervention among teenage parents and teenage parents-to-be.

Notes

1. See, for example, Melvin J. Konner, "Adolescent Pregnancy," *New York Times,* 24 September 1977, p. 21; Tony Schwartz, Mary Lord, and Ald C. Lubenow, "Pregnant Teens," *Newsweek,* 30 May 1977, pp. 54–57; Edward M. Kennedy, "Introduction to S. 2538; The National School-Age Mother and Child Health Act of 1975," *Congressional Record,* 94th Cong., 1st Session, 21 October 1975, pp. 1–4; and "Abortion Alternatives are Weighed by HEW Secretary Califano," *Wall Street Journal,* 2 September 1977, p. 1.

2. Preparation of this article was supported in part by Grants HD-11095 and HD-02274 from the National Institute of Child Health and Human Development, and by Maternal and Child Health Project No. 913 from the Bureau of Community Health Services, United States Public Health Service, Department of Health, Education and Welfare.

3. U.S. Department of Health, Education, and Welfare, National Center for Health Statistics, "Teenage Childbearing: United States, 1966–75," *Monthly Vital Statistics Report 26* (September 1977):1–15.

4. The Alan Guttmacher Institute, *Eleven Million Teenagers: What Can Be Done About the Epidemic of Adolescent Pregnancies in the United States* (New York: Planned Parenthood Federation of America, 1976), p. 10.

5. U.S. Department of Health, Education, and Welfare, National Center for Health Statistics, *Vital Statistics of the United States,* 1974 (Washington, D.C.: U.S. Government Printing Office, 1976).

6. U.S. Department of Health, Education, and Welfare, Center for Disease Control, *Abortion Surveillance,* 1974 (Atlanta: U.S. Department of Health, Education, and Welfare, 1976).

7. The Guttmacher Institute, *Eleven Million Teenagers: What Can Be Done,* p. 10.

8. Melvin Zelnick and John F. Kantner, "Sexual and Contraceptive Experience of Young Unmarried Women in the United States, 1976 and 1971," *Family Planning Perspectives,* 9 (March/April 1977):55–71.

9. William Burr Hunt, II, "Adolescent Fertility: Risks and Consequences," *Population Reports,* Series J (July 1976):157–175; and U.S. Department of Health, Education, and Welfare, "Teenage Childbearing: United States, 1966–75," pp. 7–8.

10. Jane A. Menken, "The Health and Demographic Consequences of Adolescent Pregnancy and Childbearing." Paper presented at the Conference on the Consequences of Adolescent Pregnancy and Childbearing, Center for Population Research, National Institute of Child Health and Human Development, Bethesda, Maryland, 19–30 October 1975.

11. Kristin A. Moore and Linda J. Waite, "Early Childbearing and Educational Attainment," *Family Planning Perspectives,* 9 (September/October 1977): 220–225; U.S. Department of Health, Education, and Welfare, "Teenage Childbearing: United States, 1966–75," p. 7; and T. James Trussell, "Economic Consequences of Teenage Childbearing," *Family Planning Perspectives,* 8 (July/August 1976):184–190.

12. Kristen A. Moore and Steven B. Caldwell, "The Effect of Government Policies on Out-of-Wedlock Sex and Pregnancy," *Family Planning Perspectives,* 9 (July/August 1977):164–169.

13. Kennedy, "Introduction to S. 2538: The National School-Age Mother Act," p. 2.

14. Frank F. Furstenberg, Jr., *Unplanned Parenthood: The Social Consequences of Teenage Childbearing* (New York: The Free Press, 1976), pp. 81–98.

15. Kennedy, "Introduction to S. 2538: The National School-Age Mother Act," p. 2.

16. Frank F. Furstenberg, Jr., "Preventing Unwanted Pregnancies Among Adolescents," *Journal of Health and Social Behavior,* 12 (December 1971): 340–347; and Philip M. Sarrel and Ruth W. Lidz, "Psychosocial Factors: The Unwed," in *Manual of Family Planning and Contraceptive Practice,* 2d ed., ed. Mary S. Calderone (Baltimore: Williams and Wilkins, 1970), pp. 249–264.

17. Frank F. Furstenberg, Jr., G.S. Masnick, and Susan A. Ricketts, "How Can Family Planning Programs Delay Repeat Teenage Pregnancies?" *Family Planning Perspectives,* 4 (July 1972):54–60; and James F. Jekel et al., "A Comparison of the Health of Index and Subsequent Babies Born to School Age Mothers," *American Journal of Public Health,* 65 (April 1975):370–374.

18. George Cvetkovich and Barbara Grote, "Psychosocial Development and the Social Problem of Teenage Illegitimacy." Paper presented at the Conference on Determinants of Adolescent Pregnancy and Childbearing, Center for

Population Research, National Institute of Child Health and Human Development, Elkridge, Maryland, 3–5 May 1976.

19. Nathaniel N. Wagner, "Adolescent Sexual Behavior," in *Adolescents: Readings in Behavior and Development,* ed. Ellis Evans (Hinsdale, Ill.: The Dryden Press, 1970), pp. 44–52.

20. Steven P. Schinke and Lewayne D. Gilchrist, "Adolescent Pregnancy: An Interpersonal Skill Training Approach to Prevention," *Social Work in Health Care,* 3 (Winter 1977): 159–167; and Steven P. Schinke and Sheldon D. Rose, "Interpersonal Skill Training in Groups," *Journal of Counseling Psychology,* 23 (September 1976):442–448.

21. Schinke and Rose, "Interpersonal Skill Training in Groups," pp. 442–448; and Steven P. Schinke and Sheldon D. Rose, "Assertive Training in Groups," in *Group Therapy: A Behavioral Approach,* ed. Sheldon D. Rose (Englewood Cliffs, N.J.: Prentice-Hall, 1977), pp. 182–201.

22. U.S. Department of Health, Education, and Welfare, Social and Rehabilitation Service, Assistance Payments Administration, "State Plan Provisions with Respect to AFDC Payments to an Expectant Mother in Behalf of Her Unborn Child, as of January, 1976." Unpublished report.

23. U.S. Department of Health, Education, and Welfare, "Teenage Childbearing: United States, 1966–75," p. 14.

24. Betty Russell and Sylvia Schild, "Pregnancy Counseling with College Women," *Social Casework,* 57 (May 1976): 324–329.

25. Shirley A. Nelson, personal communication cited in Frank F. Furstenberg, Jr., "The Social Consequences of Teenage Parenthood," *Family Planning Perspectives,* 8 (July/August 1976):148–164.

26. W.L. Pierce, "Child Care Arrangements in the United States in 1974." Testimony before the Subcommittee on Employment, Poverty, and Migratory Labor of the Senate Committee on Labor and Public Welfare and the Subcommittee on Select Education of the House Committee on Education and Labor, Joint Hearings on the Child and Family Services Act, 1975, 94th Cong., 1st Session, 21 February 1975.

27. Judith Bemis, Evelyn Diers, and Ruth Sharpe, "The Teen-Age Single Mother," *Child Welfare,* 55 (May 1976): 309–318.

28. Steven P. Schinke, Lewayne D. Gilchrist, and Thomas E. Smith, "Employment Application Skills of Teenage Mothers: Need Assessment and Training." Paper presented at the Second National Conference on Need Assessment in Health and Human Services, University of Louisville, Louisville, Kentucky, 28–31 March 1978.

29. See, for example, Grace C. Cooper, *Guide to Teaching Early Child Development: A Comprehensive Curriculum* (New York: Child Welfare League of America, 1975).

30. James F. Jekel, Lorraine V. Klerman, and Diccon R.E. Bancroft, "Factors Associated with Rapid Subsequent Pregnancies Among School-Age Mothers," *American Journal of Public Health,* 63 (September 1973): 769–773.

Child Maltreatment Risk among Adolescent Mothers: A Study of Reported Cases

. . . . .

F. G. Bolton, Jr., Roy H. Laner, and Sandra P. Kane

T he explosion of "official recording" that has characterized social services, medical, and law enforcement agencies in the decades of the 1960s and 1970s has provided researcher and citizen alike with an increasing volume of information about the various categories of domestic violence. The accuracy of these data has come under critical scrutiny of late[25] and has been referred to as "bureaucratic propaganda."[1] A critical issue within this "propaganda" system is the protectiveness among agencies with respect to their records. For example, as these record systems have developed, the child maltreatment record system "belongs" to the social services system through child protective services, the interspousal abuse record system belongs to the law enforcement agencies, and the adolescent pregnancy record system rests securely within the medical setting. This protectiveness and record keeping compartmentalization not only affects the treatment systems, but impairs the researcher's understanding of the relationship among these various elements of the domestic violence continuum. The objective of this study is a very tentative breaking down of these "official record" barriers through a coterminous examination of the officially reported cases to two elements of domestic violence: child maltreatment and adolescent pregnancy. More specifically, the research question guiding this work is: What is the officially reported incidence of child maltreatment when comparing two groups of mothers—

Copyright 1980 by the American Orthopsychiatric Association, Inc. Reproduced by permission. Research was supported by the Arizona Department of Economic Security and by Grant 90-1708(02) from the National Center on Child Abuse and Neglect, Children's Bureau, Office of Child Development, HEW.

women who were adolescent mothers and women who became mothers following adolescence?

Official reports of both adolescent pregnancy and child maltreatment have increased sharply during the past two decades. In the relatively recent period since the identification of the "battered child syndrome,"[14] demonstrable and rapid increases in the official reporting of child maltreatment incidence rates have been made known. Gil,[8] Light,[15] and Jenkins et al[12] have utilized nationwide central registry data and recent National Center on Child Abuse and Neglect reports to chart a pattern of increases that range from 9563 reports of physical abuse in Gil's 1967 study[8] to the current estimate of over one million children each year being subjected to all forms of maltreatment.[12] The most authoritative nonofficial survey data extrapolates from 1975 survey results to report that between 5.4 and 8.1 million children between the ages of three and 17 have been kicked, bitten, or punched; beaten-up; or had a parent use a knife or gun on them at some time in their lives.[25] Obviously, these maltreating events are not all independent; however, this unofficial report serves to point out the underestimations that characterize the official reporting of maltreatment.

Although the onset of investigation of adolescent pregnancies as an element of domestic violence has been a more recent occurrence, the official recording of this problem area suffers from "official" inadequacies similar to that of the child maltreatment recording system. In essence, the adolescent pregnancy recording system does not track adolescent pregnancy as much as it records adolescent birth and known adolescent abortion rates. Entry in this record system ordinarily implies the birth of a child or the obtaining of a legal abortion. Adolescent pregnancies that were terminated spontaneously or illegally rarely enter the data set. Despite this built-in underestimate, the rate of officially reported incidence has shown an increase similar to that of the child maltreatment rates for the past two decades.

Baldwin's[2] historical examination revealed an approximately constant rate of adolescent pregnancy between 1920 and 1945, followed by a sudden increase after World War II. This was an increasing rate that did not peak until 1960. Despite this, and despite the subsequent decline in birth rates to older adolescents, the increase in births to adolescents under the age of 17 has maintained a growth pattern.[3] The magnitude of this problem was dramatically illustrated by the Guttmacher Institute's 1976 estimate that one in ten adolescent women became pregnant each year.[16] This is a rate that translates into more than one million pregnancies and over 600,000 births to adolescents each year, and is a problem that is most severe in the school-age adolescent between 14 and 16 years old. More recently, adolescent pregnancy researchers at Johns Hopkins University determined that 35% of today's adolescent females will experience at least one pregnancy prior to their twentieth birthday.[26] It is not only the officially reported rates of growth for these problems that demonstrate a similarity, but the demographic and dynamic factors associated with each problem as well.

The demographic view of the child maltreatment situation has been described by a set of variables that may be easily seen as containing the potential to introduce stress and crisis into the parent-child relationship. Most indicative, perhaps, of the potential stress in these families is the over-representation of lower socioeconomic status families within officially reported maltreatment situations.[8] This is a factor supported in self-reports of child maltreatment.[25] In many parent-child relationships thought to contain a high risk for maltreatment, the risk may be exacerbated not only by the reduced level of financial security, but by the accompanying social stresses of parents' youth,[23] unemployment,[11] underemployment,[25] and limited communication between the adult members of the family.[10] The inability to resolve conflict and crisis, sometimes referred to as "relationship stress,"[25] may contribute to the disproportionately large numbers of single-parent female-headed households within the population of officially reported high risk parent-child relationships.[11]

Uncannily similar demographic findings are reported in the literature on adolescent pregnancy and parenting. The overrepresentation of youngsters from poor families within this population has been widely reported.[4,13,21,22] The additional realities of reduced educational level[7,19] and reduced capacity for satisfactory employment[20] within the pregnant and parenting adolescent group undoubtedly serve to maintain the daily logistical stresses and potential for crisis that characterize the high risk parent-child relationship. As within the officially reported maltreating population, relationship stresses and marital dysfunction abound in the adolescent parent population.

Marriage, as a means to legitimize the adolescent pregnancy, is viewed largely as a white middle-class option.[4] The lower-class adolescent female, in particular, seems more frequently to opt for single parenthood. This selection of single parenthood may serve as the impetus for the high rates of female-headed households, educational termination, and welfare dependency that is characteristic of the official reports of the adolescent pregnancy/parenting groups.[7] Dysfunction continues to follow even those adolescents who do select the marital option, as official statistics show that nearly 60% of these adolescent marriages are dissolved within a five-year period.[18] This rate of marital dissolution may serve as an additional contribution to the stresses impinging upon the adolescent parent-child relationship.

Those researchers[11,25] concerned with the effects of social factors on domestic violence provide the appropriate caution that the demographic variables associated with the high risk maltreatment population may be largely a function of inclusion in the low-income environment from which the official data are drawn. The argument must be noted in the interpretation of these data; however, the demographic similarities between the officially reported maltreating parent and the officially reported adolescent parent are too great to ignore. It is possible that an examination of the dynamic variables associated with these elements of domestic dysfunction can be of value in reaching a clearer understanding of the similarities and differences between these two groups.

Retrospective views of the lives of the maltreating parent[5] describe participation in a dysfunctional parent-child relationship that was often characterized by deprivation, rejection or the observation of violent behavior.[25] This childhood environment is thought to generate unresolved dependency needs[5,24] that may lead to an aberrant overdependence upon a child. The unresolved needs of the parent may lead to unrealistic expectations of the child which, when combined with ignorance of child care techniques, lack of knowledge of child development, and low frustration tolerance, can result in maltreatment of the child by either parent.[6,10]

It is further reported that, ultimately, the parent's isolation from peer group and social support systems combines with the individual's low self-esteem[3,7,10] to create a perception of the child as either the source or the solution of the parent's problems.[17] Either of these polarized perceptions of the parent-child relationship places this relationship at high risk for dysfunction.

Following a summary view of the literature in both areas, it is curious to note that, despite the available indications of similarities between demographic and dynamic variables associated with the problem areas of adolescent pregnancy and child maltreatment, all but a few writers in the domestic violence literature[6] appear to have considered these problems to be independent.

It is the intent of the present study to seek some evidence of complementary demographic and dynamic variables in official reports of these two groups. Although no statement regarding the veracity of the reported variables can be offered, due to the potential bias in official reporting, it is hoped that some measure of the need for further study may be reached. Additionally, it is the intent of this study to examine the cross-contributions of the adolescent parenting group to the incidence of the maltreating group within official records.

Method

The primary research question was: Is there a higher incidenceof maltreatment of natural children by adolescent mothers than by older mothers?

SAMPLE AND PROCEDURE

A sample of one-half of the child maltreatment cases referred to the Maricopa County unit of the Arizona Department of Economic Security's Child Protective Services between January 1, 1976, and December 31, 1978 was drawn from the Arizona Central Child Maltreatment Registry. This large (5098 cases) sample ensures a representative number of child maltreatment incidents, and allows some generalization to the target population of a largely urban and white-dominated county. The county sample was taken from an alphabetical file, by family name of the adult as reported on the National Clearinghouse on Child Abuse (NCCNA) Central Registry Form, where the data from every other Maricopa County incident was recorded on a computer coding sheet, and subsequently entered on a computer tape. The resulting sample of 5098 cases included 247 (4.9%) cases with incomplete information.

The working sample of 4851 was based on cases that included complete information on mother's and oldest child's age. Therefore, cases with other missing variable information were included in the working sample whenever different variables were being analyzed.

The plan for the ex post facto study was to examine the child maltreatment incidence by adolescent and adult mothers. Additionally, some record of the demographic and dynamic variables associated with these reports of maltreatment was to be gathered as an introduction to the potential for study of the relationship between these two types of variables and the possibility of interdependence in child maltreatment and adolescent parenting. Only the variables of interest to this study were recorded from the NCCNA form.

Following the entry of the data on computer tape, the Statistical Package for the Social Sciences was used to produce the frequency and cross-tabulation procedures. This large and comprehensive sample eliminated the need to statistically seek population estimates, since any differences recorded could be assumed to be real. Although the assumption of real differences was tested periodically throughout the data with the Davies Test of Proportionate Differences, the data are presented in this paper without statistical treatment by, for example, F-tests and chi-squares. Instead, percents and rankings are appropriately utilized to describe the population of interest.

DEFINITIONS OF CRUCIAL ELEMENTS

Incidence of child maltreatment. Occurs when a Child Protective Services worker initiates an NCCNA State Central Registry Form in response to a referral. The incidence includes all possible case statuses, whether substantiated or not.

Adolescent mothers. Includes all women giving birth to children prior to their twentieth birthday, and who are enumerated in an officially reported incidence of child maltreatment, regardless of their age at the time of the report.

Demographic variables. Includes subjects' age, sex, ethnicity, marital status, relationship to victim, role in the incident, case status, and income information, as reported by the individual Child Protective Service worker who conducted the intake and investigation phase of referral management.

Dynamic variables. Includes one or more of the 20 possible factors indicated upon the NCCNA Registry Form. These factors, categorized loosely as family environmental/social, and parental capacity variables, are reported by the individual Child Protective Services worker.

Findings

RATES OF CHILD MALTREATMENT

Adolescent mothers. Within the child maltreatment literature, the most frequent reference to adolescent mothers is to those mothers who bear children during their adolescence and also participate in a maltreating event directed toward that child prior to their twentieth birthday. If viewed solely from this perspective, a portion of the maltreatment occurring between mother and victim born during the mother's adolescence is lost.

The present study found 6.4% of the officially reported maltreatment to include a mother who both gave birth to a child and then was involved in abusing that child prior to her twentieth birthday, thereby fulfilling the traditional definition of maltreating adolescent mother. It is our assumption, however, that a fuller measure of child maltreatment can be found by tracing the pattern of the parent-child relationship across the full range of ages for all children who were born during their parents' adolescence.

Utilizing this expanded definition for adolescent mothers, it was found that a disproportionately high number of officially reported child maltreatment situations involved a mother who was an adolescent (*i.e.*, under 20 years of age) at the birth of at least one of her children. More than one-third (36.5%, or 1773 of 4851) of the total number of officially reported cases studied involved a mother who was, or had been, an adolescent at the birth of at least one of her children. (A cursory reading of the case description included on the form indicated that the substantiation/unsubstantiation decision did not appear to follow an immediately discernible logic or pattern. As such, the status decision seems to have been very subjective and potentially unreliable.)

Until a greater volume of comparison data becomes available (*e.g.*, percent of mothers across the county who gave birth to at least one of their children during their adolescence) any comparison measure for these data is absent. In short, the statistical significance of this one-third participation in the officially reported child maltreatment data for adolescent mothers must stand alone and be accepted at face validity. While we must not overinterpret these findings, neither should we overlook the significance of having found a single variable that is shared by more than one-third of the officially reported maltreatment events.

Child victims. Within that portion of the officially reported cases involving mothers who had been adolescents at the birth of at least one of their children, it appears that the child born during the mother's adolescence is at a modestly increased risk for maltreatment as compared to the children born later in the mother's life.

Within the sample of reported cases involving mothers who bore one of their children during adolescence, 85% of the offspring of an adolescent pregnancy were reported as having been victimized. These children accounted for 61.7% of all reported victims within these cases. The remaining 38.3% of victimized children were siblings of the adolescent-birth children or were other than a consanguineous relation; they represented 72% of all children born to these mothers later than adolescence.

The assumption of greater risk within the group of children born during their mother's adolescence demands caution, in that this factor may be indicative of little more than a high rate of single-child families (thus, being the only available victim) or some other shared factor (*e.g.*, the increased victimization of the oldest child).

Although tenuous, some confirmation of the risk faced by the child born during the mother's adolescence may be suggested by the finding that the mean age of maternal perpetrators within the sample of officially reported cases involving a mother who bore at least one of her children during adolescence was 25.1 years of age. The accompanying mean age of the natural child victim within this adolescent birth sample was 6.2 years of age. At the risk of "stretching" the data inappropriately, this finding may suggest that the "average" maternal perpetrator who had borne a child during her adolescence had subsequently victimized a child whose "average" age would place that child as having been born during the mother's adolescence.

Demographics

Race. As the data in Table 1 illustrate, the nonwhite maternal population of the county from which these official reports were drawn contributes a disproportionate share of all births when compared to the birthrate for the white population of that same county. The contribution made to officially reported levels of child maltreatment by mothers of nonwhite racial groups was not as dramatic as those differences reported in the birthrate; however, Table 2 data confirm the notion that minority group members are likely to be overrepresented in the official reporting of child maltreatment and adolescent pregnancy/parenting.

TABLE 1

Percent of mothers and births to mothers aged 15 to 39, by race (Maricopa County, Ariz., 1976–1978)

Race	All mothers		Adolescent mothers	
	Mothers	**Births**	**Mothers**	**Births**
White	95.6%	72.6%	93.3%	61.2%
Nonwhite	4.4	27.4	6.7	38.8
	100.0%	**100.0%**	**100.0%**	**100.0%**

TABLE 2

Percent of reported child maltreatment situations involving children born to adolescents and to adults, by race

Race	Adolescent mothers (*N*=1773)	Adult mothers (*N*=3078)	% County population
White	69.9%	77.5%	80.6%
Black	8.0	4.9	3.1
Hispanic	19.0	13.6	14.5
Native American	2.7	2.5	1.1
Asian	1.0	0.7	0.6
	100.0%	**100.0%**	**100.0%**

The data in Table 2 also indicate a differential contribution to the officially reported maltreatment rates that appears to relate to adolescent birth. That is, for all reported families who had not experienced an adolescent birth, the proportionate contribution by race approximates the distribution of these racial groups across the county. On the other hand, when the variable of adolescent birth is introduced independently, the contribution made to the officially reported maltreatment incidence by minority populations increases beyond their representation within the general population of the county. While the desire to draw directed inferences regarding the relationship among child maltreatment, adolescent pregnancy, and minority group participation is strong after viewing these data, any statement at this basic point of study would be tenuous. Further investigation is demanded in this and related areas, such as socioeconomic status.

Income. The entire sample of officially reported maltreating families was found to be living below the county's median annual income ($15,344). An examination of the absolute income figures for the adolescent and the adult parent groups found families who had experienced an adolescent birth to be existing on a mean annual income of $6608. That portion of the sample that had not experienced an adolescent birth was living on a larger mean annual income of $8181. Thus, while all families within the sample were experiencing a relative deprivation of financial resources, that group which had reportedly experienced an adolescent birth appeared to be more intensely affected financially.

While there may be a tendency to seek to confirm the reduced educational levels, underemployment, and welfare dependency posited for the adolescent pregnancy group, those assumptions exceed the power of these data. More simply, each of those secondary elements of reduced income (*e.g.,* welfare dependency) must be examined independently. Clear warnings against the drawing of conclusions from these income data present themselves in other sectors as well. It is mandatory that the researcher be sensitive to the increased likelihood for being reported in official records of some nature simply through inclusion in a lower socioeconomic status group. In addition, remembering that this group of reportedly maltreating families includes those 6.4% of adolescent mothers who both gave birth and perpetrated the maltreating act prior to their twentieth birthday, and is a group whose income is likely to be markedly inadequate, it is evident that the income levels of the adolescent birth group *must* be lower than those of the adult birth group. It is further possible that the higher minority group incidence within the adolescent birth group may contribute to the lower

TABLE 3

Mean annual income by race of perpetrators of substantiated child maltreatment cases

Race	Adolescent pregnancy	Adult pregnancy
White	$7224	$8926
Black	5293	6023
Hispanic	5416	6250

socioeconomic status participation. Table 3 offers some statement to these caveats.

As was predicted from the earlier review of demographic variables associated with the two social problems under study here, not only is the group of parents who had reportedly experienced an adolescent birth living at a reduced income, the added variable of minority group membership appears to reduce this financial support even more. Again, given the higher incidence of minority group membership across the adolescent birth group reported within this sample, the adolescent birth group not only shares the pressures of reduced income with the reportedly maltreating group generally, but may well feel even greater financial strain due to the undefined interaction between minority group membership and lower socioeconomic status.

Within that group of families who were officially reported as having engaged in a maltreating act that was substantiated, the variables of financial status, adolescent birth experience, and minority group participation continue to interact, as Table 4 illustrates. As can be seen from these data, while there is a greater proportion of Hispanic families living at or below the poverty level than either the black or white group, the introduction of adolescent pregnancy as a variable appears to have the smallest impact upon this group. The introduction of a reported adolescent birth experience seems to have a marked impact upon leading the black and white groups further into poverty. There are two suggestions for this effect that merit ongoing study: *1)* Within this officially reported sample of maltreating families at least, the level of Hispanic families already living at or below the poverty level is sufficiently high to prevent major increases in this rate through the addition of related social variables. *2)* The black family within the reportedly substantiated maltreatment group seems to be that family most harmed when the factor of an adolescent birth experience compounds an already low income level. Ultimately, the entire sample of families whose maltreatment report was officially substantiated was pressed by poverty, as evidenced by these families' enrollment rates in public assistance and income supplement programs.

TABLE 4
Families involved in substantiated child maltreatment cases living at or below the poverty level, by race

Race	Adolescent pregnancy	Adult pregnancy
White	55.0%	42.7%
Black	73.2	56.0
Hispanic	73.7	67.7

Some 40% of families were *1)* involved in substantiated child maltreatment cases, *2)* involved in an adolescent birth during their parenting career, and *3)* receiving public assistance of some nature. This rate is not markedly different from the 34% of families reportedly involved in substantiated child maltreatment who had not experienced an adolescent birth.

Keeping in mind that officially substantiated cases constituted approximately 40% of the total sample and may not be representative of all families studied, the variable minority group membership appears related to the likelihood of receiving public assistance. Among those who had experienced an adolescent birth, the 23% of nonwhites accounted for 46.9% of the public assistance received. This was a somewhat larger proportion than within the adult birth group, among whom the 26.1% nonwhite segment of the sample accounted for 37.9% of the public assistance received. Once again, the variable of adolescent birth appears to introduce some increased financial stress, and this stress is felt most intensely by minority group members. In summary, there are strong indications that there is a continuous interaction among race, socioeconomic status, and adolescent birth.

Marital status. Child maltreatment and adolescent pregnancy literature both posit an increased rate of marital disruption. Tables 5 and 6 demonstrate a relatively high rate of marital disruption and single parenthood among both the group that had experienced an adolescent birth and the group that had not. The overall rate of unmarried persons within both the adolescent and adult pregnancy groups exceeds that of the county from which these data were drawn. Examination of these two tables also confirms that it is not only more likely for a white member of either group to be married, it is also more likely for a minority member of the adult group to be married than a minority member of the adolescent group. These findings are consistent with research reports cited previously. It remains possible that the high rate of divorce that characterizes the reported child maltreatment group has not fully affected the adolescent birth group within this sample at this time as a result of the young mean age of those subjects. This high rate of divorce, however, would seem to be offset by the 6.4% of mothers under the age of 20 who would be predicted to be higher in the "never married" category. This variance may suggest a difference in the dynamics of these two groups, as will be explored in the following section.

TABLE 5

Race and marital status of adolescent mothers involved in child maltreatment cases

Marital status	White	Nonwhite
Married	53.0%	38.0%
Unmarried	47.0	62.0
	100.0%	100.0%

TABLE 6

Race and marital status of adult mothers involved in child maltreatment cases

Marital status	White	Nonwhite
Married	62.0%	46.0%
Unmarried	38.0	54.0
	100.0%	100.0%

DYNAMICS

Table 7 presents 20 factors that could represent a significant problem within the life of the substantiated child maltreater, as reported by the Child Protective Services worker. The data describe how these dynamic factors were perceived to be interacting within the lives of this sample of child maltreating families, by use of both percent and rank for each factor. (Note that more than one of the 20 factors could have been chosen by the worker in any substantiated incident.) As had been anticipated, there were no major differences found between the adolescent and adult pregnancy groups. In fact, the same set of five factors—*broken family, family discord, insufficient income, continuous child care responsibility, and lack of tolerance*

TABLE 7

Percent and rank of dynamic variables in the lives of adolescent pregnancy and adult pregnancy child maltreatment cases

Factor	Adolescent pregnancy		Adult pregnancy	
	Incidence	Rank	Incidence	Rank
Family Factors				
Broken family	11.9%	1	11.2%	1
Family discord	8.7	4	10.8	2
Insufficient income/misuse of adequate income	11.2	2	9.0	3
New baby in home/pregnancy	5.5	7[a]	2.9	16
Heavy continuous child care responsibility	10.5	3	8.4	4
Physical abuse of spouse/fighting	3.0	13	3.0	12[a]
Parental history of abuse as a child	3.8	12	3.0	12[a]
Environmental/Social Factors				
Recent relocation	5.6	6	4.6	9
Inadequate housing	4.8	11	4.0	11
Social isolation	5.5	7[a]	6.4	7
Parental Capacity Factors				
Loss of control during discipline	5.0	9[a]	5.6	8
Lack of tolerance of child's disobedience/provocation	6.7	5	7.8	5
Incapacity due to physical handicap/chronic illness	0.8	19	1.7	18
Alcohol dependence	2.8	14	4.4	10
Drug dependence	1.7	18	1.1	19
Mental retardation	0.5	20	1.0	20
Mental health problem	5.0	9[a]	6.9	6
Police/court record	1.9	17	2.0	17
Authoritarian method of discipline	2.4	16	3.0	12[a]
Lack of parenting skills	2.7	15	3.0	12[a]
	100.0%		**99.8%**[b]	

[a] Indicates tied ranks.
[b] Totals less than 100% due to rounding.

of child's disobedience—accounted for nearly half the reported factors in both groups: 47.2% of the adolescent sample and 49.0% of the adult pregnancy group. They contributed almost half of the responses, but constituted only 25% (5 of 20) of the factors.

In grouping the factors in "family," "environmental/social" and "parental capacity" categories (see Table 8), the following differences resulted: Families that had experienced an adolescent pregnancy demonstrated some increased incidence on such predictable factors as *insufficient income, new baby in the home, continuous child care responsibility, and parental history of abuse as a child*. The incidence of these factors is in keeping with the picture of the mother involved in adolescent pregnancy as having these characteristics: financially insecure; more children more closely birth-spaced, a factor that assures the presence of a young child in the home; birth of children over a longer period of time, creating the heavy and continuous child care situation; and more frequent participation in an abusive environment as a child.

TABLE 8

Percent of factor grouping present in substantiated child maltreatment, by adolescent and adult pregnancy cases

Factor Grouping	Adolescent Pregnancy	Adult Pregnancy
Family factors	54.6%	48.3%
Environmental/social factors	15.9	15.0
Parental capacity factors	29.5	36.5
	100.0%	**99.8%**[a]

[a] Totals less than 100%, due to rounding.

Families that had not experienced an adolescent pregnancy seemed to find their problems concentrated within the areas of: *loss of control during discipline, lack of tolerance of child's disobedience, physical handicap or chronic illness, alcohol dependence, and mental health problems*. Many of these factors were related to the relatively greater age (a mean age of 34.2 years as opposed to 25.1 years for the adolescent pregnancy group) of this group, as well as the differences in behavior of the older child.

Generally speaking, however, the comparison of the dynamics between the group of families that had experienced an adolescent pregnancy and those that had not did not demonstrate a measurable difference. The pattern of dynamics, at least within the scope of those alternatives presented within this study, must be considered alike pending more in-depth empirical examination.

Discussion

Data sources. The data utilized in this study were drawn from a standardized form completed in the reporting process for each suspected child maltreatment situation coming to the attention of the Maricopa County unit of Child Protective Services system. This places these forms in the category of "official records" and allows for a degree of question about their validity.

In overview, it is likely that these records are subject to the same sort of external errors (*e.g.*, selectively identifying the powerless groups more often) that plague official records of all types. In a positive vein, these records are not perceived by the Child Protective Services workers as impinging upon evaluations of their own performance, or by supervisors as being utilized in the determination of staffing or funding patterns. Removing the evaluative onus of these records may eliminate some distortion. The records are viewed, however, as a "necessary evil" and may be subject to some internal distortion as a result of cursory completion with selective accuracy in categories considered "important" by the individual worker.[1] In addition, the reported age breakdowns for families centered about five-year intervals (*i.e.*, 20, 25, 30), suggesting some significant "rounding" or guesswork on the part of workers. Finally, for families other than those being evaluated for eligibility, the workers freely admit to guessing about income categories.

This does not completely negate the value of the data within these records. Indeed, a large proportion of family violence research in general is drawn from official records. This is research that has served to motivate specific areas of study in survey research of a more reliable nature.[25] This motivation for greater study, then, may be seen as the primary utility of these data; the present report does not aspire to a thorough answering of difficult social questions in the absence of the capacity to validate the available data.

Data analysis. The presentation of the data within this paper is the most basic aggregation of data by categories that might be studied. That is, the paper was not intended to represent a comprehensive or in-depth analysis of the problems under study. Despite security in the size of the sample, the absence of a control group and normative data for the population residing in the area from which the data were drawn limit the certainty and scope of the conclusions; the present findings are tentative and in need of additional examination.

Child maltreatment incidence. The original assumption directing this work was that there would be an increased incidence of child maltreatment within that group of officially reported maltreatment cases involving adolescent mothers. Although this preliminary examination of that assumption recognizes the 36.5% contribution made to the overall child maltreatment incidence within these records provided by adolescent mothers (utilizing the expanded definition of adolescent mother), the meaning of this contribution remains elusive.

To a degree at least, the data must be seen as no more than suggestive of causality or even interdependence. That is, the influence of similar social variables within the adolescent pregnancy and child maltreatment reports studied here may serve to skew relationships (*e.g.*, minority group membership, poverty, single-parenthood). As an example of that demographic loading, the minority population of the county from which these data were drawn contributes a disproportionately large number of the adolescent births in that county (38.8%). The officially reported child maltreatment cases studied also contain a disproportionately high number of minority families. Therefore, the adolescent pregnancy disproportion within minority groups could be transmitted into the child maltreatment population studies simply through the primary vehicle of differential likelihood of being reported. In the absence of the ability to measure this skewed contribution directly, the conclusions drawn regarding the contribution made to child maltreatment by adolescent parents must also be considered tentative.

Defining the "adolescent mother." It appears from these data that the traditional researcher's view of the adolescent parent's contribution to child maltreatment is too restrictive. While we recognize the independent contribution made to child maltreatment rates by adolescent parents (including the understudied adolescent father) who both give birth to their child and perpetrate a maltreating event prior to their twentieth birthday, and recognize the clear need for study of this group, there remains an additional "adolescent parent" group that demands consideration. The expanded definition of adolescent parent proposed by this study would include all parents who bore a child during their adolescent years, irrespective of the child's age or their own at the time of the maltreating event. Through study of this expanded adolescent parent group, a truer measure of the interrelationship between adolescent parenting and child maltreatment may be assessed.

The need for an expanded definition of adolescent parent is supported by the suggestion in the present study that the child born during the parent's adolescence may be at some increased risk for becoming the victim of a maltreating act, as compared to siblings not born during the perpetrator's adolescence. Giving full recognition to other variables associated with family constellation (*e.g.,* being the oldest child), social factors, and unknown factors intervening between the parent's adolescence and the maltreating event, this adolescent birth factor remains of value in the study of the child maltreatment problem. Although this stage of study allows little beyond speculation, the data may suggest that the "special child," who frequently becomes a target for maltreatment, may trace that unique position within the family back to the adolescent birth. This speculation follows the increased concern with mother-infant bonding and the major influences that the child has upon its caregiver from birth. It is possible that, like the premature child, the premature (adolescent) parent may experience bonding difficulty.

Demographic factors. The review of demographic characteristics of the adolescent maltreatment group present within the official records studied here indicates that *1)* minority overrepresentation, *2)* financial stress, and *3)* marital disruption or single parenthood are parallel elements in the environments of the maltreating parent and the adolescent parent who has been reported for maltreatment. Within these officially reported cases, when the variables of minority group participation and adolescent parenting are placed in juxtaposition, the intensity of the financial stress on marital disruption or single parenthood is exacerbated.

The combination of *1)* the absence of normative data for the larger population of the county from which these data were drawn, and *2)* the strong tendency for official reporting to focus somewhat selectively upon families of lower socioeconomic status raises questions about any conclusions in this regard. However, while further study is required, it can be suggested that the minority adolescent parent may be at increased risk for the negative demographic variables that have been found to be associated with the development of child maltreatment.

Dynamic variables. The dynamic variables most frequently associated with the maltreating environment were found to be present in the lives of both the adolescent and the adult maltreating parent with nearly equal regularity. Unfortunately, the 20 dynamic variables available on the official record not only form a "forced choice" selection, but consist of those known to be common among families with maltreatment potential. This limitation led to the results of this study being too similar to allow substantive statements as to differences between the two groups. If differential dynamics appear in any form through this research, they appear to suggest that the pressures within the life of the adolescent parent-maltreater focus upon family problems that would be logically associated with the adolescent parenting role *(i.e., insufficient income, new baby in the home, continuous child care responsibility, and parental history of abuse as a child).* The dynamic pressures confronting the adult maltreater are, on the other hand, focused about life problems providing stress to the maltreating individual *(i.e., loss of control, lack of tolerance for child, physical handicap, alcohol dependence, and mental health problems).* There is some hint in these results, then, that the adolescent parent-maltreater is more motivated toward maltreatment as a function of situational variables, while the general maltreating group is responsive to personal and individual problem areas. This would suggest the need for sound environmental manipulations for the potential adolescent maltreater, while the more psychodynamically-oriented programs may be of greater utility to the older maltreating parent.

A final caution. At the risk of belaboring the point, additional caution in viewing the results of this study is required. While the data presented seem to indicate the predicted higher rates of adolescent parent-perpetrated child maltreatment, comparison data were not readily available to confirm this assumption through an absolute view of adolescent parenting in the population at large. (While adolescent birth rates were known, there was no way to determine how many parents had borne their children in other areas and relocated in Arizona as adolescent parents, nor was there any reliable means to determine the pervasiveness of adolescent parenting across the population who were no longer adolescents.)

Additionally, while the demographic and dynamic variables ordinarily associated with child maltreatment seem to provide a near-perfect "fit" between the adolescent parent and general maltreating group, it is not known at this point to what degree the presence of these variables is a function of the "officially reported" nature of the sample. In short, this work cannot completely answer the question: Which occurs first—the adolescent parenting, the child maltreatment, or participation in an environment characterized by the stressful demographic and dynamic variables studied?

A summary view of this work would suggest that interaction effects are taking place between adolescent pregnancy and child maltreatment. What remains as an immediate need, however, is a replication of this work utilizing child maltreatment data drawn from other areas of the country. In addition, studies of this type must be taken outside of the realm of official reporting and begin to rely upon the difficult area of self-report. It is only through continued study, utilizing both official and non-official data, that the true position of the adolescent parent within the spectrum of maltreatment can be understood.

References

1. Altheide, D., & Johnson, J. 1980. *Bureaucratic Propaganda*. Allyn and Bacon, Boston.

2. Baldwin, W. 1976. *Adolescent Pregnancy and Childbearing: Growing Concern for Americans*. Population Reference Bureau, Washington, D.C.

3. Chilman, C. 1979. *Adolescent Sexuality in a Changing Society: Social and Psychological Perspectives*. DHEW Publication No. (NIH) 79-1426, Washington, D.C.

4. Cutright, P. 1972. Illegitimacy in the U.S., 1920–1968. In *Demographic and Social Aspects of Population Growth*, C. Westoff and R. Parks, eds. U.S. Government Printing Office, Washington, D.C.

5. Daniels, A. 1969. Reaching unwed mothers. *Amer. J. Nurs.* 69(2):332–335.

6. Delissovoy, V. 1973. Child care by adolescent parents. *Children Today* 2:22–25.

7. Furstenberg, F. 1976. *Unplanned Parenthood: The Social Consequences of Teenage Childbearing*. Free Press, New York.

8. Gil, D. 1970. *Violence Against Children*. Harvard University Press, Cambridge, Mass.

9. Helfer, R. 1978. *Childhood Comes First: A Crash Course in Childhood for Adults* (First Evaluation Edition). Ray E. Helfer, East Lansing, Mich.

10. Helfer, R. 1975. *The Diagnostic Process and Treatment Programs*. DHEW Publication No. (OHD) 75–69, Washington, D.C.

11. Holmes, M. 1978. *Child Abuse and Neglect Programs: Practice and Theory*. DHEW Publication No. (ADM) 78-344, Washington, D.C.

12. Jenkins, J., Salus, M., and Schultze, G. 1979. *Child Protective Services: A Guide for Workers*. DHEW Publication No. (OHDS) 79-30203, Washington, D.C.

13. Kantner, J., and Zelnick, M. 1978. Contraceptive patterns and premarital pregnancy among women aged 15–19 in 1976. *Fam. Plan. Perspect.* 10:135–142.

14. Kempe, C., et al. 1962. The battered child syndrome. *JAMA* 181:17.

15. Light, R. 1973. Abused and neglected children in America: A study of alternative policies. *Harvard Ed. Rev.* 43:556–598.

16. Lincoln, R., Jaffe, F., and Ambrose, A. 1976. *11 Million Teenagers*. Alan Guttmacher Institute, New York.

17. Martin, H. 1976. *The Abused Child: A Multidisciplinary Approach to Developmental Issues and Treatment*. Ballinger, Cambridge, Mass.

18. Nye, I. 1976. *School Age Parenthood*. Extension Bulletin 667, Cooperative Extension Service, Washington State University, Pullman, Wash.

19. Osofsky, H. 1968. *The Pregnant Teenager*. Charles C. Thomas, Springfield, Ill.

20. Presser, H. 1974. Early motherhood: Ignorance or bliss? *Fam. Plan. Perspect.* 6(2):8–14.

21. Rains, P. 1971. *Becoming an Unwed Mother*. Aldine, Chicago.

22. Reiss, I. 1976. *Family Systems in America*, 2nd Ed. Dryden Press, Hinsdale, Ill.

23. Smith, S., Hanson, R., and Nobles, S. 1973. Parents of battered babies: A controlled study. *Brit. Med. J.* 4(5889):388–391.

24. Steele, B. 1975. *Working With Abusive Parents from a Psychiatric Point of View*. DHEW Publication No. (OHD) 75–70, Washington, D.C.

25. Straus, M., Gelles, R., and Steinmetz, S. 1980. *Behind Closed Doors: Violence in the American Family*. Anchor Press/Doubleday, New York.

26. Zelnick, M., Young, J., and Kantner, J. 1979. Probabilities of intercourse and conception among U.S. teenage women, 1971 and 1976. *Fam. Plan. Perspect.* 113:177–183.

Teenage Parenting and Child Abuse: Are They Related?

· · · · ·

E. Milling Kinard and Lorraine V. Klerman

ith the recognition of adolescent pregnancy as a major national health and social problem, the consequences of early parenthood have increasingly become the subject of theoretical speculation and empirical investigation. Most reports have focused on the short-term or long-term medical and social consequences of early pregnancy for the mother.[4,7,10–12] Little is known, however, about the psychological and social impact on the child of having a mother who is herself still a child.

Paralleling the attention to adolescent pregnancy has been a growing concern with the problem of child abuse.* Many writers in the child abuse field have proposed a link between the two problems: that adolescent parents may be more likely than older parents to abuse their children. Varied opinions have been offered in equally varied publications. Some educational materials, such as *Florida's Tale of Woe,*[3] prepared by the Florida Department of Health and Rehabilitative Services, and a brochure from The Population Institute,[16] state unequivocally that teenage mothers are likely to abuse their children.

Child abuse research, however, provides conflicting evidence. Some researchers, such as Gil[5] and Elmer,[2] have found no evidence of an associa-

---

*The term "abuse" will be used as a generic term encompassing physical and emotional abuse, physical and emotional neglect, and sexual abuse. Specific forms of abuse will be noted when necessary.

Research was supported by an NIMH Individual Research Service Fellowship Award (5-F31-MH05134) and by a Brandeis-NIH Biomedical Research Support Grant.

tion between parental age and child abuse; others, such as Lynch and Roberts,[8], Sills et al,[14] and Smith et al,[15] report an unusually high proportion of teenage mothers in abusing families. The disparity in these findings may be more apparent than real; variations in definitions of terms may lead to differing conclusions. In fact, few methodologically rigorous investigations are available that can either confirm or refute the hypothesized link. The present paper will first discuss three methodological problems that complicate any attempt to assess the relationship between child abuse and teenage parenting, and then describe four data sets that shed light on the issue.

Methodological Problems

MOTHER'S AGE

The first methodological problem involves the definition of mother's age. Three possibilities exist for calculating age of the mother: 1) at the time of abuse, 2) at the time of birth of the abused child, or 3) at the time of birth of the first child. Most child abuse studies report mother's age at the time of abuse. Conclusions based on this calculation are misleading, since the abused child could have been born when the mother was a teenager but abused when the mother was 20 or older. Calculating mother's age at the time of the abused child's birth would seem to remedy this defect, but the abused child is not always the oldest child in a family. Consequently, this second method of defining mother's age would exclude mothers who were teenagers at the birth of the first child but who were no longer teenagers at the birth of the abused child. Assuming that it is the stress produced by pregnancy, childbirth, and parenting in the teenage years that can ultimately lead to child abuse, then the third method—calculating age at the time of birth of the first child—provides the most complete data for exploring the relationship between teenage parenting and child abuse.

PERPETRATOR

The second methodological problem concerns whose age to examine. Although children are most often abused by their parents, they may be abused by other caretakers as well. In order to assess the relationship between teenage parenting and child abuse, however, the relevant population consists of natural parents living with the child at the time of abuse. Children abused in foster homes or residential care facilities are not appropriate for this kind of study. But even for children abused while living with their natural parents, there remains a question of which parent's age to examine. Birth dates for both parents are desirable, but this information is often unavailable for fathers, particularly when the mother is unmarried.

The ages of both parents should be examined, regardless of whether the parents were perpetrators of the abuse. The potential relationship between teenage parenting and child abuse is not limited to the teenage parent as abuser. Parents may contribute indirectly to the abuse of a child, even though they do not actually inflict the injuries themselves. For instance, the immaturity of teenage parents may lead to a poor choice of baby sitters, resulting in injury to the child.

COMPARISON GROUPS

The third methodological issue concerns the selection of appropriate comparison groups for determining whether teenage parents, particularly mothers, are at greater risk than older mothers of having abused children. Two methods are available: *1)* comparing the proportion of teenage mothers in a given study of abused children to national natality statistics for the corresponding time periods; *2)* comparing the proportion of teenage mothers in a given study of abused children to a matched control group. The second method is preferable because control groups can be matched with abuse groups on variables, such as socioeconomic status, that may confound the comparability between abuse samples and national statistics.

Review of Research

Four studies of child abuse illustrate these methodological problems and provide new evidence on the relationship between adolescent childbearing and child abuse: *1)* a reanalysis of Gil's 1967 nationwide epidemiological study;[5] *2)* an analysis of abuse reports for 1976 from 28 states and three U.S. territories conducted by the American Humane Association;[1] *3)* an analysis of abuse reports for the state of Georgia from July 1975 through June 1978, conducted by McCarthy;[9] and *4)* a study of child abuse conducted in 1976 by the senior author, using a sample of abused children and a matched group of nonabused children.[6]

GIL'S DATA REANALYZED

In 1967, Gil conducted a comprehensive study of all cases of physical abuse reported during that year in 39 selected cities and counties. He reported that only 9.3% of the mothers and 2.8% of the fathers were under 20 at the time of the abuse incident, commenting that:

> This age distribution does not support the observation of many earlier studies of physically abused children and their families, according to which the parents tend to be extremely young.[5]

However, Gil examined only the age of the parents at the time of the abuse incident and included both natural parents and parent substitutes.

A reanalysis of the data was therefore performed, using parental age at the time of the abused child's birth, since the data set did not include parent's age at the birth of the first child. This reanalysis was restricted to cases in which the abused child was living with one or both natural parents at the time of the abuse incident. The elimination of cases in which the abused child was living with parent substitutes and cases in which the necessary information was not available reduced the sample size to 1104 natural mothers and 577 natural fathers. In 37.9% (*N*=418) of the sample, the mother was under 20 at the time of the abused child's birth. In 11.4% (*N*=66) of the sample, the father was under 20 at the time of the abused child's birth.

These findings were compared to the age distributions at the time of the children's births of mothers and fathers in the general population. The ages of the abused children in Gil's sample cohort ranged from less than six months to 19 years, but nearly 90% were from one through 15 years of age. Most of these children, then, would have been born between 1952 and 1966. A review of vital statistics in the United States [17] revealed a striking contrast to Gil's data: teenage mothers constituted 37.9% of Gil's sample, but only 11.5% to 17.5% of the general population during the comparable time period; teenage fathers constituted 11.4% of Gil's sample, but only 2.1% to 4.5% of the general population during the same time period. This reanalysis suggests that Gil's original conclusion about the absence of a relationship between teenage parenting and child abuse was erroneous.

On the other hand, mothers under 20 at the time of the abused child's birth were no more likely to be the perpetrator than those 20 or over at the time of the child's birth: 49.3% of those under 20 were perpetrators, compared to 49.6% of those 20 and over. Fathers under 20 at the time of the abused child's birth were somewhat more likely to be the perpetrator than those 20 and over at the time of the child's birth: 65.2% of those under 20 were perpetrators, compared to 57.9% of those 20 and over.

AMERICAN HUMANE ASSOCIATION

The most recent large-scale study of the relationship between child abuse and early parenting has been conducted by the American Humane Association.[1] The AHA analysis is based on 36,822 validated cases of abuse and neglect reported for 1976 in 28 states and three U.S. territories. The age of the mother at the birth of the oldest child living in the family was tabulated by type of abuse and by whether the mother was the perpetrator.

For all types of cases, 39.3% of the mothers had given birth when they were under the age of 20. For cases of abuse only (N=11,445), 37.5% became mothers as teenagers. For reports of neglect only (N=21,812), 40.1% were teenage mothers. For cases of both abuse and neglect (N=3565), 40.3% were teenage mothers. Thus, regardless of the type of abuse, approximately two-fifths of the natural mothers studied first became parents when they were less than 20 years of age. This proportion is nearly identical to that found in Gil's study for age of mother at the birth of the abused child.

Since the analysis of abuse reports used mother's age at the time of birth of the oldest child, the comparison base for population data was first-order births. Although the exact years of birth for the oldest children in the abusing families were not available, the percentage of teenage mothers among all first-order births in the general population has changed very little during the past 17 years (1960 through 1976), raging from a low of 33.4% in 1976 to a high of 38.6% in 1966. (Though the figures shift slightly each year, there is no discernible pattern as there is with the consistently increasing proportion of total births to teenage mothers.) The percentages for the national population are only slightly lower than those for the AHA study. Thus, teenage mothers do not appear to be overrepresented among abusing families.

Within the subgroup of mothers who were teenagers at the birth of the oldest child, the percentages of mothers who were perpetrators of the abuse were calculated for each type of abuse. Overall, 81.1% of the teenage mothers were perpetrators. For cases of abuse only, 51.8% of the teenage mothers were perpetrators. For neglect only, the figure was 94.7%, while for cases of both abuse and neglect, it was 86.2%. Each of these percentages was approximately the same as the corresponding percentage for mothers age 20 and over who were perpetrators (78.1% overall; 50.7% for abuse only; 92.4% for neglect only; 82.8% for abuse and neglect), thus indicating that teenage mothers are not at greater risk than older mothers of abusing their children. However, it does appear that mothers, whether under 20 or over, are more likely to be perpetrators in cases involving neglect than in cases involving abuse.

McCARTHY'S FINDINGS

Reports of physical or sexual abuse to the Georgia Child Abuse Registry for the three-year period from July 1975 through June 1978 were analyzed by McCarthy.[9] From a total of 2436 confirmed reports, cases in which age of the mother was unknown or the natural mother was not present in the abused child's household were excluded, resulting in a sample size of 1903.

Mother's age at the time of birth of the first child was determined by subtracting age of the oldest child in the household from age of the mother. In 51.7% (N=983) of the sample, the mothers had given birth when they were teenagers. This percentage is higher than the Gil and AHA figures.

As in the AHA analysis, a comparison was made with population data for first-order births from 1960 through 1976.* The proportion of first births to teenage mothers in the general population ranged from 33.4% to 38.6% during this 17-year period. However, the proportion of teenage mothers in McCarthy's study is higher, thus indicating that teenage mothers are over-represented among reported cases of abuse.

For mothers who were under 20 at the birth of the first child, 40.3% (N=396) were perpetrators of the abuse, while for mothers 20 or older, 35.0% (N=322) were perpetrators. The difference is small, but it suggests that teenage mothers may be more likely than older mothers to be perpetrators of abuse.

KINARD'S STUDY

In contrast to the other three previous studies, which relied exclusively on comparisons with national natality data, a recent study by Kinard[6] used both of the comparison methods mentioned earlier: population data and a control group. The study groups consisted of a sample of 30 physically abused children and a control group of 30 nonabused children, matched on several variables including age and birth order of the child and family socioeconomic status. The families in both groups were predominantly lower

---

* Natality statistics for the general population were not available for 1977 and 1978.

class: 70% of each group were AFDC recipients, while the remainder did not receive this assistance but had low incomes.

Since birth dates for all family members living in the household were known, mother's age at the time of birth of the oldest child living in the household was calculated. For the abused group, 51.7% (*N*=15) of the mothers were teenagers at the birth of the oldest child; for the control group, the percentage was even higher (60.0%, *N*=18). Both of these figures are higher than the Gil and AHA statistics, but the figure for the abused group is identical to that reported by McCarthy.

These figures were compared with general population natality statistics for first-order births. During the years the study children were born (1965 to 1971), the percentage of first births to mothers under 20 ranged from 35% to 38.6%. For both the abused and control groups, then, the proportion of mothers who gave birth to their first child as teenagers was considerably higher than that in the general population. This overrepresentation of teenage mothers in both groups may reflect a tendency for childbearing to begin at an earlier age among mothers from lower socioeconomic backgrounds than among those of higher socioeconomic status.

Of the 13 mothers who were teenagers at the birth of the first child, six (46.2%) were perpetrators of the abuse, while for the 13 mothers 20 or older, eight (61.5%) were perpetrators.* Again, it would appear that teenage mothers are not at greater risk of being perpetrators of abuse.

A summary of the results of the four studies is given in Table 1. Examining Table 1 by columns shows that the studies are remarkably similar in the proportion of mothers who were under 20 years of age at each of the times when mother's age was calculated.

TABLE 1
Relationship between teenage childbearing and child abuse in four studies of child abuse

| Study | N | Mothers under 20 years of age | | |
		At time of abuse	At birth of abused child	At birth of first child
Gil[5]	1,104	9.29%	37.9%	
AHA[1]	36,822			39.3% overall
				37.5% abuse only
				40.1% neglect only
				40.3% abuse/neglect
McCarthy	1,903	8.00%	34.8%	51.7%
Kinard[6]	30	3.45%	34.5%	51.7%

Table 2 Indicates that the evidence on the tendency for teenage mothers to be perpetrators of abuse is conflicting. Despite differences among the

* Information on perpetrator was unknown for three cases and age of mothers was unknown for one.

studies, however, the findings suggest that teenage mothers are no more likely than older mothers to be perpetrators of maltreatment.

TABLE 2

Mothers as perpetrators of child abuse in four studies of child abuse

Study	Mother's age at birth of abused child		Mother's age at birth of first child	
	Under 20	20 & over	Under 20	20 & over
Gil[5]	49.3%	49.6%		
AHA[1]			81.1% overall	78.1% overall
			51.8% abuse only	50.7% abuse only
			94.7% neglect only	92.4% neglect only
			86.2% abuse/neglect	82.8% abuse/neglect
McCarthy[9]	41.7%	35.6%	40.3%	35.0%
Kinard[6]	37.5%	61.1%	46.2%	61.5%

Conclusions

The relationship between teenage parenting and child abuse has been examined by comparing data from four studies of child abuse to illustrate three methodological problems in research linking the two phenomena. The evidence presented in this paper indicates that the proportion of mothers who gave birth as teenagers is higher in child abusing families than in the general population, thus suggesting an association between adolescent pregnancy and child abuse. When low-income abusing families were compared with matching control families, however, the proportion of teenage mothers in the abusing group was in fact lower than that in the control group.

This finding suggests that the hypothesized link between teenage parenting and child abuse may be confounded by the relationship of each variable to other preceding and possibly more significant factors. For example, many studies suggest that both births to adolescents and reported cases of child abuse are more common among lower socioeconomic status families. Poverty may contribute to early pregnancy, by providing few other outlets for creative energy, as well as to child abuse, by serving as a source of frustration and anger. Studies of child abusers report social background characteristics similar to those often cited for adolescent parents: one-parent families; family history of alcohol abuse; parental depression; parental rejection; and premature infants.

The importance of social background characteristics is supported by the findings from a recent investigation of the influence of social history variables on child maltreatment.[13] According to the data analysis, level of social disorganization was the most significant predictor of maltreatment, while age of the mother at the birth of the first child was not a significant predictor.

Though the link between teenage parenting and child abuse may not be causal, but may be due instead to the association of both phenomena with impoverished backgrounds and disturbed family life, it suggest a series of intervention strategies that might reduce the incidence of both problems. These include attempts to prevent early pregnancy, such as sex education, contraception, and abortion; and efforts to reduce the negative consequences of early childbearing, such as education courses in family life and child development, as well as anticipatory guidance and close supervision for pregnant women and young parents.

References

1. American Humane Association. 1978. *National Analysis of Official Child Neglect and Abuse Reporting: An Executive Summary.* American Humane Association, Englewood, Colo.

2. Elmer, E. 1967. *Children in Jeopardy.* University of Pittsburgh Press, Pittsburgh.

3. *Florida's Tale of Woe.* Florida Department of Health and Rehabilitative Services. (undated)

4. Furstenberg, F. 1976. *Unplanned Parenthood.* Free Press, New York.

5. Gil, D. 1970. *Violence Against Children.* Harvard University Press, Cambridge, Massachusetts.

6. Kinard, E. 1978. *Emotional Development in Physically Abused Children: A Study of Self-Concept and Aggression.* Ph.D. dissertation, University Microfilms, Ann Arbor, Mich.

7. Klerman, L., and Jekel, J. 1973. *School-Age Mothers: Problems, Programs and Policy.* Linnet Books, Hamden, Conn.

8. Lynch, M., and Roberts, J. 1977. Predicting child abuse: signs of bonding failure in the maternity hospital. *Brit. Med. J.* 1(6061):624–626.

9. McCarthy, B. 1978. Unpublished data, Center for Disease Control, DHEW, Atlanta.

10. Menken, J. 1978. Health and demographic consequences of adolescent pregnancy and childbearing. *In Teenage Childbearing: Recent Research on the Determinants and Consequences,* C. Chilman, ed. Government Printing Office, Washington, D.C.

11. Moore, K., and Caldwell, S. 1977. The effect of government policies on out-of-wedlock sex and pregnancy. *Fam. Plan. Perspect.* 9(4):164–169.

12. Moore, K. and Waite, L. 1977. Early childbearing and educational attainment. *Fam. Plan. Perspect.* 9(5):220–225.

13. Ory, M., and Earp, J. 1978. The influence of teenage childbearing on child maltreatment: the role of intervening factors. Presented to the American Public Health Association, Los Angeles.

14. Sills, J., Thomas, L., and Rosenbloom, L. 1977. Non-accidental injury: a two-year study in Central Liverpool. *Develpm. Med. Child Neuerol.* 19:26–33.

15. Smith, S., Hanson, R., and Noble, S. 1974. Social aspects of the battered baby syndrome. *Brit. J. Psychiat.* 125:568–582.

16. The Population Institute. Undated fundraising letter.

17. U.S. Dept. of Health, Education, and Welfare. 1952–1966. *Vital Statistics of the United States: Volume I-Natality.* Public Health Service, National Center for Health Statistics, Rockville, Md.

Child Maltreatment
and Teenage First Births:
A Relationship
Mediated by Chronic
Sociodemographic Stress?

· · · · ·

Susan J. Zuravin

Teenage motherhood and child maltreatment are two of America's most talked about social problems. Are they related? Life course theory (Baltes & Brim, 1979; Elder, 1978) suggests that they are. This sociological model predicts that

> …deviations from the normative life script place individuals out of step with major social institutions and other members of their cohort, generating psychological, economic, and social consequences for the rest of their lives (McLaughlin & Micklin, 1983).

Teen motherhood is a prime example of "deviation from the normative life script." Consequently, it seems reasonable to predict that among its social ramifications are immediate and delayed adverse effects on maternal child care adequacy.

Accounting for immediate negative effects are a host of factors, all of which might be subsumed under two headings, "life experience" (Conger, McCarty, Yang, Lahey, & Burgess, 1984) and "social support" (Baldwin, 1983). Life experience factors include lack of knowledge about what to expect from and how to care for a child, and conflict between the developmental tasks of adolescence and the tasks required of a mother. Philliber and Graham (1981) probably best summarize the rationale for the latter factor with the following statement:

Copyright 1988 by The American Orthopsychiatric Association, Inc. Reproduced by permission.
Preparation of this paper was partially supported by grant FPR 000028-01-0 from the Office of Population Affairs.

92

If young mothers are striving to develop constructive expressions of emotion and to learn to face up to and solve conflict, can they simultaneously cope with anger towards a child and develop adequate techniques for discipline? Can young mothers be expected to understand the needs of a child for stability and security when their own needs are so similar?

Social support factors include lack of as well as failure to use support networks, particularly those that include family members. Given the life experience deficits of these young mothers, social support or its lack is highly likely to have a tremendous impact on maternal child care adequacy (Baldwin & Cain, 1980). Its absence may well lead to child maltreatment.

The delayed negative effects of teenage first birth on parental behavior are the result of a long list of factors, all of which might be said to contribute to the creation and maintenance of "chronic stress" (Conger *et al.*, 1984). Underlying this rationale is the notion that teenage motherhood has a long-term adverse effect on various social and psychological aspects of the mother's life—availability and use of social support, employment history, economic status, marital experiences, educational achievement, fertility outcomes, feelings of personal efficacy, and so forth— in such a way as to result in chronic stress. In turn, the chronic stress undercuts the mother's ability to be an effective parent.

It is likely that the antecedents and maintainers of chronic stress—low economic status, single parenthood, low self-esteem, etc.—have a complex interrelationship. Despite this, social support is probably one of the most important mediating common denominators in the intricate sequence from teenage first births to child maltreatment. This sequence is the frequent consequence of such antecedents as low self-esteem, unemployment, single parenthood, and an unmanageable number of children. In addition, it is an important and well-documented correlate of all types of child maltreatment (Baltes & Brim, 1979; Hunter, Kilstrom, Kraybill & Loda, 1978; Wolock & Horowitz, 1977) as well as an important predictor of child care adequacy among teenage mothers (Baldwin, 1983).

The hypothesized immediate effect of teenage first birth on child care adequacy has been the subject of much research attention. Generally speaking, studies agree that, independent of socioeconomic status, teenage mothers: *a)* are less responsive and sensitive to their infants than older mothers (Elster & McAnarney, 1980; Jones, Green & Krauss, 1980; McAnarney, Lawrence, & Aten, 1979; Ragozin, Basham, Crnic, Greenberg, & Robinson, 1982); *b)* have less desirable child-rearing attitudes and expectations (Field, Widmayer, Stringer, & Ignatoff, 1980; Ragozin *et al.*, 1982); and *c)* do provide more adequate care when supported socially and emotionally by family members (Baldwin & Cain, 1980). Yet, despite the less than optimal care and attitudes, the bulk of evidence does not support the hypothesis that teen mothers are at higher immediate risk for child abuse and neglect than are older mothers (Altmeier, O'Connor, Vietze, Sandler, & Sherrod, 1984; Bolton, Laner, & Kane, 1980; Hunter et al., 1978; Miller, 1984). Conceivably, this may stem from the greater amount of family social support and institutional material support that is often given to teenage mothers, particularly those with their first child.

On the other hand, there is considerable evidence of a delayed relationship between teenage motherhood and child maltreatment (Bolton & Laner, 1981; Creighton, 1985; Conger et al., 1984; Herrenkohl & Herrenkohl, 1979; Kent, 1973; Leventhal, 1981; Zuravin, 1987). Creighton's study (1985) of more than 5,000 reported incidents of child maltreatment occurring in England during the years 1977 to 1982 found motherhood prior to 20 years of age significantly overrepresented among families reported for both abuse and neglect: 35.3% of the mothers of abused children and 30% of the mothers of neglected children, compared to 10.7% of mothers of families belonging to the blue collar classes, were less than 20 years old when they became mothers. Herrenkohl and Herrenkohl's (1979) child protective service case record study of 328 maltreating families found maternal age of less than 20 at birth of the maltreated child to be a predictor of recidivism for both physical abuse and neglect. Zuravin's (1987) study of 518 urban, single parent, public welfare mothers found that young age at first birth (18 years or less) is an important risk factor for both child abuse and neglect, independent of age, race, lifetime marital status, lifetime employment status, and educational achievement.

Given some persuasive retrospective evidence of a delayed relationship between teenage motherhood and child maltreatment, it is important to identify the specific factors that mediate this relationship. Such information is highly significant from theoretical, empirical, and practical points of view. Currently, the child maltreatment literature is replete with studies that have assessed relationships between maltreatment and any of a vast array of individual demographic, social and psychological characteristics. Unfortunately, however, it is almost devoid of studies that test hypotheses about the relationships among these many different correlates of abuse and neglect. Until investigators start formulating and testing such hypotheses, theoretical and empirical knowledge about child maltreatment will remain at a very primitive level and be of limited practical value in the development of policies and programs aimed at preventing child abuse and neglect.

To the best of our knowledge, the child maltreatment literature includes not a single study which actually tests the hypothesis that chronic stress mediates the relationship between teenage motherhood and either child abuse or child neglect. Conger and colleagues' (1984) study of the relationship between age at first birth and maternal affective behavior comes the closest. The investigators identified several relevant relationships: 1) They found a negative association between age at first birth and chronic stress (measured on an index including five dichotomous variables: low income, Aid to Families of Dependent Children (AFDC) recipiency, excess numbers of children, single parenthood, and low educational achievement)—the younger the age at first birth, the greater the subsequent chronic stress. 2) They found age at first birth and chronic stress to have the same relationship to maternal affective behavior: both are negatively associated with positive maternal behavior and positively associated with negative behavior. Suggestive as these findings are, however, they do not merit the conclusion that chronic stress mediates or partially mediates the relationship between teenage motherhood and either child abuse or child neglect. Tests to establish the presence or absence of such a relationship are clearly warranted.

The study presented in this paper had two purposes: *1)* to examine the hypothesis that chronic stress mediates the delayed relationship between teenage motherhood and each of two types of child maltreatment—child physical abuse and child neglect, and *2)* to identify which (if any) of three sociodemographic markers of chronic stress—excess live births, low educational achievement, or a life history of unemployment—mediate the relationships.

Methods

SUBJECTS

Data for this three-group, retrospective study were collected from 518 women. During the sampling month, January of 1984, each respondent was a Baltimore (Maryland) resident, a member of the cohort of families receiving AFDC, known to have at least one natural child of 12 years or under, and a single parent (not living with a legally wedded spouse).

CHILD ABUSE AND NEGLECT SAMPLES

The 118 abusive respondents were self-selected from an original sample of 152 abusive mothers and the 119 neglectful respondents were self-selected from a sample of 164 neglectful mothers. Both samples were selected from sampling frames prepared from a cohort of 1,744 families receiving child protective services (CPS) from the Baltimore City Department of Social Services (BCDSS) during the sampling month. To be included in either sampling frame a family had to meet the four general study criteria and one of the following operational definitions of child maltreatment.

Definition of physical abuse. All members of the abuse sampling frame, according to the best judgment of the child protective service caseworkers involved with the family, met the following definition: had at least one natural child who was the victim of "excessive or inappropriate physical force" from the respondent herself or another caretaker and as a result of the force had sustained injuries at a minimum severity level of four on the six-point Magura-Moses Physical Discipline Scale (Magura & Moses, 1986). A Severity Level Four injury refers to bruises, welts, cuts, abrasions, or first degree burns localized in one or two areas of the body and involving no more than broken skin. This definition of physical abuse does not preclude the possibility that the respondent's children were known victims of neglect or sexual victimization.

Definition of neglect. All members of the neglect sampling frame, according to the best judgment of the caseworkers involved with the family, met the following definition: had personally neglected one or more children in at least one of the following eight areas—physical health care, mental health care, nutrition-diet, personal hygiene, household sanitation, physical safety in the home, supervision of activities, and arrangements for substitute child care *and* had no natural children who met the study definition for physical abuse. Eligibility for the sample required a minimum rating of three on any of the remaining seven Magura Moses scales (Magura & Moses, 1986). This operational definition of neglect does not preclude the possibility that one (or more) of the respondent's children was known to have been sexually victimized.

CONTROL SAMPLE

The 281 control respondents were self-selected from a sample of 376 female AFDC recipients. This sample was screened into the study from a 2.1% systematic sample (every 46th family, beginning with a random start, was selected) of the 37,158 families who were receiving AFDC but not child protective services during January 1984. To be screened into the control sample a family had to meet, during the sampling month, two sets of criteria: the four general study criteria, and the following operational definition of no child maltreatment.

Definition of no child maltreatment. All members of the no maltreatment (control) sampling frame, according to records maintained by the BCDSS Master File Division, met the following definition: had never had a child who was the subject of a report of physical abuse and had never been a recipient of any of the child welfare services provided by BCDSS, including child protective services, foster care, services to families with children, or single parent services.

PROCEDURES

Recruitment. All 692 members of the three samples were initially approached by letter. Any respondent who did not contact us within two weeks of the first letter received a follow-up letter. Those who did not respond to the second letter were contacted in person by a study interviewer. Each respondent received $15.00 for participating in the study. Up to six separate callbacks led to a total interview completion rate of 74.2% and a final total sample size of 518. Seventy-five percent of the maltreatment sample members and 74.7% of the control sample members self-selected into the final study group. Of the 174 sample members who were not interviewed, 32% refused to participate, 43.6% could not be located, and 24.2% had moved out of Baltimore.

Interview. Respondents were interviewed in their homes during the period September 1984 through June 1985 by one of ten trained interviewers, unaware of the child maltreatment status of their respondents. A questionnaire containing 1,372 closed end items was administered by the interviewer after the respondent signed the study's confidentiality and permission statement. The average interview required about 90 minutes.

VARIABLES

Dependent variables. The two dependent variables are child neglect status and child abuse status. Both are categorical variables and similarly coded: no maltreatment is coded zero and maltreatment (child abuse or neglect) is coded one. Definitions of the levels are discussed above.

Independent variable. This variable, the age at first birth, was constructed by subtracting the date of birth for each respondent's first live birth from the respondent's date of birth.

Mediating variables. Indicators of chronic sociodemographic stress were represented by three variables: *1)* family size measured by number of live births; *2)* educational achievement measured by last grade completed before stopping school; and *3)* employment history measured by a dichotomous variable where "ever employed" is coded one and "never employed" is coded zero. Information on age at first birth and number of live births was gathered with a set of questions which focused on gathering data about every live birth born to respondents. These questions were taken verbatim from the National Survey of Family Growth (NSFG) Cycle III (National Center for Health Statistics, 1981). A live birth was defined as any baby who is born alive even if death occurs shortly after birth. Information on the remaining three variables was gathered with relevant questions also taken from the NSFG, Cycle III.

Controlled variables. Given statistically significant differences ($p<.05$) among the three study groups relative to chronological age and racial origin, all analyses controlled for these two factors. Such control helps to rule out the possibility that the findings have been confounded between these two variables and the independent variable or any of the hypothesized mediating variables.

DATA ANALYSIS

The statistical procedure was logistic regression analysis (Walker & Duncan, 1967). All analyses were carried out with the SAS Logist procedure (Harrell, 1983). Logistical regression is the statistical technique of choice when the dependent variable is measured at the categorical level. It is preferable to discriminant analysis because it does not require that independent or predictor variables have a multivariate normal distribution. All analysis included two control variables—chronological age and race. The actual data analysis strategy was divided into two parts. Part 1 focused on determining if either child abuse or child neglect is associated with age at first birth or any of the three indicators of chronic stress. Part 2 focused on examining, together as well as separately, the mediating effects of the three chronic stress indicators.

Results

AGE AT FIRST BIRTH and the three indicators of chronic stress:
Are they individually associated with child abuse or child neglect?

To answer this question, four separate multiple logistic regression analyses were carried out. Each involved regressing child maltreatment status (either abuse or neglect) on one of the four variables—age at first birth, educational achievement, employment history, or number of live births—and the two control variables, age and race. Findings reveal that the independent variable, age at first birth, as well as each of the three indicators of chronic stress are significantly associated at the .01 level or better with both child abuse and child neglect.

The maltreating mothers were younger teenagers at first birth than the control mothers. The average age at first birth for the neglectful mother was 17.9 (SD=2.6), for the abusive mother 18.3 (SD=2.8), and for the control mother 19.5 (SD=3.1). In addition, both types of maltreating mothers, independent of chronological age and race, had more live births, achieved fewer grades in school prior to quitting, and were less likely to have ever been employed than the adequate mothers. The average neglectful mothers had 3.9 live births (SD=2.1) and completed 9.8 grades (SD=1.8); the average abusive mother had 3.0 live births (SD=1.5) and completed 10.4 grades (SD=1.8); and the average adequate mother had 1.9 live births (SD=1.2) and completed 11.1 grades (SD=1.7). Thirty-seven percent of the no maltreatment group compared to 50% of the abusive group and 55% of the neglectful group had never been employed.

CHRONIC STRESS: Does it mediate the relationship between teenage first births and either type of child maltreatment?

To identify a mediating variable or set of mediating variables when logistic regression analysis is the statistical technique, two regression analyses are required. *Analysis 1,* for this particular study, requires regressing the dependent variable (child abuse or child neglect status) on age at first birth (plus control variables). *Analysis 2* involves regressing the dependent variable on both age at first birth and the hypothesized mediating variables (plus control variables).

To conclude that a variable or set of variables mediates the relationship between two other variables, in this case age at first birth and child maltreatment, two criteria must be met: *1)* The Analysis 2 chi square value associated with prediction of maltreatment from age at first birth must be smaller than the comparable Analysis 1 chi square value. *2)* The difference between the two relevant chi squares must be statistically significant given degrees of freedom equivalent to the difference in number of independent variables (Knoke & Burke, 1983). Further, if the chi square value from Analysis 2 is reduced to statistical insignificance, it suggests that the intervening variable(s) may completely mediate the relationship; if the chi square is significantly reduced but not to insignificance, it suggests that the intervening variable(s) plays no mediating role.

To test the study hypothesis that chronic stress mediates the relationship between teenage first birth and child maltreatment, two regression analyses were executed using the SAS Logist procedure (Harrell, 1983). Analysis 1 is described above. Analysis 2 involved regressing each dependent variable on six variables, the three variables included in Analysis 1 (chronological age, race, and age at first birth) plus the three chronic stress indicators (number of live births, educational achievement, and employment history).

Findings displayed in Table 1 reveal that, together, the three indicators of chronic stress significantly mediate the relationship between age at first birth and each type of child maltreatment at the .00001 level or better.

With regard to child neglect, the three variables completely mediate the relationship. In other words, the significant relationship between teenage first birth and child neglect, is reduced to insignificance when the three mediating variables are controlled. All necessary criteria are met. The Analysis 2 chi square associated with the partial regression coefficient for predicting neglect from age at first birth is smaller than the comparable Analysis 1 chi square, 31.29 to 1.37 (see Table 1, rows 1 and 2). The difference between Analyses' 1 and 2 chi squares, 29.92 (see Table 1, row 3), is statistically significant at the .00001 level given three degrees of freedom. The Analysis 2 chi square value associated with the age at first birth partial regression coefficient is no longer statistically significant (see Table 1, row 2).

TABLE 1

Chi squares associated with age at first birth from two logistic regression models focused on identifying whether chronic sociodemographic stress mediates the delayed relationship between age at first birth and either child abuse or child neglect

Variables in model	Variables added to model	Neglect status (n=400)	Abuse status (n=399)
(1) *A, R, AFB*		31.29**	20.36**
(2)	*LB, ED, EM*	1.37	4.01*
(3)		Difference 29.92**	16.35**

R=race, *A*=age, *AFB*=age first born, *ED*=education, *LB*=number of live births, *EM*=employment history. *p<.05; **p<.00001.

With regard to child abuse, the three variables partially mediate the relationship. In other words, the significant relationship between teenage first birth and child abuse is significantly reduced but not to insignificance when the three mediating variables are controlled. All necessary criteria are met. The Analysis 2 chi square associated with the partial regression coefficient for predicting abuse from age at first birth is smaller than the comparable Analysis 1 chi square, 20.36 to 4.01 (see Table 1, rows 1 and 2). The difference between Analysis' 1 and 2 chi squares, 16.35 (see Table 1, row 3), is statistically significant at the .00001 level given three degrees of freedom. The Analysis 2 chi square value associated with the age at first birth partial regression coefficient remains statistically significant (see Table 1, row 2).

In summary, this set of analyses reveals that, together, the three sociodemographic variables mediate the relationship between age at first birth and both types of child maltreatment. That the variables completely mediate the relationship for neglect but only partially mediate it for abuse suggests that these particular stresses may be more important intervening influences for neglect than abuse. The next step in the data analyses focuses on identifying which of the three indicators are significant mediators.

WHICH OF THE THREE INDICATORS of chronic stress are significant individual mediators of the relationship between age at first birth and either physical abuse or neglect?

To answer this question, three different Analysis 2 regressions were required. These analyses involved regressing each dependent variable on four variables, the three variables included in Analysis 1 (age at first birth, race, and chronological age) plus each of the three hypothesized mediating variables (family size, educational achievement, and employment history).

Child neglect findings. Two of the three hypothesized mediating variables, education and number of live births, significantly mediate the relationship between age at first birth and child neglect (see Table 2, rows 6 and 9). Education is an at least partial individual mediator of the relationship; all necessary statistical criteria are met. The chi square associated with the prediction of child neglect from age at first birth independent of chronological age, race, and educational achievement is smaller than the comparable Analysis 1 chi square value—25.06 compared to 31.29 (see Table 2, rows 5 and 4). The change in chi square from Analysis 1 to Analysis 2, 6.23, is statistically significant given one degree of freedom (see Table 2, row 6). The relationship between age at first birth and neglect is not reduced to statistical insignificance once education is controlled. The partial regression coefficient for the prediction of child neglect from age at first birth is significant at the .00001 level (see Table 2, row 5).

Number of live births completely mediates the relationship between age at first birth and child neglect: all necessary statistical criteria are met. The Analysis 2 chi square value associated with the partial regression coefficient for prediction of child neglect from age at first birth independent of chronological age, race, and number of live births is smaller than the comparable Analysis 1 chi square value—2.43 compared to 31.29 (see Table 2, rows 8 and 7). The change in chi square from Analysis 1 to Analysis 2, 28.86, is statistically significant given one degree of freedom (see Table 2, row 9). The relationship between age at first birth and neglect is significantly reduced once number of live births is controlled (see Table 2, row 8). The partial regression coefficient for prediction of child neglect from age at first birth is no longer statistically significant.

Child abuse findings. Only one of the three hypothesized variables is a statistically significant individual mediator of the relationship between age at first birth and child abuse. Number of live births partially mediates the relationship: all necessary statistical criteria are met. The Analysis 2 chi square value associated with the partial regression coefficient for prediction of child abuse from age at first birth independent of chronological age, race, and number of live births is smaller than the comparable Analysis 1 chi square value—5.17 compared to 20.36 (see Table 2, rows 7 and 8). The change in chi square from Analysis 1 to Analysis 2, 14.19 (see Table 2, row 8), is statistically significant given one degree of freedom. The relationship between age at first birth and abuse *is not* reduced to statistical insignificance once number of live births is controlled: the partial regression coefficient for prediction of child abuse from age at first birth is significant at the .05 level.

TABLE 2

Chi squares associated with age at first birth from logistic regression models focused on identifying which of three markers of chronic sociodemographic stress mediate the delayed relationship between age at first birth and either child abuse or child neglect

Variables in model	Variables added to model	Neglect status (n=400)	Abuse status (n=399)
(1) *A, R, AFB*		31.29**	20.36**
(2)	*EM*	29.12**	17.78**
(3)		Difference 2.17	2.58
(4) *A, R, AFB*		31.29**	20.36**
(5)	*ED*	25.06**	17.41**
(6)		Difference 6.23*	2.95
(7) *A, R, AFB*		31.29**	20.36**
(8)	*LB*	2.43	5.17*
(9)		Difference 28.86**	14.19**

R=race, *A*=age, *AFB*=age first birth, *ED*=education, *LB*=number of live births, *EM*=employment history. *p<.05; **p<.00001

In summary, this set of analyses reveals some possible differences between child abuse and neglect. Two of the three chronic stress indicators—number of live births and educational achievement—are mediators of the relationship for neglect while only one—number of live births—is a mediator for abuse. Employment history was not a mediator for either abuse or neglect. The next step in the data analysis focuses on identifying which of the significant individual mediators mediate the relationship independently of the remaining two markers of stress.

WHICH OF THE SIGNIFICANT individual mediators have significant mediating effects independent of the other two chronic stress indicators?

When answers to this question are interpreted in light of answers to the previous question about individual mediators, it is possible to generate hypotheses about possible causal sequences among the set of mediating variables. For example, if education has significant individual mediating power but no significant mediating power apart from the other two stress indicators, then it is reasonable to hypothesize that the effects of low educational achievement on maltreatment could be through its impact on number of live births or employment history.

To answer this question for *child neglect*, two regressions were necessary because two of the three indicators of chronic stress were found to be significant individual mediators. One involved regressing child neglect status on age at first birth, the two control variables, and both employment and education, the other involved regressing child neglect status on age at first birth, the two control variables, and both employment and number of live births. To answer this question for *child abuse*, only one regression was required because only one of the three chronic stress indicators was found to be a significant individual mediator. It involved regressing child abuse status on age at first birth, the two control variables, and both employment and education.

Findings. Findings displayed in Table 3 reveal that, of the two individual mediators of the relationship between age at first birth and child neglect, only number of live births is a statistically significant mediator after controlling for the other two chronic stress indicators—education and employment. Its mediation of the relationship is complete—the Analysis 2 chi square associated with the partial regression coefficient for age at first birth is not statistically significant (see Table 3, row 2). Failure to find that education is a significant mediating variable suggests that its impact on maltreatment could be through its effect on number of live births and employment history.

TABLE 3

Chi squares associated with age at first birth from logistic regression models focused on identifying whether number of live births and educational status mediate the delayed relationship between age at first birth and either child abuse or child neglect independent of the other chronic stress markers

Variables in model	Variables added to model	Neglect status (n=400)	Abuse status (n=399)
Number live births			
(1) R, A, AFB, EM, ED		24.73**	16.21**
(2)	LB	1.37	4.01*
(3)		Difference 23.36**	12.20**
Education			
(4) R, A, AFB, LB, EM		2.28	
(5)	ED	1.37	
(6)		Difference .91	

R=race, A=age, AFB=age first birth, ED=education, LB=number of live births, EM=employment history. *$p<.05$; **$p<.00001$.

For child abuse, number of live births is also a statistically significant mediator of the relationship independent of the other two chronic stress indicators. However, its mediation of the relationship is partial rather than complete. While the partial regression coefficient for age at first live birth is significantly reduced once number of live births is added to the analysis, it remains statistically significant.

In summary, this set of analyses reveals that, for both types of child maltreatment, number of live births mediates their relationship with age at first birth, independent of the other two stress indicators. For child neglect, failure of education to persist as a significant mediator independent of number of live births and employment history suggests that its effect on neglect is through its impact on the other two stress indicators, particularly number of live births.

Discussion

Overall, study findings are consistent with the hypothesis that chronic sociodemographic stress mediates the relationship between young age at first birth and both child physical abuse and neglect. Together, the three markers of sociodemographic stress completely mediate the relationship between age at first birth and child neglect and, at least partially, mediate the relationship for child physical abuse. Examination of the mediating potential of each of the three markers of sociodemographic stress reveals that the two types of maltreatment are 1) similar in that number of live births is the only stress marker that mediates the relationship independent of the other two markers; 2) similar in that employment history does not mediate the relationship; and 3) different with respect to the mediating influence of educational achievement. For child abuse, educational achievement plays no mediating role while, for child neglect, its impact on child care adequacy appears to be funneled through number of live births and, possibly, employment history.

IMPLICATIONS FOR EMPIRICAL LITERATURE

Study results support and extend existing findings from both the maternal behavior and the adolescent childbearing literatures and provide some new meaning for findings from the child maltreatment literature. Currently, the maternal behavior literature includes only one study (Conger et al., 1984) that has addressed the issue of variables that mediate the relationship between early age at first birth and maternal behavior of any kind. Findings from this study hinted that chronic sociodemographic stress may mediate the relationship between young age at first birth and maternal affective behavior. Conger and colleagues found statistically significant individual relationships between age at first birth and chronic sociodemographic stress. Results of our investigation, which followed up on Conger et al.'s study by testing the chronic stress hypothesis, extend knowledge about maternal behavior by showing that 1) sociodemographic stress does mediate the relationship between young age at first birth and maternal behavior and 2) of three stressors, number of live births appears to be the most important mediator for the population of very low-income, single-parent mothers. Findings also suggest that, at least for child neglect, the effect of low educational achievement on maternal child care adequacy may be through family size.

The adolescent childbearing literature is an extensive and fairly sophisticated body of knowledge. Investigators have repeatedly documented that young maternal age at first birth has 1) both immediate and delayed negative sociodemographic consequences for the mother herself, i.e., higher completed fertility, close spacing of offspring, low educational achievement, unemployment and underemployment, etc. (Baldwin, 1983); 2) delayed negative consequences for the social, emotional, and developmental progress of the mother's children (Baldwin & Cain, 1980); and 3) immediate negative consequences for various affective dimensions of the mother's caretaking behavior. Interestingly enough, this literature includes very little information about the delayed effects of young maternal age on caretaking behavior and little direct information on the longer term consequences of the excess fertility and low educational achievement that are so typical of women who had early first births. Findings from this study add to this literature by showing that young age at first birth can have delayed, highly negative effects on maternal behavior for very low-income, single-parent women and that these negative effects are, at least in part, a consequence of the excess fertility that is so characteristic of many women who began childbearing during their teens.

Knowledge about child maltreatment is in a very early developmental state. It consists of dozens of fairly well-documented individual findings but almost no results regarding relationships among the many correlates of maltreatment. The four variables examined for this study have all been found to have highly significant individual relationships with both abuse and neglect (Creighton, 1985; Herronkohl & Herrenkohl, 1979; Wolock & Horowitz, 1977). In addition, family size has been found to be a particularly important predictor of child neglect relative to other well-established correlates like social isolation, adverse growing up experience, low educational achievement, low material level of living, and so forth (Wolock & Horowitz, 1977; Zuravin, 1980). This study adds to knowledge about child abuse and neglect not by identifying new correlates but by exploring how well- established correlates relate to each other. For example, with regard to child abuse, study findings suggest that educational achievement and lifetime employment status, significant predictors of child abuse for study respondents, do not play a role in the mediation of the relationship between age at first birth and child abuse whereas excess fertility does. On the other hand, with regard to child neglect, findings suggest that educational achievement does play some kind of role in mediating the relationship. Conceivably, low educational achievement is partially responsible for the excess live births which, in turn and through still other variables, lead to neglect.

IMPLICATIONS FOR THEORY AND RESEARCH

Child abuse and neglect are complex phenomena with multiple causes, the end result of two-directional interactions among variables from many different levels including the individual parent and child, the family, the neighborhood, the society, and the culture (Belsky, 1980). Findings from this study have the most implications for variables at the level of the individual parent and the family. They suggest that abuse and neglect of low-income children, may be explained, at least in part, as a delayed as well as an indirect consequence of the low-income teenagers' deviation from the normal adolescent life script, i.e., having a first child at a young age, during the mid-teens. Of the three chronic stress indicators included in this study, a large number of live births appears to be the most important chronic stressor, the main source of the delayed relationship between teenage first births and both child abuse and neglect. For many reasons, it makes sense that excess children would function as a major stressor. Every additional child *1)* means having to divide limited material and emotional resources into smaller and smaller parcels; *2)* decreases the likelihood of remarrying and as a result obtaining social support from a spouse; and *3)* lessens the probability that others, including both informal and formal providers of support, will be available to help with the children.

With regard to future research, findings underscore the merit of testing other hypothesized mediators as well as attempting to construct and test more comprehensive models of the relationship between age at first birth and child maltreatment. Perhaps the most important model to test next is one that not only examines the mediating influence of social support networks but also asks whether the mediating power of number of live births is channeled through its impact on the availability and use of social support networks.

POLICY, PROGRAM, AND RESEARCH RECOMMENDATIONS

Findings from this study suggest that family planning-oriented approaches to the prevention of both child abuse and child neglect may have merit. First, and most generally, they suggest that money spent on designing and implementing high-quality family planning programs specifically for low-income teenagers may well bring about a lower rate of both physical abuse and neglect. Second, and more specifically, they suggest that to have a maximum impact on child maltreatment rates it is important that teenage family planning programs pay particular attention to *a)* helping the young, low-income teenage girl avoid teenage parenthood and *b)* helping the young, low-income teenager who already has a child to better plan subsequent children.

Conclusions

Findings from the study reported in this paper support the "life course" hypothesis that chronic sociodemographic stress mediates the observed delayed relationship between young age at first birth and two types of child maltreatment: physical abuse and neglect. Of the three markers of chronic stress, large number of live births is a mediator for both types of maltreatment, failure to ever be employed is a mediator for neither type of maltreatment, and low educational achievement is a mediator for neglect but not abuse. Overall findings underscore the possible explanatory value of the life course hypotheses and suggest that further testing is in order.

References

Altemeier, W., O'Connor, S., Vietze, P., Sandler, H., & Sherrod, K. (1984). Prediction of child abuse: A prospective study of feasibility. *Child Abuse and Neglect*, 8, 393–400.

Baldwin, W. (1983). *Trends and consequences of adolescent child-bearing in the United States*. Statement before the Select Committee on Children, Youth, and Families. Bethesda, MD: National Institute of Child Health and Human Development, Center for Population Research.

Baldwin, W., & Cain, V.S. (1980). The children of teenage parents. *Family Planning Perspectives*, 12, 34–43.

Baltes, P.B., & Brim, O.G., Jr. (Eds.) (1979). *Life span development and behavior* (Vol. 2). New York: Academic Press.

Belsky, J. (1980). Child maltreatment: An ecological integration. *American Psychologist*, 35, 320–335.

Bolton, F., Jr., & Laner, R. (1981). Maternal maturity and maltreatment. *Journal of Family Issues*, 2(4), 485–508.

Bolton, F., Jr., Laner, R., & Kane, S. (1980). Child maltreatment risk among adolescent mothers: A study of reported cases. *American Journal of Orthopsychiatry*, 50, 489–504.

Conger, R., McCarty, J., Yang, R., Lahey, B., & Burgess, R. (1984). Mother's age as a predictor of observed maternal behavior in three independent samples of families. *Journal of Marriage and the Family*, 46, 411–423.

Creighton, S. (1985). Epidemiological study of abused children and their families in the United Kingdom between 1977 and 1982. *Child Abuse and Neglect*, 9, 441–448.

Elder, G. (1978). Family history and the life course. In T.K. Hareven (Ed.), *Transitions: The family and the life course in historical perspective*. New York: Academic Press.

Elster, A., & McAnarney, E. (1980). Medical and psychosocial risks of pregnancy and childbearing during adolescence. *Pediatric Annals*, 9(3), 11–20.

Field, T., Widmayer, S., Stringer, S., & Ignatoff, E. (1980). Teenage, lower-class, black mothers and their preterm infants: An intervention and developmental follow-up. *Child Development*, 51, 426–436.

Harrell, F.E., Jr. (1983). The logist procedure. In SAS Institute, Inc. (Eds.) *SUGI Supplemental Library User's Guide*. Cary, NC: SAS Institute.

Herrenkohl, E., & Herrenkohl, R. (1979). A comparison of abused children and their nonabused siblings. *Journal of the American Academy of Child Psychiatry*, 18, 260–269.

Hunter, R., Kilstrom, N., Kraybill, E., & Loda, F. (1978). Antecedents of child abuse and neglect in premature infants: A prospective study in a newborn intensive care unit. *Pediatrics*, 61(4), 629–635.

Jones, F., Green, V., & Krauss, D. (1980). Maternal responsiveness of primiparous mothers during the postpartum period: Age differences. *Pediatrics*, 65(3), 579–584.

Kent, J. (1973). *Follow-up study of abused children*. Los Angeles: Department of Public Social Services and Children's Hospital Los Angeles, Division of Psychiatry.

Knoke, D., & Burke, P. (1983). *Log linear models*. Sage University Paper, Series on Quantitative Applications in the Social Sciences, Number 20. Beverly Hills, CA: Sage Publications.

Leventhal, James. (1981). Risk factors to child abuse: Methodologic standards in case control studies. *Child Abuse and Neglect*, 6, 113–123.

Magura, S., & Moses, B. (1986). *Outcome Measures for Child Welfare Services*. New York: Child Welfare League of America.

McAnarney, E., Lawrence, R., & Aten, M. (1979). A preliminary report of adolescent mother-infant interaction. *Pediatric Research*, 13, 328.

McLaughlin, S., & Micklin, M. (1983). The timing of the first birth and changes in personal efficacy. *Journal of Marriage and the Family*, 45, 47–55.

Miller, S. (1984). The relationship between adolescent childbearing and child maltreatment. *Child Welfare*, 63, 553–557.

National Center for Health Statistics. (1981). *National Survey of Family Growth Cycle III Under 25 Questionnaire*. Washington, D.C. National Center for Health and Statistics.

Philliber, S., & Graham, E. (1981). The impact of age of mother on mother-child interaction patterns. *Journal of Marriage and the Family*, 43, 109–115.

Ragozin, A., Basham, R., Crnic, K., Greenberg, M., & Robinson, N. (1982). Effects of maternal age on parenting role. *Developmental Psychology*, 18, 627–634.

Walker, S., & Duncan, D. (1967). Estimation of the probability of an event as a function of several independent variables. *Biometrika*, 54, 167–169.

Wolock, I., & Horowitz, B. (1977). *Factors relating to levels of child care among families receiving public assistance in New Jersey*. Final report to the National Center on Child Abuse and Neglect (DHEW Grant 9-C-418). Washington, D.C.: National Clearinghouse on Child Abuse and Neglect Information.

Zuravin, S. (1980). *Child neglect among the poor: A comparative study*. Unpublished doctoral dissertation, University of Maryland, College Park.

———. (1987). *Fertility patterns: Their relationship to child maltreatment*. Unpublished manuscript.

Family Support: Helping Teenage Mothers to Cope

. . . . .

**Frank F. Furstenberg, Jr.
and Albert G. Crawford**

Even under the most propitious circumstances, the formation of a new family is a complex transition. A growing body of research suggests that adolescent childbearing greatly complicates the process.[1] Early parenthood creates an immediate crisis for teenage parents and their families, and often initiates a chain of events which may result in long-term disadvantage for the young parents and their offspring. With increasing precision, researchers have been able to document the commonsensical notion that early and unscheduled childbearing curtails the life chances of the young mother, especially her prospects for educational, economic and marital well-being.[2] Less evidence exists on the impact of early childbearing on the father, but there are strong indications that the male's economic and family position may be damaged as well.[3] Carefully designed studies of the consequences of teenage childbearing for the offspring are extremely rare, though scattered results from related research point in the expected direction: The child of an adolescent parent is more likely to be physically and socially handicapped than are his peers.[4]

Researchers examining the situation of adolescent parents and their offspring have generally overlooked, however, the social context in which early childbearing takes place. There has been almost no analysis of how the family

Reprinted with permission from *Family Planning Perspectives*, vol. 10, No. 6, Nov./Dec. 1988. The Alan Guttmacher Institute.
Material for this article was drawn from a background report prepared for a Conference on Perspectives on Policy Toward Teenage Pregnancy sponsored by the Family Impact Seminar. Seminar papers were commissioned by a grant from the Mott Foundation. The data were originally collected under a grant from MCHS (MC-R-420117-05-05) and the reanalysis was made possible by a contract from NICHD (NOI-HD-72822) to the Center for Reasearch on the Acts of Man.

as a social unit is affected by an early pregnancy. It is widely assumed that many young mothers, even those who marry before or shortly after childbirth, but especially those who become single parents, rely on their own families to provide economic assistance, child-care services and psychological support.[5] It is believed that parents, siblings and, not infrequently, relatives outside the immediate family are drawn into the problematic life situation of the teenage mother.

Some researchers have suggested that early and out-of-wedlock child-bearing is prevalent among low-income blacks because this pattern of family formation is more or less congruent with the matrifocal form of the family.[6] Relatives, so the argument goes, are willing to shoulder some of the responsibility for child care and child support in return for the adolescent's allegiance to the mother-centered household, for the economic resources she contributes through earnings or welfare, and for a share of the gratifications of childrearing.

None of these speculations has been tested empirically with systematic data. Whether or not they are correct, these hypotheses about the functional character of adolescent pregnancy direct our attention from an exclusive concern with individuals to a concern for collectivities. We shall consider how the family as an entity may be involved in helping the adolescent to cope with parenthood.

In addressing this issue, we hope to correct another short-coming of existing studies on early childbearing. Researchers have been so preoccupied with demonstrating that early childbearing creates serious disadvantages that they have generally overlooked the fact that some young mothers overcome the obstacles associated with premature parenthood and even derive psychological benefits from the experience. Without minimizing the difficulties, we need to explore the circumstances which contribute to the successful management of adolescent parenthood.

This investigation represents a first step in that direction. In the following analysis, we look into the role played by kin in providing support and assistance to the young mother and her offspring. Our aim is to examine the proposition that the outcome of early childbearing is mediated by the family's involvement in the transition to parenthood.

Data and Methods

In 1966–1967, under the auspices of Sinai Hospital in Baltimore, a study was undertaken to evaluate the effectiveness of a comprehensive service program for adolescent mothers and their offspring. Though the initial purpose of this research was to assess the program, the study, even as it was originally conceived, was concerned with how the pregnancy affected the life situation of the young mother and her family. At the outset, data were obtained from both the adolescents and their mothers on the social and economic status of the family and on the structure of the household. Our sample consisted primarily of lower and working-class individuals. Most of the families had incomes near or below the poverty level; the median annual income was $3,000–$4,000. One out of four families was receiving welfare assistance at the time of the initial interview (1966–1967). Most of the families were black. About 50 percent of the adolescent mothers' families were headed by two parents, 40 percent by the mother, and the rest by another relative.*

Early parenthood was not an unfamiliar event in the families of the young women in the sample: Nearly one-half of the prospective grandmothers had borne their first child when they were younger than 18, and at least one-quarter had borne a child out of wedlock. Many of the siblings of the adolescents in the sample had also become pregnant while they were in their early teens.

All women younger than 18 who entered the hospital program were interviewed at the time of registration; their parents were interviewed in the home shortly thereafter. The initial interviews were conducted with 404 pregnant adolescents, of whom 87 percent were black, and with 350 of the prospective grandmothers. Nearly 95 percent of the adolescents were reinterviewed one year later (1967–68), when the program evaluation had been completed. Because so little was known about the long-term careers of adolescent parents and their children, further funding was obtained to trace the impact of the teenage birth on educational, economic, marital and fertility behavior three years and five years after delivery. Data were also collected from a sample of former classmates of the adolescent mothers who did not get pregnant as teenagers (or did so later than the teenage mothers). The classmates were first interviewed in 1970, when the young mothers were interviewed for the third time (approximately three years after delivery) and again in 1972, when the final interview with the adolescent mothers took place. Sample attrition remained quite low throughout the study; nearly 82 percent of the original participants were reinterviewed at the five-year follow-up.

The interviews conducted three and five years after delivery provided additional data on the family situation of the young mother and her child (including an account of her residential situation), as well as selected information on economic aid provided by the family, participation by kin in child care, and psychological support, advice and information offered by relatives. An assessment of the impact of early childbearing on the organization of the family can be made by comparing the respective situations of the young mothers and their classmates at the final interview.

What makes the Baltimore data attractive is the longitudinal perspective they afford on the changing role of kin during the period of family formation. As the data make clear, provision of assistance by the family changes markedly over time. Consequently, a snapshot view at any point in time yields an

---

* Because the sample is a purposive one, it is not easy to determine whether it provides a basis for generalization to the larger population of adolescent mothers in Baltimore. Efforts were made to compare the characteristics of our sample with those of teenagers who delivered in other Baltimore hospitals during the same period. In general, the results were reassuring. Our sample appeared to resemble the population of other teenagers below the age of 18 who delivered a child in Baltimore. The socioeconomic profiles of the families of our sample were also similar to the characteristics of the larger black population as reflected in census data on low-income families in the city. A detailed description of the sample, study design and content of the interviews can be found in F.F. Furstenberg, Jr., 1976 (see reference 2).

incomplete picture of the aid rendered by the family. Only by tracing the changing pattern of family involvement do we begin to develop a sense of the flow of family assistance.

Having noted the advantages of the Baltimore data, we should also mention certain of their limitations. The principal defect is that the study was not designed to examine the questions posed in this article. Little systematic information was collected on the extent of the kinship involvement, especially in the early stages of the study; consequently, we are forced to make do with less than ideal indicators of family assistance. We do have careful records of household composition, and our analysis is based on this feature of the family support system. But even here we are confronted with certain difficulties. We have observations of the young mothers' household arrangements only at four separate points in time. No records exist of young mothers who moved out of and back into the same household during an interim period or who changed residential situations more than once in any given interval. Therefore, our results inevitably understate the changes that actually took place in family situations during the five-year period following delivery.

With these restrictions in mind, we may proceed to a consideration of what can be learned from the Baltimore study about the assistance rendered by the family and its consequences for the young mothers' adaptation to parenthood.

Attitudes Toward Family Formation

The conventional sequence for forming a family in our society begins with the departure from one's family of origin, typically before, but sometimes concurrent with, entrance into marriage. Generally, marriage precedes parenthood, though in fact a substantial number of marriages have been and continue to be precipitated by pregnancy.* Establishment of a separate household generally happens before or at the same time as marriage, and infrequently succeeds childbearing.

Most of the teenage mothers in our study endorsed, at least verbally, this conventional schedule for family formation. In the final interview, when their median age was 21, nearly two-thirds said that becoming premaritally pregnant probably harms a couple's prospects for a successful marriage (although most approved of premarital sexual activity). Virtually all (96 percent) stated that living with relatives after marriage is likely to hurt a couple's chances for marital success. Almost no one regarded a premarital pregnancy or a postmarital extended-family arrangement as a desirable prelude to married

---

* The rate of births conceived premaritally in the 1970s is lower than in the immediately preceding decades, owing to the greater availability of abortion, but still, one-third of all teenage births occurring within marriage in 1972 were conceived out of wedlock. (See: P.J. Placek, "Trends in Legitimate, Legitimated by Marriage and Illegitimate First Births: United States, 1964–1966 and 1972," paper presented at the annual meeting of the American Statistical Association, Aug. 14–17, 1978, San Diego.)

life. Moreover, the young mothers' standards were the same as those of their nonpregnant classmates, whose opinions, in turn, resembled the general values of the larger population of young adults regarding the appropriate schedule for family formation.

In practice, however, the young mothers' experience departed from the ideal pattern of family formation. Almost all became pregnant before marriage, thus disarranging and complicating the conventional sequence of family formation. What ensued were a number of distinct strategies for coping with these complications, which, as we shall see, reflect both personal predilections and the availability of material and psychological resources from family members.

Household Change Over Time

Households were classified* according to whether the adolescent mothers were married or unmarried, living with parents or other kin, or living alone or with their husbands in a separate household, or with their husbands in the family's home. The resulting fourfold typology is presented in Table 1, which displays the household arrangements of the young mothers at the four

---

TABLE 1.

Percentage distribution of adolescent mothers and a comparison group of classmates, by marital status and type of household in which they resided, 1966–1967 to 1972.

Marital status and household type	Adolescent mothers				Classmates, 1972	
	1966–1967 (N=370)	1967–1968 (N=374)	1970 (N=347)	1972 (N=312)	Early pregnancy (N=42)	No early pregnancy (N=158)
Currently unmarried						
Total	85	72	64	66	66	69
Never-married	85	64	48	36	57	58
Alone	2	5	8	11	21	9
With parents or kin	83	59	40	25	36	49
Ever-married	0	8	16	30	9	11
Alone	0	2	4	15	7	2
With parents or kin	0	6	12	15	2	9
Currently married						
Total	15	28	36	33	33	31
With spouse only	10	16	25	27	19	22
With spouse and parents or kin	5	12	11	6	14	9

Note: The *N*s in this and the following tables vary because all questions were not answered by all respondents or because responses were unclear. Percents in this and subsequent tables may not add to 100 because of rounding.

---

* No standard formulation for classifying the household arrangements of family members exists other than the one developed by the Census Bureau. We use a modification of this scheme, adapted to the information available from the interviews.

interview points, as well as the classmates' residential situations at the five-year follow-up in 1972. The data, when arrayed over time, point to several developments.

During the period from pregnancy to the five-year postpartum interview, a growing proportion of the young mothers predictably made their way out of the household of their parents. In 1966–1967, 88 percent of the pregnant adolescents (including both the married and the unmarried) were living with one or both parents, and/or other relatives. We suspect that the two percent of expectant mothers who were living alone had only moved from their families' household after becoming pregnant, although data to demonstrate this theory are not available. In effect, then, before childbirth, virtually all the pregnant adolescents resided with their parents or a parent surrogate and/or a spouse. In view of their youth, any other arrangement would have been surprising. It is noteworthy that few adolescents used the occasion of the pregnancy to leave their family of origin, probably because few were in an economic or psychological position to do so.

The second interview (1967–1968) takes us to the period approximately one year after delivery, and reveals the impact of childbirth on the residential situation of the young mothers. As the table shows, a large but diminished proportion of the young mothers continued to live in their parents' or relatives' home (77 percent compared with 88 percent the previous year). Although 28 percent of the young mothers were currently married at this time (compared with 15 percent the year before), 43 percent of all those currently married were still living with parents (usually the woman's), an even larger proportion than the year before. Overall, the rate of marriage was even greater (36 percent had ever been married), but 22 percent of all marriages had already been dissolved. The breakup of marriage resulted either in the return of the young mother to her former household (six mothers) or in her establishment of a separate household (four mothers). Despite the frequency of marital breakup, only seven percent of the young mothers were living alone at the one-year follow-up. In contrast to the conventional pattern of family formation, disengagement from the parental household seldom took place among adolescent parents even *after* matrimony or childbearing.

About two years later, in 1970, there is evidence of some change, although the household constellations remain basically similar to those in previous periods. By this time, most of the young mothers were in their late teens and early 20s and 52 percent had been married (36 percent were currently married and an additional 16 percent were separated). Nonetheless, 63 percent of the entire sample continued to reside with one or both parents or other relatives. Of course, not all lived continuously with their family of origin since the outset of the study (as we shall see shortly from the longitudinal analysis), but residence with parents remained the modal arrangement. The number currently married had risen, but 31 percent of these couples continued to live with parents, again usually the woman's. Only a small proportion, 12 percent, of all the women had set up independent households.

At the final interview, when most young mothers were in their early 20s, a further shift had taken place in residential situation. By then, as the table shows, the proportion still living with their families had dropped to 46 percent, including married couples. The decline of this type of household arrangement did not result from a growth in the marriage rate, however. Indeed, the proportion of young mothers who were currently married actually decreased slightly during this period, from 36 percent to 33 percent. It has been reported elsewhere that there is a sharp rise in the proportion of women in comparable age and socioeconomic status who are currently married at this stage of life.[7] But in the Baltimore sample, we observe a sizable increase in the proportion of women living alone, and only a slight increase in the proportion currently living with their spouses. The proportion of women living alone more than doubled between 1970 and 1972. Thus, the loss of parental assistance was not usually offset by a gain in conjugal support.

The extent to which early childbearing accelerates the movement away from the parental household, contributing to a separation from the family of origin, is highlighted by contrasting the residential situations of the young mothers with those of 200 of their classmates at the five-year follow-up. We have subdivided the classmates into two groups: those who, like the young mothers, had become parents during adolescence, but at a later age (constituting 21 percent of the sample); and the remainder, who either had not yet become pregnant or had waited to do so until they were at least in their early 20s.* Data on these two subgroups of classmates are located in the last two columns of Table 1.

Now compare the early childbearers with the classmates who had not become pregnant or who had experienced a conception only after adolescence.** Virtually the same proportion of the classmates as of the young mothers were currently married at the five-year follow-up. (However, 63 percent of the young mothers had ever been married by this time, compared with just 42 percent of the classmates.) What distinguishes the women who delayed childbearing from the adolescent mothers was not their current marital situations but the residential situations of those who had remained single. A much greater proportion of those who had deferred childbearing were living with parents or other family members at the final interview. Fifty-eight percent were unwed and resided with parents at the final interview, compared with 38 percent of the early-childbearing classmates and 40 percent of the women in the clinic sample.

---

* In most respects, the 42 classmates who were teenage childbearers are virtually indistinguishable from the young mothers drawn from the clinic population. A higher proportion of the currently married classmates with children were still living with relatives, probably because their pregnancies had occurred more recently, allowing less time for a separate marital unit to be established.

** We grouped together the nulliparous classmates with those who delayed their first pregnancies until their 20s, as most of the latter had married prior to delivery, unlike the teenage childbearers. Moreover, the never-pregnant and later-pregnant women had similar household situations in 1972.

One other important difference emerges when we compare the early childbearers with their classmates who delayed conception. Only 11 percent of the childless classmates and those who had deferred childbearing were living alone, compared with 28 percent of the classmates who had had children later in adolescence, and 26 percent of the early childbearers. At least at this stage of life, teenage parenthood seems to result in an earlier establishment of a separate household unit, perhaps removing individuals from the amount of parental and family support which they might otherwise obtain.

Residence Patterns/Family Support

A pivotal problem, but one that we can only partially resolve, is what these early residential patterns imply for the subsequent flow of family assistance. We did not inquire about the specific provision of family support until the three-year follow-up; moreover, we neglected to collect detailed information on this subject until the final interview, making it impossible to examine data on the provision of family assistance over time. Incomplete as it is, however, the available evidence confirms the common sense assumption that family support is more available to the young mother who remains with her parents or other relatives. Certain avenues of financial and emotional support are closed off to the young mother who leaves the family context; or, perhaps (as we shall later show) she departs because family support is not available to her.

At the one-year follow-up, the mothers were asked three questions relating to sources of child-care advice in particular and psychological support in general.* As the responses to these items were highly intercorrelated, they were combined into a single index, measuring the level of dependency on parents. Table 2 shows the extent of dependency expressed by the young mothers in the different residential contexts. According to expectation, the unmarried young mothers living with their parents or kin were more likely to be highly reliant on them than were the young mothers residing alone.

The unmarried young mother's parents and other kin play a key role in the determination of whether she will resume her education or go to work outside the home. At the one-year follow-up, when the young mothers were asked if they had received any help from their parents or kin in returning to school, none of the unmarried women living apart from their parents reported that they had received such help, while 12 percent of the women living with

---

* The questions asked were as follows:

> "A lot of teenagers have personal problems from time to time. Suppose you had a serious personal problem, who would you go to for advice?"

> "Suppose you wanted some information about how to feed your baby, who would you go to for advice?"

> "Suppose your baby were ill, who then would you go to for advice about what to do?"

TABLE 2

Among young mothers living in various types of households, percentage who obtained support from parents and other kin, by type of support; various years.

Indicator of support	Household type			
	Alone	With parents or kin	With spouse	With spouse and parents or kin
Substantial reliance on parents or kin, 1967–1968				
(*N*)	(25)	(243)	(61)	(45)
%	12	25	7	9
Help from kin in returning to school, 1967–1968				
(*N*)	(25)	(243)	(61)	(45)
%	0	12	2	0
Not working because of lack of child care, 1970				
(*N*)	(40)	(182)	(88)	(37)
%	42	22	38	35
Various child-care arrangements, 1972				
(*N*)	(79)	(116)	(77)	(16)
Adolescent mother most (%)	52	43	53	62
Grandmother or other kin most or equally (%)	33	43	32	25
Other (friend, babysitter, day-care center) most or equally (%)	15	14	16	12
Receiving money from parents or kin, 1972				
(*N*)	(82)	(127)	(85)	(18)
%	18	20	12	22
Nonfinancial contributions from parents or kin, 1972				
(*N*)	(82)	(127)	(85)	(18)
%	12	64	6	33

their parents said they had received this assistance. Virtually none of the married women had received such aid, regardless of their residential situation.

Access to child-care support has significant consequences for the likelihood of finding stable employment.[8] At the three-year follow-up, the single young mothers living alone were almost twice as likely as those residing with parents or kin (42 percent vs. 22 percent) to say that they were not working because they had no one to care for their child. No such difference occurred, however, between the two groups of married young mothers.

In response to a question asked at the five-year follow-up about who spent the most time caring for their children, the unmarried respondents revealed that those who lived with their parents or other kin typically received more assistance from them than those living apart from them. In order to develop a measure which tapped various levels of support, we combined those cases where the grandmother or another female relative assumed greater child-care responsibility with the cases where the adolescent mother and that other woman assumed equal responsibility. Thus, we found that 43 percent of the unmarried mothers living with parents or other relatives reported that another woman was a principal caretaker; 33 percent of those no longer living with parents or relatives relied on them for child-care support. The young mothers living alone were correspondingly more likely than those living with family to take responsibility for child care themselves (52 percent vs. 43 percent), rather than to adapt by using other kinds of child care (15 percent vs. 14 percent). Their situation most closely resembled that of the married women, who received the least assistance with child care from relatives.

In the final interview, the women were asked whether they were currently receiving any financial assistance from their parents. Whether or not they responded affirmatively, they were also questioned about other forms of material aid provided by their parents, such as food, clothing or personal effects. Obviously, this open-ended question failed to yield complete information on assistance rendered, for many respondents undoubtedly neglected to report occasional gifts or forms of help that were taken for granted, such as room and board.

Very few of the young mothers, regardless of their residential situation, were receiving direct financial contributions from their parents at the five-year follow-up. Only 17 percent reported any form of cash allowance. And there was only a slight difference by household type in the unmarried women's chances of receiving such aid. Married women living with their parents or kin were more apt to receive money from them than were women living with their spouses alone (22 percent compared with 12 percent).

In addition to financial assistance, 33 percent of the women listed other forms of material support. Women living with their families were more likely to receive such assistance. Only six percent of the married women living in separate households with their husbands reported regular assistance from their families, whereas 33 percent of the married women residing with their parents or kin stated that they got regular help. Twelve percent of unmarried women living by themselves reported nonfinancial support, compared with 64 percent of the single women who were living with a relative. Thus, while moving out of the home does not totally preclude receiving material assistance from parents, it certainly is associated with a decreased likelihood of receiving such aid.

In summary, we have found some consistent differences in the availability of family support by residential situation. Unmarried women living with their parents or other kin are generally more reliant on them for advice and support; their parents provide more aid, such as food, clothing and child care; and the young mothers take advantage of such aid in order to continue their educational and occupational careers. While some differences hold also for the married women, the differences are typically greater among the unmarried women, suggesting that marriage attenuates the supply of parental aid, perhaps because a spouse is able to provide the aid which otherwise comes from parents.

Differences in the availability of family support between women who remain in the household and those who leave their family of origin are probably sharpest around the time of delivery. Once patterns of child care and material assistance are initiated, they may continue even after the adolescent establishes a separate household. No doubt, many young mothers, both married and single, remain near their family of origin even after they move out of the household, and that proximity enables an exchange of services to continue.

Transitions in Family Formation

Having demonstrated that young mothers residing with their kin received greater benefits from their families in the form of advice, material aid and child care, we now face the task of explaining the circumstances which governed the residential careers of the young mothers. There are many ways of approaching this question, but we find it useful to begin our analysis with a longitudinal inspection of the data we presented earlier in our section on changes in residential situation over time. This longitudinal perspective provides a view of the dynamics of household change and an opportunity to pick up certain clues about the conditions underlying residential movement.

We have already learned from Table 1 that a sizable proportion of the young mothers altered their living situation during the course of the study, and that the pace of movement picked up slightly in the later phases of the study. By cross-tabulating the residential situation at each point in time with that at the successive point in time, we can introduce an element of animation into the four snapshot pictures depicted earlier. The text which follows

TABLE 3.

Percentage of young mothers living in various types of households at the one-year follow-up who were living in the same or different type of household at the five-year follow-up, by type of household

Household at five-year follow-up	Mothers at five year follow-up		% of mothers, by household at one-year follow-up			
	%	N	Alone (N=19)	With parents or kin (N=205)	With spouse (N=46)	With spouse and parents or kin (N=38)
Total	100	308	6	67	15	12
Alone	26	80	53	24	22	29
With parents or kin	41	126	21	49	17	34
With spouse	27	84	21	21	56	26
With spouse and parents or kin	6	18	5	5	4	11

* The figures in the table are related to but are not identical with the amount of geographic movement that took place, for we are only recording residential movement which involved a change in household type.

summarizes the results of this analysis; however, for the sake of simplicity, we shall not show each separate turnover table. We present, instead, a summary table (Table 3) showing the pattern of movement from the one-year follow-up to the five-year follow-up. It captures most of the important residential changes that took place during the course of the study.*

While there is no simple way of summarizing in statistical terms the rate of movement from one interval to the next, some idea of the level of change which occurs can be obtained merely by examining the diagonal cells of the table, which represent stability. Between the one-year follow-up and the five-year follow-up, there was a modest level of residential stability, around 50 percent, in all but one of the four household arrangements (those who lived with spouse and parents). Among the women living alone, more than half, 53 percent, remained in that position. Just under half, 49 percent, of the unmarried women living with parents or other kin had the same living arrangement four years later. And more than half, 56 percent, of the married women living only with their spouses remained in this residential situation at the final follow-up. However, among the married women living with their spouses and parents or relatives at the one-year follow-up, only four out of 38, 11 percent, remained in that kind of household. Apparently, this arrangement was a temporary convenience, permitting marriage to occur earlier than it otherwise could if a separate household had to be established prior to matrimony. Among the women who were married and living only with their spouses at the one-year follow-up, hardly any, four percent, were living with their relatives at the five-year follow-up interview.

One other finding not shown in Table 3 is of some importance. Single women who lived with families augmented by extended kin were no more likely to move out, either to marry or to establish an independent household, after their child was born, than were those who lived in nuclear arrangements. However, movement from households with parents and kin occurred soon after the birth, suggesting that an additional family member may have placed more immediate strain on existing resources when the household was already augmented. In sum, the residential careers of single women were not greatly affected by their living arrangements when delivery occurred.

In a rather abbreviated fashion, we have tried to feature what may be thought of as typical transitions in family formation among the young mothers in our sample. As we found above in our cross-sectional analysis, almost all of the young mothers started out in the parental household and most remained there even after their child was born. The move to independent household headship did not occur for most even by the end of the study, although more than three out of five had ever married by this time. It bears reporting that marriage did not invariably mean departure from the family of origin. Throughout the study, particularly in the early phases, a substantial proportion of the married couples continued to reside with their parents, and the women whose marriages broke up frequently returned to live with their parents.

A Typology of Residential Careers

Although it was theoretically possible for the young mothers to live in some 80 different residential situations in the course of the study, more than half of them followed one of four residential careers, two-thirds followed one of seven, and more than four-fifths followed one of 12 careers.*

The most common residential arrangement was for the young mother to be living with one or both parents or other kin throughout the first five years after delivery. Twenty-nine percent of the sample were sharing a household with their parents at each of the four interviews. While some may have spent a brief time outside the parents' or relatives' household during one or another interval, the young women in this category generally experienced a high degree of continuity in their residential situation.

The second most common sequence was to move from living with parents or relatives to living with a spouse for the rest of the time covered by the study. Twenty-four percent followed this route, though not all, as we have already seen, departed from their parents' household as soon as marriage occurred.

As we have previously observed, a number of unmarried mothers had established their own households by the conclusion of the study: Fifteen percent of the young mothers lived with their parents for some time after childbirth before moving to their own quarters, usually in the latter phase of the study.

Three other common residential sequences involved young mothers who married during the course of the study. Half of these women were no longer residing with their spouse at the five year follow-up. Two-thirds (11 percent of the entire sample) had moved back into their parents' household, while the others had established their own separate household (four percent of the sample). A small segment of the married mothers, slightly more than six percent of the participants, were wed at the time of the initial interview and remained so throughout the study.

Only a tiny fraction of the sample, one percent, lived in independent households from the start.

Eleven percent of the sample did not conform to any of these patterns. Most of these women oscillated between a separate household, residence with parents and other kin, and marriage. While most women we studied experienced either no change in residential status (33 percent) or only one transition (40 percent) during the course of the study, all of the residual group made at least two moves and one-third of them had three recorded changes in their household situation during the five years following delivery.

The remainder of this article is devoted to an exploration of why these different residential strategies were adopted and what implications they had for adjustment to early parenthood. The initial objective of this analysis was to discover specific determinants of the young mother's decision to remain

---

* Individuals residing with both spouse and parent(s) were coded as living with spouse, and those living only with siblings, cousins or children were considered to be living alone.

with or move away from her family. This decision, we believe, was dictated by two very general considerations—a woman's need for assistance and her family's ability to render aid. Using an economic analogy, we refer to the first as *demand* and the second as *supply*.

The Demand for Assistance

One obvious explanation for the variations in residential strategies is age and the aging process. This explanation, in fact, is deceptively simple, for age has manifold cultural, psychological and sociological implications. Following pregnancy, most young mothers would experience increasing pressure to set up an independent household, and the older the young mother, the more likely she would be to assert her independence from the family. Sociological conditions should reinforce this pattern, since older women in the study would be more likely to be of "marriageable age" or, at least, be old enough to meet the economic requirements of establishing a separate household if a marriage did not take place.

As we and others have discussed in some detail in previous publications, age is an important determinant of the timing of marriage.[9] A significantly higher proportion of the young mothers who were 21 and over at the conclusion of the study than of those younger than 21 had wed (71 percent vs. 56 percent), largely because the older women were in a position to marry immediately before the child was born. Although we have already seen that marriage does not automatically remove the young mother from the parental household, it typically has this effect. (Only 10 percent of the married women remained with their families throughout the study.)

Because of the link with marriageability, then, we would expect age to be inversely associated with continuous residence with parents throughout the study, and directly related to continuous residence with a spouse. It is true that among the never-married women, those under 21 were more likely to have remained with their parents throughout the study than were those 21 or over (69 percent vs. 59 percent). Nevertheless, there were no pronounced differences by age among the ever-married women in their likelihood of being married at the end of the study (50 percent vs. 45 percent). And, among the separated women, the younger women were *less* likely to be residing with their parents (39 percent vs. 56 percent). Possibly the age spread within the Baltimore sample is too narrow to account for much variation in residential arrangements.

We are not in a strong position to examine the influence of racial differences on the flow of family assistance, owing to the small number of whites in our sample. Nonetheless, we suspect there are sharp divergences between blacks and whites in the role the family plays after childbirth. As we have described in more detail elsewhere,[10] most of the whites in our study (70 percent) married soon after becoming pregnant, while most of the blacks (84 percent) deferred marriage until after childbirth. In part, these patterns reflect the disparate social meanings of out-of-wedlock childbearing for the two racial groups, but age and economic circumstances also enter into the differing strategies of accommodation to early pregnancy. The whites in the sample were generally older, and the fathers of the children, because of their higher economic status, were in a better position to enter marriage.*

Young black women and their families frequently questioned the advantages of a rapid marriage, and with good reason, since their marriages tended to have lower rates of survival. Not only did deterrents to early marriage exist, but there were also decided incentives for remaining single. Most black parents were willing to provide subsidies to the young mother in the form of free room and board and often child care as well.

A major reason many young mothers postponed marriage was their desire to remain in school. The commitment to continuing their education was strongly voiced by both the young mothers (94 percent) and their parents (87 percent).[11] The women who stayed in school or resumed their education immediately after delivery were more likely to be living with their parents at the one-year and three-year follow-ups. It appears that the need for child-care assistance, and perhaps material support, led many young mothers to adopt a residential strategy which kept them close to their parents. In addition, our evidence suggests that aid was more likely to be provided when strong affective bonds existed between the young mother and her parents.

We mentioned earlier that an index of reliance on parents was constructed from several questions included at the one-year follow-up interviews concerning the degree to which the young mother looked to her parents for advice and support in child-rearing matters. This index predicted, rather strongly, subsequent residential patterns. Whereas 52 percent of the women who never married during the course of the study indicated that they would look to their parents for help in each of the three hypothetical situations, 35 percent of the young mothers who married expressed this same level of dependency. This result reflects the fact that women who married before or shortly after delivery were much less likely to rely on their parents, turning instead to their spouse or boyfriend, a friend, or some other relative when they needed counsel.

Even if eventual marital status is held constant, we still find that the index of reliance on parents forecasts rather clearly the residential strategies from pregnancy to the five-year follow-up. Among the single mothers, 39 percent of those who expressed a low degree of reliance on their parents remained in the parental household, compared with 79 percent of those who acknowledged a high degree of reliance. Clearly, those who felt more independent during pregnancy were more likely to move out and establish their own households soon after their child was born**

---

* Recent qualitative interviews with white families suggest that when parents are willing to provide the resources, the white adolescent may elect to defer marriage as well. (See: P.C. Glick and A.J. Norton, "Marrying, Divorcing and Living Together in the U.S. Today," *Population Bulletin*, Vol. 32, No. 5, 1977.)

**Of course, one cannot impose any one causal interpretation on these results. Very possibly, some young mothers who were highly reliant on their parents were more likely to voice their dependency precisely because they *expected* to remain in the parental household, while young mothers who had moved or were about to

Reliance on parents also had some bearing on the residential decisions of the young mothers who married and subsequently separated. Approximately 50 percent of the young mothers who scored high on the index of reliance returned to live with parents after separation, compared with 32 percent of those who were less responsive to their families' opinions.

Thus, a reason for young women's accepting support from their families can be traced to bonds which antedate the pregnancy but which are sustained and perhaps deepened when a child is born. Obviously, for the women who remain single, pregnancy complicates the process of separation during late adolescence and early adulthood by offering real incentives for staying in the parental home. But it is also clear that these same incentives operate for many married women, perhaps reducing commitment to conjugal ties.*

From the evidence we have pieced together, it seems clear that the teenager derives a number of benefits from remaining with her parents during the early years of parenthood. Few teenage parents, especially those who remain single, have the skills or resources to establish an independent household, and the family provides an alternative to a hasty marriage. With the completion of their education and a diminished need for in-the home child care, some of the young mothers in the study were ready to separate from their families by the five-year follow-up. How they felt about setting out on their own is a question that cannot be answered from the data at hand, but we have reason to suspect that pressures may have been building within the family which hastened their departure.

The Supply of Assistance

Thus far, we have considered only one side of the picture, the circumstances which increase the demand for family aid. We shall now try to show that the availability of assistance also shaped the young mothers' residential careers. In this section, we examine whether their families' desire to help and their resources to do so affected the young mothers' residential decisions.

Unfortunately, the initial interview, conducted in 1966–67, does not provide abundant information on the family's willingness or ability to provide assistance. The parents' initial reaction to the pregnancy had no effect on the residential strategies of the young mothers who never married during the course of the study. Parents who were extremely upset when the pregnancy occurred were actually slightly more likely to extend support to their daughters (70 percent vs. 66 percent)—an indication that few parents reacted punitively once the pregnancy occurred. On the other hand, among the separated young mothers, those whose parents were extremely upset about their pregnancy were less likely to return to their parents' household (38 percent vs. 52 percent). Apparently, these young mothers' marriage and

---

move into marriage accordingly gave less allegiance to their parents' views. Nevertheless, it is most certainly the case that women who experienced a high degree of dependency were less willing or able to move away from their parents.

* For a more detailed discussion of this problem, see: F.F. Furstenberg, Jr., 1978 (reference 2).

inability to succeed in that marriage estranged them from their parents, complicating further what were already strained relations between them.

When asked whether the baby should be given up for adoption, 95 percent of the grandparents favored keeping the child. The tiny minority who counseled adoption were less likely to have their daughter and her offspring in the household at the follow-up interview. This pattern, however, may have as much to do with the availability of resources as with the reaction to the pregnancy.

We found little evidence that a prior history of early childbearing in the family promoted greater dependence on parents after delivery, or that female-headed families were more receptive to maintaining the mother and child in the home. Indeed, the contrary appears to hold true. Unmarried women were actually less likely to remain with the parents when other members of the family had borne a child out of wedlock (61 percent vs. 74 percent). Such a history of out-of-wedlock childbearing was highly correlated with female-headed families; such families were less likely than couple-headed households to retain the adolescent mother if she did not marry (60 percent vs. 83 percent) or if her marriage was dissolved (43 percent vs. 56 percent). One explanation, consistent with our data, for this result is that young mothers who were living in couple-headed households were more likely to look to their parents for advice and assistance (89 percent compared with 68 percent). It is also the case, however, that couple-headed households had more to offer in the way of material benefits than did female-headed households. Many of the female heads were already living on the economic margin and probably could not provide as much material assistance to their child and grandchild as could the household with two parents.

Our data confirm the supposition that the family's economic resources are critically important in determining the long-term supply of assistance to the young mother. The economic position of the family did not predict either early or eventual marriage of the young mother, but it did strongly influence the likelihood of her remaining with the family if marriage did not occur. Table 4 shows the residential patterns of the young mothers who remained single throughout the study and of those who married but separated, by the socioeconomic position of the parents.

The better the family's economic situation at the outset of the study, the more likely the unmarried young mother was to remain in the home through the five-year follow-up. In families in which at least one of the parents worked at a skilled job, 73 percent of the unmarried young mothers remained in the household; where their parents' economic status was lower, only 57 percent of the women remained with their parents. Among the young mothers whose marriages had been dissolved, their families' economic status did not affect their likelihood of returning to live in the parental home. However, the separated women from poorer families were more likely to live alone than

---

* Families in which one or both parents worked at skilled jobs were classified as being of high socioeconomic status; families in which neither parent worked at a skilled job were classified as being of low socioeconomic status.

TABLE 4.

Percentage distribution of young mothers with various residential patterns, by parents' socioeconomic status, according to young mothers' marital status, 1972

Marital status and residential pattern	Socioeconomic status	
	High	Low
Never-married	(N=62)	(N=46)
Alone*	23	41
With parents or kin**	73	57
Other***	5	2
Separated	(N=49)	(N=38)
Alone*	16	32
With parents or kin**	47	47
Other***	37	21

* Alone throughout the study or from living with families or spouse to living alone.
** With parents or kin throughout the study or from living alone or with spouse to families.
*** Two or more residential movements not coded otherwise.

were those from families of higher economic status (32 percent vs. 16 percent).

There are too few cases to assess with any precision the independent effects of family form (that is, whether the household was headed by a couple or a single parent) and the economic position of the household(s). However, it seems likely that both headship and economic standing independently affect the long-term supply of assistance to the young mother. Intact families are generally more economically secure, and economically secure families are more stable. Hence, each condition probably reinforces and augments the other.

Perhaps intervening circumstances relating to marriage, such as the economic status of the husband or the number of children produced, play a greater role in determining the fate of women in marital or post marital situations.

Just as the transition to marriage often precipitates a move from the parental household, additional childbearing frequently forces the young mother and her family to reconsider the residential arrangement. The proportion of never-married women residing with their parents throughout the study drops from 71 percent to 62 percent when a second child is present, and declines to 50 percent when three or more children are present. Additional children also deter the formerly married from resuming residence with their parents. As in the case of the never-married mothers, the sharing of a common household declines among the formerly married women as parity increases (from 50 percent of mothers with one or two children to 29 percent of those with three or more).

Available physical space may have had a good deal to do with the residential strategies which evolved during the course of the study. Although the size of the sample does not permit a definitive test of this interpretation, additional childbearing seems to precipitate a change in household situation because of lack of space. We computed a crude measure of crowding by taking the ratio of the total number of persons in the household to the total number of rooms; we then dichotomized this variable. Where crowding was more serious, only 45 percent of the unmarried adolescent mothers remained in the household of their parents or other kin; under less crowded conditions, 75 percent of the women remained. As we pointed out earlier, crowded conditions may also have forced the breakup of extended families of procreation and eventually may have forced some young mothers to move away from their families.

Our discussion has touched on only a few of the circumstances which explain residential patterns. We have examined both demand and supply conditions which promote and restrict the flow of family assistance, discovering that both psychological factors (such as dependency on parents) and material conditions enter into the decision of where and with whom to live after the child is born. In the final section of the article, we take up the question of how those residential decisions affect the well-being of the young mother.

Consequences of Family Help

Our examination of the impact of residential careers on the life chances of the young mother and her child offers, at best, only an introduction to this topic. The information at hand is not specific enough for us to carry out a refined analysis of the causal pathways which link family assistance to the subsequent economic outcomes or psychological sequelae. Moreover, our sample is not large enough for us to disentangle the complex sequence of familial and economic events which follow delivery; nor did we collect extensive qualitative information that might aid in the interpretation of the data. Nevertheless, it is possible to explore, albeit tentatively, whether remaining with parents enhanced the social prospects of the young mother and her child. Let us first consider some of the findings and then return to the difficulties in interpreting them.

As in the previous analysis, our results are clearer when we separate the young mothers who remained single from those who wed. Looking first at those who never married, we find a clear relationship between residential strategies and economic outcomes (see Table 5). Women who remained with their parents were somewhat more likely to return to school and to be graduated from high school; a much larger proportion were employed and a much smaller proportion were on welfare. (However, among those who were employed, a larger proportion of those who lived alone held skilled jobs.) Conversely, women who moved out of the home at the time of pregnancy or after the transition to parenthood were more likely to have dropped out of school and to have failed to return, a larger proportion were unemployed, and a larger proportion were receiving welfare at the time of the final interview. (It is notable that these data give no support to the

126

conventional belief that teenagers have babies in order to get on welfare and escape from the parental home.)

TABLE 5.
Five indicators of socioeconomic achievement of young women at the five-year follow-up, by marital status and residential pattern

Indicator	Never-married women				Ever-married women							
	Alone		With parents or kin		Alone		With parents or kin		With spouse		With spouse and parents or kin	
	%	N	%	N	%	N	%	N	%	N	%	N
Proportion who returned to school (excluding those who had already completed high school)	76	33	87	71	83	23	76	41	79	76	44	23
Proportion who completed high school	47	34	62	74	43	23	45	44	55	87	36	28
Proportion who were employed	41	32	60	68	43	23	43	44	51	85	36	28
Proportion who held skilled jobs, among those who were employed	31	13	24	41	10	10	11	19	23	43	10	10
Proportion who were on welfare	65	34	43	72	61	23	59	44	12	85	56	27

For the women who married and subsequently separated, the findings are quite different. There are virtually no differences in socioeconomic status between the women who returned to live with their parents and the women who set up independent households. However, the women who remained married and lived with their spouses typically achieved somewhat higher socioeconomic levels than did the women who separated and set up independent households or who returned to the homes of their relatives.

The disparity in outcomes between the never-married and previously married lends plausibility to the interpretation that assistance from families may directly affect the economic prospects of the single mother. If the same outcome had occurred for both never- and ever-married mothers, we might have been convinced that the advantage in subsequent socioeconomic status was largely attributable to conditions that preceded the pregnancy and were associated with the family background of those women who resided with their parents. The fact that a favorable outcome occurred only among never-married women who remained with their parents throughout the study, and not among the women who returned home after marriage, suggests that the long-term provision of family assistance may have a part in shaping the economic career of the single mother. An intervening marriage, accordingly, attenuates the potential benefit of family support.

Even if we are correct in assuming that assistance from families does promote the economic well-being of unmarried mothers, we cannot say for certain why this is so. Do these women fare better because they remain with their parents? Or do they remain with their parents because they are committed to advancing their educational and occupational careers? We suspect that both conditions are true, though not in equal measure in all families. Families who strongly support their daughters' educational efforts may be more likely to help out financially or provide child care so long as the young mother remains in school. If she drops out, there is less incentive for them to help and, thus, for her to remain in the home. Similarly, women who wish to advance educationally may be more likely to seek aid from their parents.

There is some evidence to substantiate each of these interpretations. Adolescents who were more educationally ambitious were less likely to marry, and hence were more inclined to remain with their parents throughout the study. In turn, women who remained in the home were far more likely to attend school. Even at the five-year follow-up, when most had completed their education, women living with their parents were more likely to be currently enrolled in school.[12] Probably, then, the relationship between family assistance and socioeconomic achievement is a reciprocal one. Women who receive family aid are more likely to advance economically, and those who most wish to improve their position are more likely to turn to their families for help.

Finally, we must point out that although our data are longitudinal, this study describes only a small slice of time in the lives of the young mothers. All the returns are not yet in. Many of the young mothers still living with their parents at the five-year follow-up may have been on the verge of moving out. Were the more successful ones to exit, the pattern reported here would disappear. Despite this qualification, our data strongly indicate that family support of single mothers improved their chances of returning to school, entering the labor force and finding employment.

Family Assistance and Parenting

We explored whether the young mothers who received support from their families in the early years of parenthood developed greater parenting skills than did the young mothers who did not receive such help. We also examined what effect, if any, such support had on the well-being of their children. Our data show that residential careers had little influence on childrearing patterns, and there is no evidence that the provision of family support made any difference in the way the young mothers performed their maternal tasks. The quality of parent-child interaction seems not to have been affected by the child-care arrangements made by the young mothers.

Similarly, scrutiny of data gathered on the children's development showed little difference by the mothers' residential patterns. Only one measure, a test of cognitive skills, suggested that the children of unmarried mothers who resided in households with kin (usually, grandparents) outperformed those who lived with their mothers alone, even though the latter children were more apt to have gone to school. (However, the findings were not statistically significant.)

Conclusion

We have tried to show that the residential career of the teenage child-bearer provided a means, albeit an imperfect one, of monitoring the flow of family support to the adolescent mother during the transition to parenthood. Most support received by the young mother is supplied by her nuclear family—her parents and siblings—in the form of free room and board and partly or wholly subsidized child care. The availability of material support is greater when the adolescent remains in the home, though even when she separates from her parents, she may continue to receive childcare assistance from a family member.

Our analysis suggests that the assistance rendered by family members significantly alters the life chances of the young mother, enhancing her prospects of educational achievement and economic advancement. It may also contribute to the well-being of her child, though the evidence we can marshall is limited.

If other studies, using richer data sets than ours, reach the same conclusions regarding the benefits of family support in easing the transition to early parenthood, what implications will such conclusions have for policies and programs designed to ameliorate the adverse effects of early childbearing?

Present policies strike us as ill-conceived and shortsighted because many of the solutions devised for coping with early parenthood run counter to or undermine existing natural support systems. Nothing in the behavior of the young women in our study or their families suggests that they were alienated from one another. Quite the contrary, these predominantly low-income families provided support of all types, often at what must have been considerable sacrifice.

Public programs should build on the strengths inherent in these families. Financial assistance and other appropriate aid, such as child care, should be extended to families willing to help their young daughters to pick up the threads of their lives and advance their educational and occupational prospects. Assistance should go, as well, to the young fathers if they show interest in supporting the young women and their children. Assistance should be given, when needed, to young married couples to try to strengthen their marriages. Present welfare rules often guarantee the breakup of many of these marriages since assistance is usually provided only when there is no male head of household. This is shortsighted, punitive and self-defeating.

Where appropriate, support should go to those young women who desire to become independent. But the option of how to solve their residential problems should be theirs. They should not be pushed into premature independence to obtain the assistance they need.

Another illustration of the shortsightedness of public policies is in the formulation of programs intended to prepare the young mother for parenthood. There is widespread agreement among experts that the early

129

childbearer is at some disadvantage in assuming the maternal role because of her psychological immaturity. Many young mothers are themselves still experiencing the developmental tasks of adolescence, consolidating their own interpersonal skills, working out life aims and achieving some sense of personal identity. It is widely believed that many young mothers lack the experience and skills to manage the complex obligations of motherhood. Based on these presuppositions, a number of programs serving teenage mothers have developed parent education courses designed to teach mothering skills. These programs operate on the erroneous assumption that the mother is the principal, if not the only, caretaker. If the results of our study are any indication, the family and the infant's father, not just the adolescent mother, should be targets of instruction as well.

In fact, many young parents are receiving a great deal of training on the job from parents, older siblings or more distant kin. Even though they may not always be residing with the young mothers and their children, the children's fathers, or father surrogates, too, may be performing important child-rearing functions. Without taking into account the actual parenting structure, educational programs may be imparting wisdom that either cannot be applied or is ill-suited to fit the situations that young mothers typically face.

In citing ways the family adapts in order to ease the transition to early parenthood, however, we do not wish to dismiss the potential dysfunctions for the adolescent parent and her family members. These are discussed in some detail elsewhere.[13] Our data suggest that this kinship configuration may not be well designed to promote or reinforce conjugal ties. What is adaptive from one perspective, then, may be maladaptive from another. Furthermore, if we follow the logic of our longitudinal analysis, we must conclude that arrangements that are immediately functional for the young mother and her child are not always adaptive later in the life course. These qualifications serve to remind us of both the limitations of the present analysis and the urgent need for further studies of the impact of early childbearing on the family unit.

References

1. W.H. Baldwin, "Adolescent Pregnancy and Childbearing: Growing Concerns for Americans," *Population Bulletin,* Vol. 31, No. 2, 1976; and E.A. Crider, "School Age Pregnancy, Childbearing and Childrearing: A Research Review," 1976 (paper submitted to the Bureau of Elementary and Secondary Education, U.S. Office of Education, under Contract No. P00760271).

2. F.F. Furstenberg, Jr., *Unplanned Parenthood: The Social Consequences of Teenage Childbearing,* The Free Press (Macmillan), New York, 1976; —————, "Burdens and Benefits: The Impact of Early Childbearing on the Family," paper presented at the Conference on Perspectives on Policy Toward Teenage Pregnancy, Family Impact Seminar, Washington, D.C., Oct. 23-24, 1978; G.E. Hendershot and E. Eckard, "Unwanted Teenage Childbearing and Later Life Changes: Evidence from the National Survey of Family Growth," paper presented at the annual meeting of the Eastern Sociological Society, Philadelphia, Apr. 2, 1978; K. Moore, "The Social and Economic

Consequences of Teenage Childbearing," paper presented at the Conference on Young Women and Employment, Washington, D.C., May 1, 1978; and H.B. Presser, "The Social and Demographic Consequences of Teenage Childbearing for Urban Women," paper presented at the National Institute of Child Health and Human Development Workshop on the Consequences of Adolescent Pregnancy and Childbearing, Bethesda, Jan. 12–13, 1978.

3. J.J. Card and L.L. Wise, "Teenage Mothers and Teenage Fathers: The Impact of Early Childbearing on the Parents' Personal and Professional Lives," *Family Planning Perspectives,* 10:199, 1978.

4. D. Nortman, "Parental Age as a Factor in Pregnancy Outcome and Child Development," *Reports on Population/Family Planning,* No. 16, Aug. 1974.

5. H.B. Presser, "Sally's Corner," paper presented at the annual meeting of the American Sociological Association, San Francisco, Sept. 4–7, 1978.

6. J.A. Ladner, *Tomorrow's Tomorrow: The Black Woman,* Doubleday, Garden City, N.Y., 1971; and L. Rainwater, *Behind Ghetto Walls,* Aldine, Chicago, 1971.

7. A. Cherlin, "Postponing Marriage: The Influence of Schooling, Working, and Work Plans for Young Women," paper presented at the annual meeting of the American Sociological Association, San Francisco, Sept. 4–8, 1978.

8. F.F. Furstenberg, Jr., 1976, op. cit.

9. A. Cherlin, 1978, op. cit.; F.F. Furstenberg, Jr., 1976, op. cit.; J. Modell, F.F. Furstenberg, Jr., and T. Hershberg, "Social Change and Transitions to Adulthood in Historical Perspective," *Journal of Family History,* 1:7, 1976; and D. Strong, "The Timing of Marriage in the Transition to Adulthood: Continuity and Change," *American Journal of Sociology,* special issue on Turning Points: Historical and Sociological Essays on the Family (forthcoming).

10. F.F. Furstenberg, Jr., 1976, op. cit.

11. Ibid.

12. Ibid.

13. F.F. Furstenberg, Jr., 1978, op. cit.

Support Networks for Adolescent Mothers

. . . . .

**Diane de Anda
and Rosina M. Becerra**

During recent years there has been an alarming increase in the number of adolescent pregnancies. Catherine S. Chilman found that between 1967 and 1976 the birthrate for adolescents seventeen years of age and younger increased while those for all other age groups declined.[1] Furthermore, in the fifteen to nineteen year age group, premarital pregnancy rates rose from 5.6 percent in 1971 to 13.5 percent in 1979 for the white population and 25.3 to 30.0 percent for the black population.[2] The change in the illegitimate birthrate within the adolescent population has been even more dramatic, increasing 60 percent since 1965 and 300 percent since 1942.[3] While the birthrate for fifteen- to seventeen-year-olds began to plateau during the late 1970s, the illegitimacy rate has continued to rise from seventeen per thousand in 1970 and nineteen per thousand in 1976 to twenty-one per thousand in 1980.[4] Moreover, June Sklar and Beth Berkov estimate that 85 percent of today's adolescent mothers keep and raise their infants rather than place them for adoption.[5] This trend has served as an impetus for research into the needs and experiences of the growing population of adolescent mothers raising their infants.

With few exceptions, research on the adolescent mother has focused primarily on areas of risk within the population.[6] The adolescent has been described as more likely to have limited educational and occupational achievement, to suffer more medical complications related to pregnancy and

Reprinted by permission from Diane de Anda and Rosina M. Becerra, Support networks for adolescent mothers, *Social Casework: The Journal of Contemporary Social Work* 65, 172–181. Copyright 1984 Family Service America.

delivery, to indicate greater potential for child abuse, and to suffer greater rates of emotional and psychological instability, as well as higher rates of marital discord[7] (if married) than her older cohorts. This research, while informative, has primarily focused on her liabilities, with insufficient effort being given to determining factors which might serve as strengths such as arenas of social support. The exploration of social support systems as an area of potential strength is critical for the development of intervention strategies that will serve to enhance the life of the adolescent mother. A second shortcoming in this research has been the complete lack of attention to the experiences of the Hispanic adolescent, whose liabilities and strengths can both be enhanced and inhibited by the "acculturating" process.

The issue of support networks among Hispanics is of particular importance, since traditionally the extended familial system has generally acted as a source of both economic and emotional support, and the strength of this network is cited as one of the major characteristics of Hispanic culture. However, the movement of most Hispanic groups to urban centers has tended to disrupt traditional familial structures, which are now being modified to fit changing economic, social, and cultural conditions. As a result, the effects of this acculturation process may have implications for intervention strategies, particularly with adolescents, who are at the crossroads of their cultural identification, their change from adolescence to adulthood, and their move from childhood to motherhood.

The need to focus greater attention on the Hispanic adolescent mother can best be illustrated by comparative statistics of live births to the adolescent population in 1979 in Los Angeles County, California, the county with the largest Hispanic population in the United States. According to the Office of Vital Statistics in the county's Department of Health Services, of the 17,671 births to girls nineteen years of age or younger, about 52 percent were to Hispanic adolescents and about 24 percent each to black and white adolescents.

The research reported in this article examined the social support networks of adolescent mothers from a cross-cultural perspective. Its purpose was to begin to identify areas of commonalities and differences and ultimately to better develop intervention strategies that consider cultural issues. Specifically, the research addressed the following questions: Who provided social support during the adolescent's pregnancy; who is presently providing social support; what type of support is the adolescent being provided (for example, help with the infant or listening to problems); and what types of problems is the adolescent encountering in her support network?

Method

To focus on the factors most relevant to the experiences of the adolescent mother, a three-stage process was undertaken. First, a workshop was held at which professionals with several years direct experience with pregnant adolescents and adolescent mothers engaged in a structured dialogue aimed at developing a profile of the pregnant adolescent or adolescent mother, her problem areas, and her areas of strength. The workshop included individuals

133

from a broad range of professions—social work, teaching, counseling, nursing, and research. Input from this workshop, along with that provided by a review of the literature, was used to develop a detailed structured interview schedule. The second stage involved using this schedule in approximately twenty hours of in-depth interviews with adolescent mothers and pregnant adolescents. Responses provided by the subjects were then used to design a closed-ended questionnaire which was administered to subjects in Woman Infant Child (WIC) programs in the western region of Los Angeles County and in the City of Long Beach. Respondents were solicited from WIC programs throughout these areas over a two-year period, generating a participation rate of approximately 90 percent of all WIC clients in the thirteen- to twenty-year age group.

Subjects

The sample consisted of 122 adolescents in that age group who were either pregnant or who had delivered a child within the past twelve months. Forty white and eighty-two Hispanic adolescents were surveyed, with the Hispanic adolescents further identified as forty-three English-speaking and thirty-nine Spanish-speaking persons. This breakdown by language was used as an indicator of acculturation, since English-speaking ability among Hispanics is a variable explaining the greatest amount of variance in differentiating high and low acculturation levels.

The majority of subjects in all three samples indicated incomes substantially below poverty levels: 77.6 percent of the Hispanic Spanish-speaking (HSS) sample, 67.5 percent of the white respondents, and 53.3 percent of the Hispanic English-speaking (HES) subjects had yearly incomes of less than $5,500. A negligible number of respondents (2.5 percent to 4.9 percent) reported incomes over $10,000.

In the distribution of the three samples with regard to marital status (see Table 1), two-thirds of the HSS subjects were married while an equal number of the white respondents were unmarried, indicating a substantially higher illegitimacy rate among whites. The percentage of unmarried HES adolescents was lower than whites but higher than for the HSS, demonstrating

---

TABLE 1

Marital status (percentage)

	Ethnicity		
Marital status	**White Non-Hispanic**	**Hispanic English-speaking (HES)**	**Hispanic Spanish-speaking (HSS)**
Single	47.5	39.1	23.0
Engaged	22.5	19.5	10.3
Married	22.5	43.9	66.7
Separated/divorced	7.5	2.4	0.0

---

that, as the Hispanic adolescent becomes more acculturated, she also begins to behave in all ways more like the white, non-Hispanic adolescent.

The HES and white samples were very similar with regard to the years of schooling (HES=10.4; W=10.9). In contrast, the educational level of the HSS subjects was significantly ($F=26.15$; $p \le .001$) lower, with a mean of 8.2 years of schooling. Moreover, over 28 percent of the HSS sample reported an educational level of six years of schooling or less and were the group least likely to consider continuing their education.

The Support Networks

An examination of the data about living arrangements offers information concerning the potential support available to individuals within the various samples. The majority of adolescents residing with parents in all three samples were those seventeen years of age and younger. A larger number of white (52.3 percent) and HES (53.5 percent) respondents indicated that they shared living arrangements with their parents or their own or their spouse or boyfriend's relatives than did respondents in the HSS sample (35.8 percent). Part of this difference is accounted for by the fact that a significantly larger proportion of the HSS sample was married and, therefore, lived in a separate household with their husbands (71.8 percent). However, this fact does not fully explain the difference suggested by the data reported below, which repeatedly indicate similar trends with reference to the support provided by significant others.

THE MOTHER-DAUGHTER RELATIONSHIP

The subjects were asked to specify those individuals who provided support during their pregnancy and at present. Table 2 indicates the primary source of support for the white and HES samples was their mother, while, for the HSS sample, the husband served as the main provider of support. Although the HSS subjects reported their mother as a secondary source of support, the proportion indicating the mother as a source of support was significantly lower ($x^2=12.21$; $p \le .01$) for the HSS sample than for the HES or white samples. Moreover, an even greater discrepancy was noted between the amount of concrete support offered in the form of child care by the mothers of the white and HES respondents in contrast to the HSS adolescents (Table 3). While over 60 percent of the white and HES samples reported that their mothers helped with child care, a significantly ($x^2=17.29$; $p \le .001$) smaller proportion (23.7 percent) of the HSS sample indicated support from their mothers in terms of child care. Inasmuch as the HSS respondents tended to be fairly recent immigrants from Mexico, this difference may be partly explained by geographical distance from the family of origin, which probably resided in Mexico.

The quality of the mother-daughter relationship was measured by a series of questions. First, the subjects were asked to indicate along a three-point scale how often they felt their mothers listened to them. No statistically significant differences were found between the three samples. The majority

135

TABLE 2
Persons offering support during pregnancy and presently (percentage)

| Ethnicity | Source of support | | | | | |
	Mother	Father	Husband	Boy friend	Siblings	Girl friends
Hispanic English-speakers (HES)						
Pregnancy	83.7	37.2	46.5	35.9	66.7	27.9
Now	86.0	41.9	46.5	39.5	67.4	30.8
Hispanic Spanish-Speakers (HSS)						
Pregnancy	48.7	25.6	58.9	10.3	33.3	17.9
Now	56.4	35.9	61.5	5.1	33.3	7.7
White Non-Hispanics						
Pregnancy	72.5	12.5	30.0	50.0	40.0	40.0
Now	75.0	25.0	17.5	50.0	35.0	40.0

TABLE 3
Persons who do/will help care of infant (percentage)

Ethnicity	No one	Mother	Father	Husband	Boy friend	Brother/ sister	Girl friend	Husband/ boyfriend family	Other
Hispanic English-Speakers (HES)	5.1	65.1	18.6	34.9	18.6	43.6	13.95	27.9	6.98
Hispanic Spanish-Speakers (HSS)	7.7	23.1	2.6	51.3	2.6	5.1	7.7	17.9	0.0
White Non-Hispanics	10.0	62.5	5.0	22.5	45.0	30.0	27.5	20.0	10.0

of subjects felt their mothers were for the most part willing to listen to their concerns. Moreover, the adolescent saw her mother as the person in her support network most willing to listen to her. Within the HES sample, however, girl friends were similarly viewed.

To gauge the amount of conflict or extent of negative feelings toward her mother, the adolescent was asked how frequently her mother treated her unfairly. While no statistically significant differences between the three groups were found, the trend of the data suggests movement toward some degree of conflict between mother and daughter. However, the impact of this conflict may be particularly potent for this adolescent population, since the mother was viewed as the most responsive member of the support network, particularly for those who resided with their parents and were dependent upon their material support as well.

The mother's reaction to the girl's pregnancy was sought to determine the type of emotional support afforded in a crisis or (if married) important life event. For all three samples, the most frequent responses of the mothers toward the girls' pregnancies were positive, the three most frequent responses being: surprised (HES 48.9 percent; W=47.0 percent; HSS=23.0 percent); happy/excited (HSS=48.7 percent; HES=44.2 percent; W=42.5 percent); and understanding (HES=32.6 percent; W=27.5 percent; HSS=20.5 percent). Significantly fewer respondents (x^2=8.97; $p \leq .05$) in the HSS sample indicated surprise as their mother's response than did the white and HES respondents. While the frequencies for the three groups to the response "happy/excited" did not show a statistically significant difference, this was the response with the highest frequency for the HSS sample. The fact that a significantly greater proportion of the HSS population were married may account for this difference, along with the concomitant fact that a greater number of white and HES adolescents were announcing out-of-wedlock pregnancies. Most mothers' reactions were for the most part positive, with negative responses low in frequency. Few mothers reacted with anger (W=12.5 percent; HES=9.3 percent; HSS=7.7 percent), with the negative reaction showing the highest frequency being that of "very upset" (HES=23.3 percent; W=17.5 percent; HSS=7.7 percent). This again points to the mother primarily as a source of support for the adolescent mother.

Several questions tapped the extent of the mother's influence and control over her adolescent daughter. Although no statistically significant differences were found among the three groups, a comparison of the mean ranks across the support network indicates that the mother's opinion was first in importance for both the HES and HSS samples and in the white sample second only to the subject's opinion of self. Moreover, the mean rank for the mother was generally greater than that of any other person in the support network.

As a further measure of the mother's influence and control over the adolescent, subjects were asked how often they did what their mothers wanted them to do, and whose desires they followed when there was a conflict between what they wanted to do and what their mother wanted them to do. The F-test showed (F = 3.90; $p \leq .01$) that the groups differed significantly in the frequency with which they complied with their mothers' wishes, the difference being between the two Hispanic subsamples. The direction of the means indicated that the HSS were willing to comply with their mothers' wishes most often and the HES least often of the three groups. The white sample appeared in between the Hispanic subsamples but was more similar to the HES sample. Moreover, the high means indicated a relatively high degree of compliance with maternal desires across all groups. While statistical significance was not obtained between the groups, the HSS sample was the group in which the greatest number of respondents were willing to accede to their mothers' desires over their own when a disagreement occurred. Again, there was more similarity between the white and HES samples than between the Hispanic subsamples, indicating the possible effects of acculturation as measured by language dominance.

It appears then, that the mother was viewed by all groups as an important source of influence and emotional support. This seems to be the case in particular for the HSS adolescent. However, the actual support provided shows a reverse pattern, with the white and HES samples receiving substantially more concrete support from their mothers. It is not likely that this was the result of acculturation difference but was more likely due to the geographic distance of the HSS respondents from the family of origin. It is ironic that the subjects with the strongest emotional ties to their mothers were the least able to utilize their mothers as a source of support.

THE FATHER-DAUGHTER RELATIONSHIP

The emotional and physical support offered by fathers to their adolescent daughters appears relatively negligible. A comparison of the rates of support offered by various individuals in the adolescent's environment (Table 2) indicates that the percentage of fathers offering support was the second lowest for the entire support network. It also suggests that he was the person seen as least supportive among the adolescent's family members. The contrast between the low percentage of fathers viewed as offering support as compared with the high percentage for the adolescents' mothers is quite marked. This is particularly the case for the white adolescent, who indicated a significantly ($x^2=6.97$; $p \leq .05$) lower frequency for paternal support during pregnancy than did the Hispanic respondents. This may be because a greater proportion of the white sample came from single parent female homes and had become pregnant out-of-wedlock.

This trend of low paternal involvement continued with regard to assistance with child care. For all but the HES sample, the fathers offered the least amount of assistance. While the HES sample indicated a greater amount of support from their fathers than the other two samples on all indices, this support level was marginal at best from 42 percent for support in general to a mere 19 percent for help with child care.

The father-daughter relationship appeared to be weak qualitatively as well. While no statistical significance was found among the three groups, the Hispanic samples ranked the father's opinion of them third in importance while the white sample ranked his opinion fifth. Additionally, the three groups were similar with respect to the frequency with which they indicated that their fathers listened to their concerns or treated them unfairly. While the mean for the three samples ($X=2.19$) indicates that the fathers were willing to listen to their daughters' concerns "sometimes," these means were the lowest among all the individuals within the adolescent's support network. In contrast, however, the mean (2.67) indicating the frequency with which daughters perceived their fathers as treating them unfairly was the lowest among those in their interpersonal environment.

Despite what appears to be a comparatively weak emotional bond between father and daughter uniformly among the three samples, there was some difference in the amount of control exerted by the fathers over their adolescent daughters among the various groups. A statistically significant difference (F=5.42, $p \leq .01$) was found between white and HSS samples in the frequency with which the respondents did what their fathers wanted or thought they should do, the HSS sample acceding to their father's wishes more frequently. The mean for the HES sample fell between the two samples, indicating the effects of acculturation on the respondents. However, when the adolescents disagreed with their fathers, very few were willing to accede to his wishes over their own (W=10.0 percent; HES=27.9 percent; HSS=25.6 percent). A greater percentage were willing to accede to their mothers' and husbands' wishes over their own than to their fathers'.

The responses of the fathers to the announcement of the pregnancy were similar for the HES and white samples, the three most frequent responses being: surprised (W=34.9 percent; HES=25.0 percent); understanding (W= 34.9 percent; HES=22.5 percent); and happy/excited (W=11.6 percent; HES =22.5 percent). While the rates for the HSS sample were comparable for the reaction of surprise (20.5 percent) and understanding (17.9 percent), a significantly (x^2=10.03; $p \leq .01$) greater number of fathers were reported to express the response "happy/excited" (41.0 percent). Again this may be due to the fact that a greater proportion of the HSS sample were married and, therefore, were announcing legitimate pregnancies.

In general, the findings indicate that the adolescent's father held a very low profile in the support network, exerting minimal influence and providing little nurturance and support.

RELATIONSHIP WITH HUSBAND OR BOY FRIEND

Inasmuch as a large percentage, particularly of the white sample, were not married, the data for both husband and boy friend will be discussed together. When the rates for support offered by the boy friend and husband were combined, the amount of support for the most part equaled or sur- passed that of the mother (Table 2). The patterns of support, however, appear somewhat different for each sample. For the HES sample, the mother and husband or boy friend provided approximately equal amounts of support both during pregnancy and at present. For the HSS sample, the reverse was the case, with the husband serving as the adolescent's major source of support. While the white respondents indicated that their husband or boy friend provided the greatest amount of support during pregnancy, there was a sharp drop in the husband's support at the present time, leaving the mother as the primary source of support.

In terms of assistance in caring for infants, the HES and HSS samples had almost identical rates, with over 53 percent of the respondents indicating support from their spouse or boy friend in this area. However, while the husband was the principal source of assistance in child care for the HSS sample, the HES sample also indicated support from their mothers in this area and at a higher rate. A larger percentage of the white sample (67.5 percent) reported help with infant care from their husband or boy friend than did the Hispanic samples. With the high percentage of white respondents also indicating assistance from their mothers (Table 3), this group appears to have the greatest amount of assistance with child care of the three samples. This substantial amount of both emotional and physical support offered by partners is contrary to the literature on adolescent pregnancy, which stresses the tenuousness of the marital relationship for adolescents.

Questions regarding the extent to which the adolescents believed their spouse or boy friends listened to their concerns and treated them unfairly offers information regarding the quality of the relationship. The great majority of respondents in all three groups reported that their spouses or boy friends were for the most part willing to listen to their concerns; 67.4 percent of the HES sample, 56.4 percent of the HSS sample, and 57.5 percent of the white sample indicated that this was the case "most of the time." Only 5 percent of the white and HES samples indicated that their husbands or boy friends rarely or never listened to them, with a slightly higher (12.8 percent), but nonsignificant, rate for the HSS sample. For the HSS sample, they were the second person most likely to listen to them (after their mothers), while for the white and HES samples, the husbands or boy friends ran a very close third following mothers and girl friends.

There does not appear to be a serious amount of conflict between the adolescent and her spouse or boy friend, as a very small percentage of the respondents (W=5.0 percent, HES=9.3 percent, HSS=12.8 percent) reported that their spouses or boy friends treated them unfairly with great frequency. The fact that some amount of ill feelings did exist was intimated, however, by the percentage of respondents who reported that their husbands or boy friends treated them unfairly at least some of the time (W=47.5 percent, HES =39.5 percent, HSS=25.6 percent).

Taking into account the differences in marital status among the three samples, there appears to be some variation in the ranking of the husband's or boy friend's opinions of the adolescent. The greatest importance placed on these opinions was that given by the HSS sample, ranking their husbands' opinions second in importance after their mothers'. The white sample ranked their boy friends' opinions third in importance, following their own and their mothers' opinions. Finally, the HES sample ranked their husbands' opinions fourth in importance following (and only .1 percent lower than) their fathers' opinions of them.

Husbands or boy friends appeared to exert a considerable amount of influence over a large proportion of the three groups sampled, with 41 to 51 percent of the respondents reporting that they did what their spouses or boy friends wanted them to do most of the time. The white and HES samples were likely to comply with these wishes more often than with those of anyone else in the support network and the HSS only slightly less often (.2 percent) than with those of their mothers. Moreover, when they disagreed with their husbands or boy friends, a notably large number of respondents complied with their desires over their own (white=55.0 percent, HES=39.5 percent, HSS =41.0 percent). It appears, then, that for a substantial proportion of the three samples, husbands or boy friends served as a significant source of support and influence.

Significant differences were found between the amount of support offered by brothers and sisters of HES subjects in comparison to those of white or HSS respondents. Over two thirds of the HES sample reported receiving support from their siblings both during pregnancy (x^2=6.48; p≤.05) and at present (x^2=11.92; p≤.01), in contrast to only a little over one third of the HSS and white samples. When, however, support by providing child care was reported, there was an over 20 to nearly 30 percent drop in the rates for the Hispanic samples to 43.6 percent for the HES and 5.1 percent for the HSS groups. The white sample indicated an approximately 5 percentage point drop to 30 percent. The rates may be low because many of the adolescents' siblings might have been minor children and, therefore, not able to offer assistance with child care. Again, the HSS sample appears to have the smallest support network available of the three groups, which may be the result of the extended family being geographically distant.

There was a significant difference (x^2=7.60; p≤.05) between the Hispanic and white samples regarding the frequency with which "happy/excited" was given as the siblings' response to the pregnancy. "Happy/excited" was the most frequently occurring response for the HSS (56.4 percent) and HES (60.5 percent) samples; it was a much lower rated second (30.0 percent) for the white sample. The most frequently reported response for the white sample was "surprise" (72.5 percent). "Surprise" was rated second in frequency for the HES sample (51.2 percent). The HSS sample reported a significantly (x^2=8.48; p≤.01) lower frequency (25.6 percent) for the response. These differences may be because a greater percentage of the HSS subjects were married and pregnancy was, therefore, more likely to have been expected.

The data further indicate that the relationship between siblings appeared positive for the majority of respondents. All three samples reported relatively good communication between themselves and their siblings, with the overwhelming majority (W=77.5 percent, HES=81.4 percent, HSS=71.8 percent) of the respondents reporting that their brothers and sisters listened to their concerns sometimes or most of the time. By the same token, few respondents reported any substantial amount of conflict with siblings; that is, few thought their siblings treated them unfairly "most of the time" (HES=11.6 percent, HSS =12.8 percent, W=7.5 percent). However, a third to a half of the respondents felt their siblings treated them unfairly some of the time, suggesting that the relationship was not completely conflict free.

Although siblings seemed to offer a great deal of emotional support, their influence and control appeared relatively weak. While 43 to 53 percent of the total respondents were willing to do what their brothers and sisters wished some of the time, only 14 percent or less were willing to consider this frequently. Moreover, approximately 7 percent of the white and HES sample would accede to their siblings' wishes over their own. While 23.1 percent of the HSS respondents reported they would comply with their siblings' wishes over their own, the difference among the groups was not statistically significant. Finally, the siblings' opinion of the adolescent ranked fourth or lower in importance among those in the support network.

RELATIONSHIP WITH PEERS (GIRL FRIENDS)

Pregnancy and the birth of a child appear to have weakened and reduced peer relationships for the majority of the adolescents sampled, particularly for the HES group. All groups were similar with respect to the frequency with which they saw their friends prior to pregnancy, the mean being a few times a week. After they became pregnant, the frequency of contact dropped for all groups to once a week for the white and HSS respondents and to a significantly (F=4.01; $p \leq .05$) lower rate—a few times per month—for the HES sample. Moreover, with the passage of time, the contact with peers continued to diminish, the difference being significantly greater (F=3.35; $p \leq .05$) between the white and HES samples. The white respondents maintained the most frequent contact with peers, as even telephone contact (averaging about once a week) was significantly more frequent (F =5.62; $p \leq .01$) than that of the Hispanic samples.

Beyond mere contact with friends, the amount of support offered by peers also showed significant differences in frequency (x^2=10.67; $p \leq .01$) between the ethnic groups, with the white respondents indicating the highest percentage of support (40 percent) and the HSS the lowest (7.7 percent). The HES sample's rate of 30.8 percent was lower but closer to that of the white than the HSS sample. While the differences did not reach statistical significance, the same trend was found with respect to the amount of support provided by peers in terms of child care (W=27.5 percent, HES=13.9 percent, HSS=7.7 percent).

While peers offered little concrete support in terms of child care, they do appear to have offered some emotional support, at least initially. While surprise was the most frequent response for peers in the three samples (W=72.5 percent, HES=67.4 percent, HSS=43.6 percent), the response next in frequency (and equal in frequency for the HSS) was that of being "happy/excited." However, the frequency attributed to "understanding" as a response was significantly (x^2= 13.02; $p \leq .001$) higher for the white sample (35.0 percent) than for the Hispanic samples.

Not only was contact with peers somewhat limited but the information regarding the quality of the interactions with peers is unclear. Nearly two thirds of the white and HES respondents indicated that their friends were willing to listen to their concerns most of the time. While only one third of the HSS sample reported this, the bulk of the remaining respondents indicated the rate to be "sometimes." Moreover, very few (2.5 percent to 7.7 percent) respondents reported that friends rarely or never listened to them. The lower rate for the HSS sample may be because this group's contact with peers was relatively low. However, a portion of the respondents (HES=44.2 percent, W=32.5 percent, HSS=28.2 percent) felt their friends treated them unfairly some of the time. Inasmuch as friendships are generally considered reciprocal relationships offering mutual satisfactions entered into freely, this rate of conflict is somewhat puzzling. A small percentage of the adolescents alluded to serious difficulties in peer relationships: 7 to 10 percent reported feeling their peers treat them unfairly most of the time.

Moreover, in contrast to the typical preoccupation of adolescents with the opinion of peers, the opinion of girl friends ranked lowest in importance among those in the support network. Further substantiating this lack of influence exerted by peers were the findings that, when in disagreement with peers, the respondents in all three groups were least likely to accede to the desire of peers than any other individuals in their support network (2.5 percent–0.0 percent).

Discussion

While the liabilities attached to adolescent pregnancy and motherhood have been documented in the research literature, little effort has been expended in exploring areas of strength. The results of this study indicate that a considerable amount of both potential and actual support exists in the interpersonal network available to the adolescent surveyed.

The primary asset in the interpersonal environment was the adolescent's mother, particularly for the HES and white adolescent. She served as a source of emotional support both during pregnancy and after the birth of the child and was generally the most supportive in terms of providing child care. The relationship appeared to be reciprocal, with the mother showing the most interest in her daughter's concerns and offering the most positive responses to her situation, and the daughter indicating a willingness to respond positively by complying with her mother's desires and giving weight to her mother's opinion of her. Sadly ironic is the fact that while the HSS subjects indicated the strongest emotional relationship with their mothers, they were the least able to receive actual support from them. As was noted earlier, this was most probably the result of geographical distance, as a large proportion of the HSS respondents' parents were presumed to reside in Mexico. While the amount of support provided by the mother to HES and white respondents was substantial, an element of conflict should not be overlooked. Because of the importance of the relationship between mother and adolescent, the areas of conflict that do exist (as indicated by the percentage of this study who felt they were treated unfairly at times) should be further explored with the aim of strengthening an already positive relationship. The importance of enhancing this relationship has been noted by others providing direct services to this population.

Similar strengths were found for a large portion of the respondents with regard to the relationship with the husband or boy friend, particularly within the HSS sample. Probably because of the geographical distance from the family of origin, the HSS respondents were the most dependent upon their spouse as a source of emotional and physical support, which he, in turn, offered in the great majority of cases. Husbands and boy friends were also seen as supportive by the great majority of adolescents in the HES and white samples as well. Moreover, the emotional ties were expressed in terms of a willingness of the spouse or boy friend to listen to the adolescent's concerns, and, in turn, by a willingness to please the spouse by complying with his wishes. While there appears to be positive reciprocity in the relationships, there also appears to be some potential for conflict, as the husband's or boy friend's opinion of them was not among the highest ranked and there is indication of feeling unfairly treated to some extent by him. Again, it seems that a major thrust of any intervention would be one of building on the positive aspects of the relationship to develop a means of determining and dealing with the issues leading to conflict.

In sharp contrast, the relationship with fathers and peers was, at best, marginal in terms of the support they provide. While a significantly greater proportion of the HES fathers offered support to their adolescent daughters, the percentage (41.9 percent) was still relatively low. Fathers appeared the least involved with the adolescent of all persons in the family network, with even siblings offering greater emotional support. Concomitantly, the adolescent's emotional investment in her relationship with the father was also low, as the majority reported his influence to be quite low. That is, the adolescent indicated little desire to please her father by complying with his desires and little concern regarding his opinion of her. Certainly the father-daughter relationship points to an area in need of intervention in almost every respect.

While the lack of importance ascribed to peer opinion and desires may be interpreted as a strength in the population surveyed, the sharp decline in peer contact associated with pregnancy cannot be viewed so positively. It is quite apparent that pregnancy and child birth served to isolate the adolescent from her peers. While the relationship with her mother and spouse or boy friend are important to encourage, concomitant peer relationships reduce the likelihood of dependency due to a restricted support system. In any case, the adolescent appeared cut off from her peers at a point in her development when peer contact is particularly critical.

The results of this survey suggest a contrast between statistical and clinical significance. In general, the majority of the respondents generated a support system for themselves; however, the clinician must always be aware of those respondents in the remaining portion of the sample who do not have available to them the potential for the strong support networks outlined above. It is important to note that a substantial proportion of the adolescent population surveyed demonstrated significant areas of strength within their interpersonal relationships (along with areas in need of improvement); this characteristic testifies to the potential for positive intervention and supports the conclusion that adolescent pregnancy need not always signal negative expectations in all areas of the individual's functioning.

Notes

1. Catherine S. Chilman, *Adolescent Sexuality in a Changing American Society: Social and Psychological Perspectives* (Washington, DC: U.S. Government Printing Office, 1977).

2. Melvin Zelnick and John F. Kantner, "Sexual Activity, Contraceptive Use and Pregnancy among Metropolitan-Area Teenagers: 1971–1979," *Family Planning Perspectives*, 12 (September/October 1980):230–237.

3. Frank G. Bolton, *The Pregnant Adolescent* (Beverly Hills, CA: Sage Publications, 1982).

4. U.S. National Center for Health Statistics, Monthly Vital Statistics Report 31: Supplement (November 30, 1982).

5. June Sklar and Beth Berkov, "Teenage Family Formation in Postwar America," *Family Planning Perspectives*, 6 (Spring 1974):80–90.

6. Gail K. Polsby, "Unmarried Parenthood: Potential for Growth," *Adolescence*, 9 (Summer 1974):273–284.

7. See Frank J. Furstenberg, *Unplanned Parenthood* (New York: Free Press, 1976); Bernard B. Braen and Janet Bell Forbush, "School-age Parenthood, a National Overview," *Journal of School Health*, 45(1975):256–262; Howard J. Osofsky et al., "Adolescents as Mothers: An Interdisciplinary Approach to a Complex Problem," *Journal of Youth and Adolescence*, 2, No. 3 (1973):233–249; Bolton, *The Pregnant Adolescent*; Maurine LeBarre, "Emotional Crisis of School-age Girls During Pregnancy and Early Motherhood," *Journal of the American Academy of Child Psychiatry*, 11 (July 1972):537–557.

Adolescent Sexuality and Teenage Pregnancy from a Black Perspective

. . . . .

June Dobbs Butts

As a black sex educator, I find it impossible to assess the problem of teenage pregnancy unless it is set in focus, against the backdrop of history. The higher fertility rate among black adolescents as compared with whites will only be elucidated when one analyzes the historical context which produced both sets of youngsters.

I believe our nation has a disease which is systemic in nature and devastating in its consequences; thus, how we approach the problem is crucial to its solution. I feel that people who design government programs and policies have been historically myopic—merely describing the symptoms of our disease rather than defining the true causative agents.

Teenage pregnancy is one fact of life which confronts all Americans whether urban or rural, rich or poor, white or black, male or female. This disturbance is creeping into our collective consciousness from quietly contained, little Midwestern hamlets just as surely as it is staring us in the face from noisily sprawling, big-city ghettos. We see it clearly among minority groups, notably among blacks—America's largest ethnic minority—because skin color and economic impoverishment make for high visibility in a welfare-wary national economy. But the disturbance is growing steadily and stealthily also among whites—especially in the urbane, affluent class whose power heretofore has insured it privacy and protection from sensational news media coverage. So, although teenage pregnancy is a fact of modern life, it is the black teenage mother who epitomizes the crux of the problem, for it is in regard to her undeveloped, but emerging body that we find the culmination of all those abstract ideas—racism, sexism, and the stamp of despair—that are bred by grinding poverty.

And if the sight of a fourteen-year-old about to give birth is not disturbing enough, there is a convoluting problem within the problem: the offspring. What are we as a nation to do, say by the year 2000, when we are faced with a generation of unwanted, and sometimes mentally or physically defective, offspring from the kids having kids at the present?

It is my thesis that teenage pregnancy is but a vexatious symptom of a societal illness. Until America can solve the twin issues of racism and sexism, we will have a diseased country, and can expect further exacerbation of the symptoms.

I define racism as the conviction that one's own race is inherently superior to all others. The same principle applies to sexism: it is the strong belief that one's own sex is intrinsically better than the other. People who do not see other people as individuals but always view them as representatives of a particular racial group are, according to my definition, racists. And by the same token, any man who views his maleness as a reason to look down upon or to disparage all women is a sexist. And vice versa, of course.

On the personal, attitudinal level, I firmly believe that being for one group (or cause, or idea) does not imply that one is automatically against others. However, the history of our country has been permeated by such thoughts and this has led to the institutionalization of racist and sexist behavior.

I feel that the sexist bias is even more ingrained than is racism, and exists on a world wide basis. And why do men feel superior to women? I feel that men fear and/or envy the female and her ability to become pregnant, to give birth, and to suckle her young. And because of this ambivalent feeling men have historically treated women only as sex objects or as mother figures neither of which is a position of parity in the governance of society. For, if women are restricted only to the home, and men dominate outside, then each realm lacks the other's valuable perspective. But this exclusivity need not remain. Now science has given us choices. Anatomy need not be destiny for women any more than for men.

This essay will discuss several characteristics of the black experience that have relevance to teenage pregnancy. I call them principles (ideas which are valued in the black community), and urge that both the design and implementation of federally funded programs should become more sensitive to them. These principles are a sex-positive view of life, the extended family, and the historical value of fecundity.

A Sex-Positive
View of Life

I believe that blacks should be studied because we have what my colleagues in the field of sex education call a "sex-positive view" of life. This is in direct contrast with the values of white society, which are essentially sex-negative. I consider what goes on in America to be a type of sexual schizophrenia, a schism between our attitudes toward sex and our sexual behavior. Why do we as a nation glorify the family, but refer to sexual activity in the pejorative? Whence do families originate, if not from sexual encounter? How can we praise the product but not the process? Our whole country is permeated with sexual innuendo—buy this product (a car, toothpaste, anything), for it will make you "sex-y"! We allow youngsters to become supersaturated with provocative sexual stimuli while telling them that the only respectable outlet for sexual expression is heterosexual coitus performed by legally married couples. The difference between what we practice and what we preach is more than a charming little deceit—it borders on the psychopathic, and the youngsters know it. We Americans are schizoid in our attitude toward sensuality, toward sexuality, and certainly, toward fecundity.

We say that sex is natural and good, but we adults panic when teenagers seek any mode of sexual expression. Adolescents today—rich or poor, black or white, male or female—feel that having sex is "in," but they seldom use contraceptives, especially for the first time. (Research studies have told us what they do, but not why.) I feel that they get discouraged by adults. I know that when I worked in New York City as a consultant in Family Life and Sex Education to the Human Resources Administration, and when teenagers flocked into the low-cost clinics (especially during the school strike, when they were bored and frustrated) asking for advice on contraception, most of the adult outreach workers did not praise them for acting responsibly—most just said, "Don't!" Wouldn't it be great if O.J. Simpson and Jesse Jackson could appear on a TV program especially designed for teenagers, and discuss the manliness of using condoms? I am serious. If O.J. can pose for magazines that deal with sex in a titillating fashion, why not use his charisma in an edifying way, by treating sex with respect and dignity? Our young people need role models who are responsible, sexually aware human beings. They need people who are not ashamed to offer some viable alternatives to the traditional chorus of voices chanting, "Don't," and, "Thou shalt not."

A clear-cut example of this sex-positive view of life can be found in the ways blacks value sensuousness. (This is different from being told by whites that we have "natural rhythm.") Distinguishable from either sex or sexuality, sensuousness is a dominant thread in the fabric of black family life. The socialization process—the many different practices involved in nurturing and raising the young—among black families is more lenient, more child-oriented, and more sensuous than is the case in the dominant white culture, regardless of the socioeconomic class of blacks. *Sensuousness* is literally the process of living in a world of sensation and perception. It means the ability to interpret the world through one's senses: sight, sound, taste, smell, and touch. The sense modality of *touch* is one of the keenest ways of interpreting stimuli and is the one that is used most in the field of sex therapy. Perhaps it is in the touching and the enjoyment of contact with human bodies that black culture is most alive, and is introduced into the life of the growing child. The fondness for touch permeates black culture from the cradle to the grave. One need only observe the highly stylized gestures and charades of black athletes, whether teenagers on the block playing basketball or pros earning a living in contact sports, to see the fondness for human touch. What is striking to me about these men is their very physicality: they handle each other freely, good-naturedly, and as an integral part of their shared nonverbal communication. One can also see the fondness for human touch—basic sensuousness without sexual overtones—that reflects much warmth and conviviality at gatherings in which blacks take part on a regular basis, such as at church meetings. For example, the slave spirituals, and later the gospel music of the black church that help to celebrate such rites of passage as christenings, marriages, homecomings, and funerals partake of sensuousness by appealing to many senses at once.

When sexual stimuli are added to other stimuli, the information is transformed beyond the level of sensuousness into what is called the *sensual*. The sexual component is the decisive factor in changing what is mere perception into a "turn on" or into a "turn off." An excellent example of sensuality in black culture is the idiom of jazz. This is a uniquely black contribution to song and dance, although whites have made far greater economic gains from their imitations of black song and dance than have the black artists whose work was original; witness the enormous adulation accorded George Gershwin, the Beatles, Elvis Presley, and recently the Bee Gees—all of whom acknowledged their black inspiration, and all of whom the adolescent culture has venerated. There is a beat and rhythm which "turns whites on," for rhythm is natural to us all, contrary to the stereotype that holds that only blacks have "natural rhythm." This was never intended as a compliment, since it was traditionally cast in the pejorative as meaning something base and denigrating; however, this is the releasing and rejuvenating quality that young whites are seeking today, most frantically in the current disco scene.

For many whites, the expression of their basic sensuality was considered anathema according to the edicts of many of their religious bodies. The equating of sensuality with sin occurred early on in Western religious thought, for things "of the flesh" could not be considered holy. Because of a difference in religious origin, we need to assess the significance of sensuality and of sensuousness in the life of the black teenager from an historical point of view. The African roots of today's black teenagers, where religious fervor and sensuality were merged, figure in their conceptualization of sensuality and sensuousness. Of course, there were strong injunctions against casual sex in early tribal Africa, which enforced strict codes that venerated fecundity and saw sex as a pleasurable means to an end, but never as an end per se. This is an important idea to fit into the conceptual framework when analyzing the strength of the black family. Given the freedom derived from this African heritage to accept and glorify their basic sensuality, it was natural for black Americans to accept and to glorify their sexual feelings. The culture itself was sex-positive; and socialization is always facilitated by the healthy expression of one's innate sensuality. It is said that in Africa today there are virtually no people with sexual dysfunctions such as impotence or female nonorgasmic response (outside the chronically ill). And we know that experts have estimated that sexual dysfunctions occur in about half of the married popu- lace of the United States, including American blacks. That should tell us something about the puritanical ethos of our American culture. In this country, human sexuality is not accorded respect or dignity. I personally think that the current upsurge of teenage pregnancy is a misguided, pathetic attempt to correct the situation. The kids are saying, "This is my body, and it feels good; it belongs to me." They are not thinking ahead to the future of motherhood or of fathering a family, with its constant responsibilities. They are children of a "Now" culture, and they desperately need older adults to be with them, to remind them of their roots, and to give them a sense of futurity.

The Extended Family

I feel that we, as a nation, would do well to study the survival techniques of black families. Most Americans know the manner in which blacks were captured and sold in bondage into this country, and how families were so often torn apart. Few truly appreciate the will to survive that has been nourished by the bonds of the black family and its ability to forge new survival techniques, in spite of hundreds of years of institutionalized slavery, ghetto- ization, discrimination, and grinding poverty.

The sense of kinship based on African tribalism has been a bulwark in the black experience. It goes without saying that the family is a major stabilizing force for most ethnic groups—so why is the black family special? The tribalism of Africa was not extinguished by the enforced bondage of slavery. The egalitarian nature of the man/woman relationship that existed among blacks during the slave days may well have been a unique example in Western civilization. Socially and sexually, black men and women were partners, equals—when permitted to live together—and they were usually very appreciative of the chance to do so in spite of the fragility of their union. Theirs was a tenuously held bond and therefore, perhaps, all the more precious; their mutual vulnerability was to be "sold down the river" at the caprice of the master. "Family" as a means of knowing who one was, and of survival itself, became an important facet of slave life. Since names were changed, families broken up, and males often sent out to stud, it was difficult to count on blood relatives for consolation and protection. Friends who were willing to see one through hard times; to bring up the offspring of a dying or a sold-away mother; who were able to learn crafts and buy their freedom, perhaps sending for loved ones; or who were willing to take into their families the ex-slaves who had made their way North—these friends became the extended black family; and there is no parallel to this type of friendship in American history: it was all purely voluntary.

The urbanization trend accelerated, and coincided with northward mi- gration after the Civil War; it took on great impetus after World War I and II. The black family became more truncated, less "extended," but the concept has not died out by any means. It is only a bit less convenient today. Living quarters in the North were not conducive to having a flock of relatives, or even good friends, come to visit or move in for a while. So, today's young people may not have ever actually seen or lived among numerous branches of their family tree, but the concept of valuing "the family" remains quite strong in black culture.

I have seen groups of middle-class teenage black youngsters—including my own—adopt the nomenclature of family life when finding themselves in new situations—for instance, going to summer camp, or changing residences or schools. One becomes someone else's "brother," "uncle," or "mama"; and this takes the edge off inevitable disappointment when a love affair dissolves. The same phenomenon occurs with amazing regularity among black youths in prisons. Giving and receiving some type of family appellation fosters a basic sense of security, and gives purpose to one's life in unknown or trying circumstances. Thus, family provides a sense of something bigger than one's finite self—of the life force, perhaps, of which one is a part—and thus gives purpose and meaning to one's mundane travails, even when scorned by others—as when having a baby out of wedlock. The impartiality of the extended black family has traditionally bolstered up the sagging spirits of its members and flattened any inflated egos evenhandedly. The extended family has proved itself of inestimable worth in accepting and incorporating into its fold the babies of teenagers. This brings us to the third principle.

The Historical Value of Fecundity

A cursory glance at the research literature of the past generation shows that black adolescents have a proportionately higher rate of out-of-wedlock pregnancies than do white teenagers. Earlier researchers tended to write of this phenomenon in the pejorative, citing the immorality of such behavior and implying that blacks are more prone to sexual excess. Recently, the more psychoanalytically inclined researchers have dealt with teenage pregnancy from a more humane stance. Whether this is because the researchers themselves are becoming more humane, is unclear in my mind. At any rate, the ambience surrounding this subject matter is one of concern now, rather than condemnation.

Nevertheless, facts show that black youngsters are becoming pregnant more frequently than whites. What does this mean when placed in the black perspective? It tells me that the researchers have counted pregnancies rather than assessing sexual activity. White teenagers engage in more types of what we in the field of sex education call nonprocreative sex. Such behavior, by definition, cannot lead to pregnancy. Nonprocreative sex means stimulation accomplished by any means other than direct genital contact. Its source can be manual, oral, anal, autoerotic, or by artificial means, such as a vibrator. White youngsters engage in all these types of sexual activity at an earlier age and for a longer portion of their lives than do their black counterparts. I do not place a value judgment on any type of sexual activity that is performed

151

between consenting mature human beings without doing harm to either party; I only point out that some types of stimulation lead to pregnancy and others do not. It is a maladroit combination of ignorance and of innocence among black youth that encourage them to use coital patterns for "natural" sexual expression and to eschew contraceptive measures. Whites have traditionally used methods that mitigate against pregnancy, or have found it more desirable (when pregnancy not only occurred but went to term) to place the offspring up for adoption. This is a practice that is frowned upon in the black community, basically because many black people still believe in the old adage that "a baby is the future." Possibly this attitude also influences blacks' reluctance to use contraceptives effectively.

If young blacks—both male and female—today are to be persuaded to give up the myth that one proves one's worth through demonstrated fecundity, then I believe it will only come to pass when our government shows them openly and honestly that it considers them part of the nation's natural resources. They must be convinced that there is a future for them: a chance to attend school, a relevant curriculum to pursue, and a dependable chance of their finishing school and not having to drop out because of economic privation and/or unwanted pregnancy. And most important, they must be assured that the job market won't remain closed to them: that industry, the military, the arts, higher education, commerce—every branch of our country's economy counts them as an integral part of the potential labor force. When this happens, and only if it happens, our country will have gotten rid of the twin evils, sexism and racism. This, then, is my analysis of why teenage pregnancy is abroad and rampant in the land.[1] Let me now share with you the small but eloquent sample of informed opinion of black health care professionals that I garnered as back-up references offering concrete ways in which government can alter the crisis situation we now face.

The Dilemma of the Black Health Care Professional

The peculiar dilemma of the black health care professional is really no different from the dilemma of the black politician, the black school superintendent, or the black public sanitation worker: how to gain upward mobility within the system (based on one's merits and not on tokenism) while fighting to change the system.

The cruel word "genocide," which was hurled at government programs so often during the past decade and a half that the general public began to turn a deaf ear, is still heard today. The black health care professional who advocates planning and spacing one's children, who informs the public about the availability of surgical fertility control, such as vasectomy and tubal ligation, who cautions adolescents against casual sex, who upholds the rights of homosexuals, who understands the need for some people to remain "child-free" in their marriages, who sponsors and supports adoption and more stringently improved foster care networks—such a person is deeply suspect in many quarters of the larger black community. There has to be a commitment of greater valor to continue working for the good of one's people in spite of frightened reactionaries.

Approximately eight years ago in New Rochelle, New York, a gang of black men were so angry about the work of a certain Planned Parenthood Center that they broke into the local office and literally, as well as figuratively, "wrecked the joint." On Monday morning, however, a group of black women who obviously respected and needed the services of the Center showed up offering to sweep and tidy the place, and get the doors open again to the public. It is counterproductive to shame or ignore the black men who were outraged. We who have had the benefit of education and some measure of success need to listen to them, interpret what the root cause of their vast rage is, and help them restore a sense of manhood—for, indeed, what they were protesting was being stripped away by an aloof white society that callously tells them that they shouldn't father any more children. Yet, the women were right also. They wanted the contraceptive services when they needed them, under their own control, not at the dictate of some organization. So, the black health care professional is much needed as liaison, as social change agent, and as an important member of the black community. And he or she must be heard by the white power structure not as a "black authority" but as a competent health care professional who happens to be black, just as he or she happens to be male or female—neither factor should create bias for or against anyone.

As I took down the comments of my colleagues, I was struck with the similarity of many of their answers. I asked them the three questions found on page fifty of the "Interim Report" published in April 1978 by the Family Impact Seminar. We spoke on the telephone, for I felt it afforded us easier dialogue than the static quality of a written letter. The questions I asked were the same for each respondent, and they were:

Can you identify ways in which federally funded programs discriminate against certain groups—in this case, against blacks?

Can you identify ways in which federally funded programs are insensitive to, or even do damage to, certain values and attitudes of black people?

In what way could these programs build on the values, attitudes, resources and strengths of black people in order to encourage more effective family functioning?

Of my ten respondents, only one asked not to be identified by name. I could understand her reasons, and have quoted her materials anonymously. I am grateful for the cooperation of them all, and would have enlarged the sample, had time permitted. The people whom I quote now are candid and sex-positive men and women; I only hope their wisdom will be heard. The following are all too brief excerpts from their responses to my questions:

James Batts, M.D. The Director of the Department of Obstetrics and Gynecology at the Harlem Hospital Center in New York City, Batts commented:

> The welfare system, which encourages women to refrain from having their husbands live with them, is flagrant and outright discrimination. Abortion legislation is blatantly anti-poor people.
>
> Look at the Family Planning programs—they sound good at first, but the [adolescent] child is receiving charity. This encourages children to break free of parental control and to leave home. Such programs should encourage the child to inform parents and to enlist their support. Why should only broken families receive support? Turn it around and look the other way—why not give financial support to a complete or intact family, as well as or even more so than to a family on welfare? And if a man is in the family, they should help him find a job, not get rid of him.

Kenyon Burke, M.S. Associate Director for Programs with the NAACP in New York City, Burke had this to say:

> Take the welfare program: in order to qualify for eligibility, it discourages male membership. The program as it is federally funded now is completely inadequate. What's needed is more and better day care centers, training—this is all important—for the men who are entering the labor market from the low status which has been so meager up till now, and other factors, too. More black women than white women work at this lowest level, and therefore, they're at a disadvantage. Programs for reentry (for the mature woman) are much needed. The teenager also needs work, and especially the young mother.
>
> The language of the majority group toward the black family is often insensitive. They expect and are biased in favor of two parents and their children constituting a "real" family. This is not so in the black community.
>
> The strength of the extended family in the black community is not often well understood outside of the black community. Historically we've had it, and we must get back to that close intimacy again. We've gotten infected with that same independent, isolated feeling that infected white people: alienation! The black church could be a network to rebuild that sense of "family."

William A. Darity, Ph.D. Darity, Dean of the School of Health Sciences at the University of Massachusetts at Amherst, said:

> Yes, there is discrimination. To be specific, there's an insufficient number of black researchers and administrators.
>
> Most of these programs are designed for the majority group's needs, and not to meet specific needs of black families. Look at the Cancer programs. The funding for studies on the black family goes to white researchers. The Family Planning programs too often are designed to impose values on the recipients, that is, limiting family size, marital status, etc. There's never been real recognition of the validity of a one-parent family, particularly when that mother has never been married. Often religious impositions are made on individuals too.
>
> Family Planning and social welfare programs do damage to the kids, by branding them as "illegitimate," which is terrible. The economic issue plays a major role in all of this. Whites have the means, the economic means to either adopt or in some way to get rid of any evidence of sexuality; blacks don't. Those programs need black input and black implementation!

Ramona Edelin, M.S.W. Executive Assistant to the President of the Urban Coalition in Washington, D.C., Edelin said:

> Look at the welfare reform business going on now. The Medicaid-abortion issue restricts funds for poor women severely. It is obvious that ultimately it is the children who are the ones being discriminated against. Having the man in the home! There is a reform piece of legislation coming up pertaining to this. New legislation now permits another wage-earner to live in the home. There are some attempts being made which help: the Head Start program could pull the family into the picture. Also, Jesse Jackson's EXCEL (Push for Excellence) program speaks to the involvement of the family—it's too late once the kids reach adolescence. We need health, recreational and all other kinds of preventive services (like after-school, as well as in-school, programs). We could look at each governmental department and ask what they can do for the black family. They could all be asked for help.

Helen Dickens, M.D. She is Associate Dean of the School of Medicine and Professor of Obstetrics and Gynecology at the University of Pennsylvania in Philadelphia. Her comment is:

> Children do not receive their fair share of the tax dollar. The total amount of funds to children and youth through Maternal and Infant Care (MIC) programs are funded annually, but if you have more patients than their amount of dollars covers, either you can't see them all or they have to pay out of pocket. MIC funds are only for high-risk obstetrics—like the teens (or at least about two-thirds of them) whom I see. Family Planning funds—for nonpregnant teenagers—are grossly inadequate.
>
> Often the staff members are inadequate, and often they do not represent the black community at all. There may be a token or two of black representatives on the staff of these programs, but the entire programs don't reflect the thinking of the black community. Example: not paying for abortions of poor women— the Governor of Pennsylvania vetoed this during his "lame duck" session, and effectively stalled it until the next Congress.
>
> Most of these programs aren't funded to [build on the strengths of black families]. Their personnel don't understand or can't work with black families. There is no economic support for middle-class teenagers who become pregnant; so, often they marry even if they don't stay together long. For poor kids who get pregnant, often the male can't work or if he does, he can't earn much—so the female gets welfare, and then sometimes they just don't even marry. There could be changes in the way these programs are being mandated.

Elizabeth Graham, M.S.W. Graham, the Supervisor of Social Services in the Department of Obstetrics and Gynecology and Co-Director of Young Parents' Program at Columbia-Presbyterian Medical Center, New York, said:

> Aid to Families of Dependent Children (AFDC) really divides families! The whole system fails to promote the growth and development of black family members; it creates generations of dependents instead. No "self help" is built into the system. It's always the system against them. Day care programs have long waiting lists and often a fee schedule is unreasonable. There aren't enough "family day care" programs where a two-month-old infant can be cared for. They could provide a neighborhood woman to help so that the mother could go back to work. Mothers need help with their own development, life is turbulent enough.

Any program has peaks and valleys. No program that I can think of right off the bat is blatantly insensitive, but the implementation and the monitoring systems leave a lot to be desired in most of them.

So many of these programs are just designed to deal with the problems and to ignore the strengths! Some of the teenagers have great resources, and many programs could encourage and foster their strengths instead of fostering a continued sense of dependency.

Naomi T. Gray, M.S.W. Gray, the Director of Naomi Gray Associates in San Francisco, California, said:

Agencies are indifferent, don't provide for minorities to serve on their boards of directors, for example, or in similar higher decision-making capacities. The federal government hasn't monitored these agencies well at all. They simply file contracts and grants—and that is not spending wisely. And the end result is that black families aren't being served well.

Most of these programs don't understand the cultural values and the particular life styles of blacks—in fact, very few do. Most of them need black input into the planning and organizing phases of their programs, as well as during the implementation of such programs. And blacks should be paid for their advice!

The ultimate consumers of these services should be placed in peer relationships—in other words, GIVE THEM JOBS.

Mary S. Harper, Ph.D. She is Assistant Chief, Center for Minority Group Mental Health at the National Institute of Mental Health in Rockville, Maryland. Her comments included:

[Services] are fragmented—meaning there is no central theme or committed effort. Right now each branch has gone its own way, piecemeal. Therefore, government programs which help the black family really haven't yet been focused.

We need an "Inter-Agency Committee on the Family," just as we have one on children. The federal government should collaborate with private organizations (concerned with families). There are over 150 of them. Why not bring them all together and work on ways in which they can conceptualize what's going on with families, with what research is needed to improve things? Blacks would be represented in all these organizations.

Robert Staples, Ph.D. An author and Associate Professor in the Department of Social and Behavioral Sciences at the University of California at San Francisco, Staples said:

The program Aid to Families of Dependent Children (AFDC) may actually be encouraging teenage pregnancy. Also, it's a bit hazy why there were so many sterilizations in Alabama in a governmentally sponsored program a few years ago. Black input is needed! The ban on federal funds for abortion is especially bad. Black women need this option because of their economic dependence. Blacks also need more sex education in our schools—more availability of contraception, etc. One-third of blacks are now being born to teenagers! What is the future of these children?

[Programs] don't, as a rule, recognize that black families need support systems. This fact portends bad things for the next generation.

Somehow the role of the black man has to be strengthened through a variety of good outreach programs which are community based.

Anonymous Administrator in a large, Northern, federal program. This health care professional said:

In Family Planning there's a large segment of the black population which earns just above the poverty level now held as the cut-off point for receiving federal assistance and services. Regionalism makes a difference in how far one's money can be stretched. Rearing a family of four in Austin, Texas, is a lot easier than caring for such a family in Harlem, with its over- inflated rents, food, transportation, weather differences for clothing, etc. There should be a relative adjustment made for the relative cost of living.

The government is pushing voluntary fertility control without giving any consideration to other economic, social, and dental aspects of general and comprehensive health. The total person has to be considered, or it's genocide.

Community people should be employed as staff for such programs.

Just as the lives of individual men are often enriched when they can listen without bias to the observations of concerned women, so can the quality of life in white society be greatly improved when the insights of its minority members are respected and incorporated.

Notes

1. Those interested in exploring some of these themes further may want to consult the following references: Phyllis Greenacre, *Emotional growth,* vol. 1 (New York: International Universities Press, 1971); Calvin Hernton, *Sex and race in America* (Garden City, N.Y.: Doubleday, 1965); Robert B. Hill, *The strengths of black families* (New York: National Urban League, 1971); Joyce A. Ladner, *Tomorrow's tomorrow: The black woman* (New York: Doubleday, 1971); Kenneth Little, "Some urban patterns of marriage and domesticity in West Africa," *The Sociological Review* 7 (July 1959); L.P. Mair, "African Marriage and social changes," in *Survey of African marriage and family life,* ed. A. Phillips (London: Oxford University Press, 1953), p.1; ed., Robert Staples, *The black family,* rev. ed. (Chicago: Wadsworth, 1978)—see especially chapter by Alan P. Bell, "Black sexuality: Fact and fancy"; and Charles V. Willie, B.M. Karmer, and B. S. Brown, eds., *Racism and mental health* (Pittsburgh: University of Pittsburgh Press, 1973).

The Impact of Adolescent Pregnancy on Hispanic Adolescents and their Families

. . . . .

Angel Luis Martinez

> *First generation*. Pete Morales, seventeen, was born in Texas. His parents were born in Sonora, Mexico. They speak mostly Spanish. He speaks mostly English: "There ain't no jobs; school sucks; everywhere we go they lie to us. So we get high and mess around. If somebody gets pregnant, at least you have some excitement."

> *Newcomer*. Juanita Cabrera has two children, lives alone, and is unemployed. She arrived from the Dominican Republic three years ago and speaks English with apparent distaste and difficulty. She is nineteen.

> *Second generation*. Nadine Ayala doesn't speak Spanish. She takes it in school. All of her friends speak English and her boyfriend's family has never known Spanish. Her parents were born in Denver, and the family now lives in Berkeley. She is fifteen and pregnant.

In order to discuss adolescent pregnancy in the Hispanic family and community, it is necessary that we ask what we know about Hispanics, in general, and about Hispanic adolescents, in particular.[1] There are more than twelve million persons of Spanish origin who live in the United States.[2] Of these, approximately 7,200,000 are Mexican, 1,800,000 are Puerto Rican, 700,000 are Cuban, and 2,400,000 are considered "other" Hispanics. The estimate of all Hispanics, including undocumented persons, is nineteen million (See Tables 6 and 7).

Hispanic adolescents represent approximately 24 percent of this total, compared to a 20.3 percent adolescent population for the general population.[3] (These figures do not include the Bureau of Census estimate of three million people living in Puerto Rico who are American citizens.)[4]

TABLE 6

**Population of Spanish origin, by sex and type of Spanish origin
(for the United States, March 1978; number in thousands)**

Type of Spanish origin	Both sexes		Males		Females	
	Number	Percent	Number	Percent	Number	Percent
Mexican	7,151	59.4	3,528	60.3	3,623	58.5
Puerto Rican	1,823	15.1	825	14.1	997	16.1
Cuban	689	5.7	342	5.8	347	5.6
Central or So. American	863	7.2	396	6.8	467	7.5
Other Spanish	1,519	12.6	758	13.0	761	12.3
Total	**12,046**	**100.0**	**5,850**	**100.0**	**6,196**	**100.0**

Source: Department of Commerce, Bureau of the Census, *Current Population Reports,
Persons of Spanish origin in the United States,* ser. P-20, no. 328, table 2
(Washington, D.C.: GPO, March 1978), p. 5.

TABLE 7

**Total and Spanish origin population, by age and type of Spanish origin
(for the United States, March 1978)**

Age	Total population	Spanish Origin						Not of Spanish origin*
		Total	Mexican	Puerto Rican	Cuban	Central or South American	Other Spanish	
Under 5 years	7.2	12.6	13.9	11.3	5.7	9.4	13.4	6.8
5 to 9 years	7.9	11.5	11.8	13.6	6.8	9.2	10.6	7.7
10 to 17 years	14.5	17.7	17.3	21.1	13.4	14.8	18.9	14.4
18 to 20 years	5.8	6.2	6.6	5.2	5.2	5.8	6.1	5.8
21 to 24 years	7.1	7.8	8.4	6.2	5.4	6.7	8.1	7.1
25 to 34 years	15.4	15.7	16.1	16.4	11.4	21.2	12.4	15.5
35 to 44 years	11.1	11.0	10.2	11.5	14.4	16.6	10.0	11.1
45 to 54 years	10.8	8.4	7.8	8.2	15.3	8.1	8.6	10.9
55 to 64 years	9.6	4.8	4.2	4.4	9.2	5.1	5.8	9.9
65 years and over	10.5	4.3	3.7	2.3	13.3	3.1	6.1	10.9
18 years and under	70.4	58.3	57.0	54.0	74.1	66.7	57.1	71.1
21 years and over	64.6	52.1	50.4	48.8	68.9	60.8	51.0	65.3
Median age (years)	29.5	22.1	21.3	20.3	36.5	26.8	21.5	30.0
All ages (thousands)	*214,159*	*12,046*	*7,151*	*1,823*	*689*	*863*	*1,519*	*202,113*
Percent	**100.0**	**100.0**	**100.0**	**100.0**	**100.0**	**100.0**	**100.0**	**100.0**

Source: Department of Commerce, Bureau of the Census, *Current Population* Reports,
Persons of Spanish origin in the United States, ser. P-20, no. 328, table 2 (Washington, D.C.:
GPO, March 1978), p. 5.

* Includes persons who did not know or did not report on origin.

More precise numbers are difficult to arrive at because of poor available sources, and because no figures exist on the number of "undocumented" or "uncounted" Hispanics in this country—adult, adolescent, or child. Within this population, a Nadine Ayala may have more in common with a Marie Osmond than with a Juanita Cabrera. In reality, we know very little about either Nadine or Juanita, or even how many of each there are in the general population. However, when Hispanic young people are spoken about, when they are considered by social service agencies, or when they are deplored in the media, they are usually spoken of generically.

The stereotypical adolescent is a media creation. A preponderance of printed media and of television programming, dealing with adolescents or adolescent concerns, focuses basically on problems: alcoholism, prostitution, runaways, pregnancy, and status offenders. Teenagers as able, responsible, and talented people are not often seen.

Behind the overall negative image of adolescents lie the images of minority adolescents. Hispanic youth, who, with black youth, are made media-visual as problems whenever they gather in groups of more than one, are also generally portrayed as linguistically maladroit and morally deficient.

The programs providing services to Hispanic young people that attract media attention are, of course, the ones that deal with problems. As a result, the picture that America gets is one of drug addicts that need rehabilitation, pregnant girls that need care, and troublemakers who seem to be in the news all the time. It is a bleak and distorted picture. And the created myopia has become a real deficiency of discernment. We know so little, yet we make so many judgments.

Within every group of Latin American people in the United States there is a heterogeneous adolescent population—newcomers, oldtimers, and the degrees in between. We know that as a whole they are the least employed, earn the least when they are employed, are the least educated,[5] and have conflicts with legal authorities out of proportion to their numbers.

But we know very little about their lifestyles. We don't know whether recently arrived Puerto Rican, Mexican, or other Hispanic young people have more in common with each other, or with members of their own nationality who have either lived in this country for years or were born here. We don't know or understand how they are affected by cultural displacement, or the conflicts they experience between their families' cultural expectations and external values of American society.

Economics

> If I don't go to school, I can't work,
> if I work I can't go to school.
> What are you, crazy, or what?
>
> —Pete, seventeen

Almost one-half of Hispanics are under the age of eighteen;[6] and one out of three lives at or below poverty levels. About one-half live in the inner cities of America. One-half have completed high school; one out of five holds a white collar job.[7]

Families headed by Hispanic women are twice as likely to have incomes below the poverty level as those headed by Hispanic men; and Hispanic women are less likely to participate in the labor force than are men. Hispanics account for about 5 percent of the total population, 4 percent of the civilian labor force, and 6 percent of the unemployed.[8]

The situation for Hispanic youth is even more precarious. Although youths account for only one-quarter of the labor force, they represent half of all unemployed persons![9] It is almost impossible to do any real economic analysis on Hispanic youth unemployment because there are only poor, misleading, and discriminatory data available. A recent example is the report published by the Congressional Budget Office entitled *Youth unemployment: The outlook and some policy strategies.* For Hispanics, the data are not very useful because in the report, "unless otherwise noted, the term 'white' applies to Caucasians including those of Hispanic heritage. The term 'non-white' applies to blacks (which may include some persons of Hispanic heritage), American Indians, and Orientals."[10] Result: no data on Hispanic youth.

In June 1976, Public Law 94-311 was enacted; it directs federal agencies to expand the collection, analysis, and publication of statistics that will indicate the social, health, and economic conditions of Americans of Spanish origin or descent. The Departments of Labor and Commerce were given major responsibility for the collection and analysis of labor force and population data.

In May of 1978, the Commission on Civil Rights published a report entitled *Improving Hispanic Unemployment Data: The Department of Labor's Continuing Obligation,* which charged that "eighteen months after enactment of the law [P.L. 94-311] most of the Department of Labor's efforts were in the planning stages and the department did not know when it would publish the expanded data...Moreover, it did not plan to publish Hispanic unemployment data monthly, as it does for blacks and whites. It planned to separate Hispanic unemployment data for only a very few states and for no local areas with large Hispanic population."[11]

By the mid-1980s, it is expected that Hispanics will represent the largest minority population in the United States. Without accurate data for all economic, social, and health indices to reflect the true situation of Hispanics, no comprehensive action can be taken to identify strategies that will address any of the problems faced by this population, including teenage pregnancy.

The Hispanic population in America is a very youthful one; the median age is 20.5, as compared to 28 for the overall population. In addition, the percentage of youth under eighteen within the Hispanic population is 44.2 percent, compared to 42.3 percent within the black population, and 33.2 percent within the white population. By contrast, the percentage of elderly (sixty-five years and older) within the Hispanic population is only 4.4 percent, as opposed to 7.0 percent within the black population, and 10.3 percent within the white population.[12] Hence, while the overall declining birthrate in America means a future decline in youth unemployment generally, the Hispanic youth population will continue to increase over the next decade, and, by extrapolation, will account for a larger percentage of unemployed youth, and of adolescent problems generally.

As Jones and Placek have pointed out, major sources of data relating to adolescent fertility do not separately break out pregnancy and births to Hispanics (which are included in the "white and other" category). Furthermore, there are virtually no research reports on Hispanic adolescent fertility in the United States. Thus, a discussion of teenage pregnancy in the Hispanic community has to rely on anecdotal impressions, experiences, and conjecture.

It seems reasonable to assume that the fertility rate among Hispanic teenagers is at least comparable to that of white youngsters, and may be as high as blacks. The extent of the problem of teenage pregnancy among Hispanic populations is partly indicated in the report of some preliminary analyses of new data collected from the 1979 National Longitudinal Survey on youth. These data indicate that Hispanics drop out of school much more frequently than whites or blacks; and among the major reasons cited are pregnancy, getting married, and home responsibilities. (Only 6.9 percent of whites ages eighteen to twenty-two are school dropouts who left school for these reasons, while the number for blacks is 14.7 percent, and for Hispanics, 19.6 percent.)[13]

Furthermore, there are serious implications in the high youth unemployment rate and poor employment prospects of Hispanics. Clearly, Hispanic youth, already at a socioeconomic disadvantage, will be further victimized by pregnancies. With one out of three already living in poverty, the chances for socioeconomic betterment will be limited, at best. A Hispanic child born of a teenage pregnancy has a very high likelihood of being locked into poverty.

The Hispanic youth who decides to bear and raise a child is likely to live below the poverty level. The young Hispanic parent is probably poorly educated, lives in the inner city, and lacks job skills, and in general, will exert pressure on existing family resources. She will be even less job-ready than her white American counterpart, because Hispanic women with children are less likely to work. The social cost, still unmeasured, is borne directly by the Hispanic family.

Old Traditions and New Pressures

> ...The moral bit, you know.
> My mother said, "You've got to get married.
> You can't disgrace the family.
>
> —Rosa Maria, sixteen

Although Hispanics in the United States are not a homogeneous population, many cultural, linguistic, and traditional values are held in common.

162

If we are going to attempt to influence Hispanic young persons' sexual and reproductive behavior, we should keep in mind that the evidence is that the educational and health programs for Hispanics that have been tried so far show that we have failed rather miserably.

Some of the causes lie in our lack of knowledge and understanding of the cultural world in which Hispanic adolescents live. For most white Americans and for a majority of blacks, the old traditions are *old* traditions. For them, "old traditions" is a term used to recall those values that are perceived almost as historical relics rather than active values. One example might be the family; within the old traditional values, this meant a nuclear grouping with a working male head, and concern for and care of the grandparent generation. Another "oldie" is the preeminence of parental authority over all matters affecting their children. These and other traditional values have changed radically in America, so that now their mention is generally within a context of wistfulness, or of a return to times gone by.

For large numbers of Hispanics, however, most of these traditional values have not changed; the modifier "old" does not apply. It is important to note that Hispanic families are more likely than either whites or blacks to be two-parent, male-headed families (78 percent, as compared with 77 percent and 63 percent in 1969, respectively).[14] Furthermore, there exists a sense of *familia* that encompasses an extended family (e.g., grandparents, aunts, uncles, and cousins), and identifies the older adults as persons with family position, authority, and relevance. If you're an Hispanic teenager, and a relative arrives from "over there" to live in your home, your life changes. When you go to visit "over there," your life changes. It happens because they are *familia*. The fact that the traditions and values are active can be seen in the threat that some parents use with teenagers who are not "behaving"; they are told that if they don't shape up they'll be sent "over there." For the parent this implies that cultural sanctions will have a stronger impact there. (Somewhat similar to the black youngster being sent "down South.") The school, the law, other adults, all receive more respect in Latin America by teenagers than they do in the United States.

The slow but generally continuous contact that occurs between Hispanics in the United States and relatives from Latin America acts as a protector and promoter of values, among them sexual values, that differ from the current values in the United States. It is not within the scope of this paper to document these differences—bibliographies are available. However, Hispanic teenagers are easily recognizable as being the group most "on the line" in this conflict of values. They identify as Latins, as coming from a distinct national group, as newcomer or oldtimer, as family; and as teenagers caught between these cultural roots and the barrage of images, ideals, and models presented sometimes by their American schools, sometimes by their surrounding community, and always by the media.

We do not know how all these experiences affect Hispanic adolescents. Or how in turn these adolescents affect their families and community. We do know that the attitudes and values in the United States regarding adolescent sex, sexuality, and parenting are contradictory, dishonest, and, at times, immoral. If we are to reach Hispanic adolescents and provide them with the skills, values and education necessary to help them make personally responsible sexual decisions, there is much that needs to be considered.

The Hispanic family has traditionally been, and is, what much of the Anglo family in this country has ceased to be. The intrinsic values of an Hispanic family are difficult to understand for anyone who exists in a milieu that has essentially disavowed the value of intergenerational living and the emotional strength of the extended family.

It would be irrational to base policy or programs aimed at Hispanic families on data gathered from non-Hispanic populations. For example, where the male in the American family plays an increasingly nebulous role, this cannot be said of Hispanics. This issue alone has major implications that affect not only the man's role but also those of "wife" or "mother." In a study of the reasons for, and consequences of adolescent pregnancies, these issues are not to be easily dismissed.

In a social milieu where parenting is increasingly being called an "alternative optional lifestyle," the Hispanic woman lives in a context in which the role of mother has an extremely high social value. When contrasted to an existence of high unemployment, inadequate education, and low social value, which is the lot of so many Hispanic adolescents, that so-called "alternative" may become a highly desirable one.

Family Relations

Wilma Montanez of the San Francisco General Hospital Perinatal Unit has conducted interviews with Hispanic adolescent women, their parents, siblings, and friends. The following comments are excerpted from her notes:

> The really interesting sight is that of grandmothers walking arm in arm with their teenage granddaughters who are obviously pregnant. It's easy to tell that she is proud that she will be a great-grandmother soon. At the same time it is clear that she is confused and somewhat bewildered at the new morals and the new configurations that her family is taking in the United States. Yes, she was pregnant when she was a teenager, but she was married first.

The confusion of the grandmother is often shared by her daughter, the teenager's mother. Doris was forty when the second of her teenaged daughters became pregnant.

> I never thought of it happening to me. I let them have boyfriends at a young age so they wouldn't have to sneak around behind my back. I figured if I gave them permission they wouldn't have sex. When the two got pregnant, I was hurt and very embarrassed at the same time.

The family, Montanez states, provides the basic support system for the pregnant Hispanic adolescent. If there is no supportive sister, the next in line is the mother. However, even here some teenagers find walls. For example,

Eva, fourteen years old, confessed: "I waited for her to ask me. I had the feeling that as my mother she knew all the time. I knew she was going to be hurt, but it never crossed my mind that she would say, 'You've got to get out of the house.'"

Montanez found that most of the girls she interviewed expressed that fathers left it up to the mothers to handle the situation—fathers were the least supportive.

> Rose Maria said, "When I went home and told my parents I was pregnant, my father, he really blew it. He asked me if I was going to get married. I said no and he didn't speak to me for about four to five months after that. That was pressure on me during that time. He was completely ignoring me. I still had to respect him and serve him. My older brother blew it too. He threatened me and said, 'You get married.'"

Younger brothers, however, tend to be more supportive in these situations. Eva shared how her brothers played a dad role for her child and her sister's. "They babysat our babies, they changed diapers. They even got sick like us during our pregnancies."

The male partner in adolescent pregnancies generally plays an uncertain role. Most do not know what they can do or what is expected of them. Socially they're seldom given any direction, nor is there a sense of what the role is, besides contributing to conception, that they are to play as males. The images are confusing, to say the least. When asked how he felt when he first found out that his girlfriend was pregnant, a seventeen-year-old Hispanic replied, "One half of me said 'Wow,' and one half said 'Oh shit.'"

"He was hurt and embarrassed. Mostly hurt," says a teenage boy's mother. Lorena, fourteen, says of her seventeen-year-old boyfriend: "He just got happy and didn't say nothing. That's all. He keeps calling every day. He wants to take me to my clinic appointments. He just wants to help me."

There can be no doubt, however, that the most profound impact of an adolescent pregnancy is on the pregnant young woman. She is ultimately alone in the shock, the amazement, the unknown. She has to confront decisions— perhaps for the first time in a lifetime where decisions have always been made for her, at times even the decision to have intercourse:

> Lorena, fourteen: "At first I was happy. When it was too late, I thought, 'What do I want a baby for?'"

> Rosa Maria, sixteen: "I just felt very stupid, hopeless. I was mad at my parents. I was totally restricted. They were scared of reality."

> Cookie, sixteen: "I always had problems with my period. So I thought at first that it was a problem with my period. When I felt kicking I knew it wasn't no period."

All of these young women are Hispanic; the information being gathered from them and their families will do much to help us understand how Hispanic families are affected by the occurrence of an unplanned pregnancy of a teenager. It will then be possible to provide the services most needed.

There are obvious needs for education and preventive services—much of the current intervention, however, comes after the fact.

Educational Concerns

"Pregnancy," says Alfred Moran, Executive Vice President of Planned Parenthood of New York City, "is the major factor in the dropout rate among junior and senior high school girls."

We do not have data for the incidence of pregnancy among Hispanic girls in junior and senior high schools. However, we do have evidence that many do not finish high school.[15] Whether they are dropouts or pushed-outs, these young women, if they are not pregnant, become very much at risk of pregnancy. Where school provided at least some sort of structured time, unemployment offers no such benefits.

Hispanic adolescent boys and girls find themselves in an educational system that offers them very little in terms of realistic education or preparation for life. Reports from national organizations representing Mexican-Americans, Puerto Ricans, and other Hispanics all point to the fact that schools are simply not meeting the basic needs of Hispanics.

Rosemary Samalot, a New York City social worker and pregnancy counselor, states:

> They all get wasted. The boys don't know what to do with themselves and neither do the girls. They end up being trapped into playing house. Inevitably the girl gets pregnant and the cycle has been completed and started again. The status for both the male and the female is then essentially settled. He is unemployed and ill educated—she is even less so. For the female, the status evolved binds her to raising a child and, almost invariably, getting pregnant again.

Josefina A. Card and Lauress L. Wise found that the repercussions of teenage childbearing are long lasting: "The young parents acquire less education than their contemporaries; they are often limited to less prestigious jobs, and the women to more dead-end ones.[16] Their marriages are less stable than those of their contemporaries who postponed childbearing." For the Hispanic family—with low education, income, and unemployment—the combined problems of dropout and pregnancy among adolescents present some major concerns.

Postscript

"Implicit in many discussions by political leaders, human service professionals, and the media—and explicit in some—is the assumption that teenage pregnancy is a problem because adolescents are acting 'irresponsibly,'" states the 1976 annual report of the Alan Guttmacher Institute (AGI).[17] However, in a recent television program about teenagers, a writer quit and a minor flap ensued when he divulged that the network's censors would not allow a teenage boy to use the word "responsible" in reference to birth control. "This is not something a fifteen-year-old should think about," said the network censor. What are we telling young people?

The AGI report adds, "A recent statement on adolescent health and pregnancy by an agency of the HEW described sexually active unmarried teenaged women as 'acting out,' which is a professional term for deviant, if not pathological behavior. Since 35 percent of unmarried teenage women are sexually active, the description has two immediate results: it defines more than one-third of United States teenagers as sick, and it implies that the problem of teenage pregnancy is largely insoluble."[18]

If there is confusion for the adolescent, it seems that it merely mirrors that of their adult counterparts. For Hispanic families, the realities of the impact caused by adolescents remain family secrets. The lack of common information regarding major issues affecting their lives limits the possibilities of action. It seems likely to remain that way unless strong action is taken to enact considerable economic, social, and attitudinal changes in this society.

Having considered the factors which may affect Hispanic adolescents and their families—population, traditions, social pressures, stereotypes, economics, family relationships, and education—and the lack of information about them, it is clear that few, if any, conclusions or recommendations can be drawn regarding the impact on Hispanic families of adolescent pregnancies.

However, in addition to the suggestions presented earlier, we can list the areas on which we need information or action:

We must strive to understand the impact of a very young and fast-growing population in Latin America on the Hispanic population in the United States.

We must secure information on the knowledge, attitudes, and opinions of Hispanic children and youth, and their families regarding sex, sexuality, parenting, and general health issues. We need to carefully examine significant differences and similarities among Hispanics with different national origins.

We must make policy studies that accurately reflect the effect of minimum wage laws and tax incentive initiatives on Hispanics. Through these, manpower plans can be developed that deal with the group with the highest unemployment rate—youth.

We must improve access to health careers for Hispanics. (The United States Statistical Abstract for 1977, detailing American Medical Association licensure statistics for health professionals, offers no data on the number of Hispanics in health professions.)

Churches must provide avenues for data and for educational leadership. James R. Brockman, S.J., associate editor of *America* magazine, has written that from one-fourth to one-third of the Catholic Church's members are Spanish-speaking and of Hispanic culture.

We must know the extent of involvement of United States Hispanics with the Roman Catholic Church. Are they influenced more by the Church and its doctrines than the total United States Catholic population? If so, what are the implications regarding birth control, preventive services, and educational programs? The recent papal visits to Latin America and the United States, and their consequences have not been lost on the Hispanics. (During recent private discussions in Mexico City, the author learned that officials are still evaluating the impact of the Pontiff's visit on family planning efforts. It may serve us well to monitor their findings as useful indicators for American policy and programming of family planning efforts for Hispanics.) Essentially, it would be counterproductive to ignore the influence of the Church and its revitalization in the world of *Latinos*.

Programs for teenage parents, such as the New Futures School in Albuquerque, where Hispanics represent more than one-half of the enrolled population, must be adequately evaluated so that they might serve as planning models for similar ventures in areas of high Hispanic population.

Studies must also be performed which address the following questions:

1. What are the causes of adolescent sexual behavior among Hispanic young people within their cultural context?

2. What are the consequences of this behavior in terms of education, health, economic, and social status?

3. How do the differing cultural attitudes regarding sexual behavior and expectations affect Hispanic young people? How are these reconciled? How do they affect parenting? Pregnancy?

4. What are the relationships between Hispanic unemployment, school dropout, and drug or alcohol use, and adolescent sexual behavior?

5. What are the prevailing attitudes toward abortion among Hispanic young people, compared to practice?

6. What are the immediate and long term effects of early parenting and/or marriage on these young people?

7. What percentage of women of Hispanic origin have children? What is their age breakdown? What are their national origins?

8. To what extent are Hispanic families changing or moving away from extended families?

9. What programs and policies should we develop to provide adequate health and education programs for Hispanic young people?

We can provide education that is honest and significant to the needs and questions of young people—but in order to do this we have to prepare ourselves as parents, teachers, health care providers, and human beings.

Simply saying, "You're too young to know that," has not worked. To say in its place, "We can't talk about that, but there's a contraceptive brochure in the library," I fear, would be equally dishonest. We must not fall into the trap of trying to find simplistic or purely technological (i.e., contraceptive) solutions. We must provide the kind of education and example that takes into account not only the minority who "get in trouble," but also the majority that do not, and give them support when they choose to say, "No, I'm not ready yet." Basically we should live our lives as an example to young people of what we say we believe.

Notes

1. This paper was prepared in collaboration with: Wilma Montanez, Health Educator, San Francisco General Hospital; Arturo Riera, OBECA Arriba Juntos, San Francisco.

2. Department of Commerce, Bureau of the Census, Current Population Reports, *Persons of Spanish origin in the United States,* ser. P-20, No. 328, Table 2 (Washington, D.C.: GPO, March 1978), p. 5.

3. Ibid.

4. Commission on Civil Rights, *Puerto Ricans in the continental United States: An uncertain future.* (Washington, D.C.: GPO, Oct. 1976), p. 5.

5. Commission on Civil Rights, *Improving Hispanic unemployment data: The Department of Labor's continuing obligation.* (Washington, D.C.: GPO, May 1978), p. 12; Commission on Civil Rights, *Puerto Ricans,* Table 27, p. 93

6. Department of Commerce, *Persons of Spanish origin,* p. 1.

7. Department of Labor, Bureau of Labor Statistics, *Workers of Spanish origin: A chartbook* (Bul. 1970: 1978), Chart 31, p. 46; Chart 2, p. 6; Chart 5, p. 9. See also "MexAmerica," *Washington Post* (5-pt. ser.), March 26 and 30, 1978; Department of Labor, *Workers of Spanish origin,* chart 19, p. 29.

8. Department of Labor, *Workers of Spanish origin,* Chart 23, p. 34; Chart 6, p. 10; summary indicators, p. 1.

9. Congressional Budget Office, *Youth unemployment: The outlook and some policy strategies* (Washington, D.C.: GPO, April 1978), p. xiii.

10. Ibid., p. ii, n.

11. Commission on Civil Rights, *Improving Hispanic unemployment data,* letter of transmittal, p. ii.

12. Bureau of the Census, *Census of Population: 1970,* vol. 1, Characteristics of the Population, Pt. 1, Section 1, U.S. Summary, chap. C, "General Social and Economic Characteristics," Negro Population 1970, PC(2)-1B, Persons of Spanish Origin 1970, PC(2)-1C, and U.S. Summary, Detailed Characteristics 1970, PC(1)- D-1 (Washington, D.C.:GPO, 1972).

13. Barbara Gomez-Day, "Hispanic youth and education," chap. 4 in *A profile of Hispanic youth,* Youth Knowledge Development report 10.2, Office of Youth Programs, HEW, April 1980.

14. Bureau of the Census, final report PC(1)-C1, United States Summary.

15. Department of Commerce, *Persons of Spanish origin*, Table 5, p. 7.

16. Josefina Card and L. Wise, "Teenage mothers and teenage fathers: The impact of early childbearing on the parents' personal and professional lives," *Family Planning Perspectives, 10,* no. 4 (July/Aug. 1978):199–207.

17. Alan Guttmacher Institute, "Annual Report: 1976" (Washington, D.C.: Alan Guttmacher Institute, 1976), pp. 3–5.

18. Ibid.

Teenage Pregnancy from the Father's Perspective

· · · · ·

Bryan E. Robinson

At an average age of 16, seven million males and five million females in the United States are sexually active (Alan Guttmacher Institute, 1982). While adolescent males are responsible for a portion of the 1.1 million unintentional teenage pregnancies each year, the exact number of teenage fathers is difficult to determine because many mothers refuse to identify the father; nor has his age been a statistic of common interest in the past. Numerous studies have indicated, however, that most males who father children by adolescent mothers are two or three years older than their partners (Brown, 1983; McCoy & Tyler, 1985; Nakashima & Camp, 1984; Rivara, 1981; Westney, Cole, & Mumford, 1986). It has been reported, in fact, that the incidence of teenage fatherhood is not as wide-spread as that of adolescent motherhood, since nearly one-half (47%) of the babies born to adolescent females have fathers who are 20 years of age or older (Sonenstein, 1986). Even so, the number of teenage fathers is still high. During 1981, for example, more than 129,336 live births were fathered by males less than 20 years of age (National Center for Health Statistics, 1983). This number is probably low since it does not include those teenage fathers whose ages were omitted from birth registration forms. It has been suggested by some authorities that one in 10 to 20 teenage boys will be responsible for a premarital pregnancy (Elster & Panzarine, 1983).

Myths About Teenage Fathers

Scientific study of adolescent fathers has lagged far behind that of mothers, as has service delivery to these young men. They have been depicted in books and movies as roughnecks, interested primarily in sexual gratification (Robinson & Barret, 1987). These and numerous other myths about teenage fathers can be traced to the early writings of the 1940s when all unwed fathers, regardless of age, were lumped together for analysis and discussion (Futterman & Livermore, 1947; Kasanin & Handschin, 1941; Reider, 1948). Influenced by insufficient data, a handful of anecdotal cases, historical stigma, and the media, five commonly-held myths were born of the sociological context in which laws were made and research conducted (Robinson, 1987). 1) The "Super Stud" myth: he is worldly wise and knows more about sex and sexuality than most teenage boys. 2) The Don Juan myth: he sexually exploits unsuspecting and helpless adolescent females by taking advantage of them. 3) The macho myth: he feels psychologically inadequate, has no inner control and, unlike other adolescent boys his age, has a psychological need to prove his masculinity. 4) The Mr. Cool myth: he usually has a fleeting, casual relationship with the young mother and has few emotions about the pregnancy. 5) The phantom father myth: absent and rarely involved in the support and rearing of his children, he leaves his partner and offspring to fend for themselves.

Ultimately, research may show some truth in some of these myths, but no current evidence exists for any of these stereotypes. Studies have shown, in fact, that throughout the premature pregnancy teenage fathers typically remain involved—either physically or psychologically—and have intimate feelings toward both mother and baby. The educational and economic setbacks for the young fathers are serious and often cause anxiety; nevertheless, they are seldom severe enough to warrant different psychological characterization from their nonfather contemporaries (Earls & Siegal, 1980; Robinson, 1987).

Sexual Knowledge and Behavior

Studies have shown that teenage fathers are uninformed about sex, sexuality, and reproductive physiology (Barret & Robinson, 1982; Brown, 1983; Finkel & Finkel, 1975; Howard, 1975; Johnson & Staples, 1979). Their knowledge of sex, pregnancy, and perceived effectiveness of contraception, however, is no more deficient than that of their nonfather peers (Rivara, Sweeney, & Henderson, 1985). Teenage fathers either do not use contraception or use it inconsistently (Alan Guttmacher Institute, 1982; Barret & Robinson). Both fathers and nonfathers often have unprotected intercourse several times a month (Rivara et al., 1985).

Fathers differ significantly from nonfathers on their views about illegitimacy and are significantly more likely to accept teenage pregnancy in their families as a common occurrence and minimally disruptive to their current and future lives (Rivara et al., 1985). Numerous investigations have found that teenage fathers have many role models for unwed pregnancies. They are more likely than nonfathers to be children of teenage parents themselves

(Card, 1981; McCoy & Tyler, 1985; Rivara et al, 1985; Robbins & Lynn, 1973), to have a sibling born out of wedlock (Elster & Panzarine, 1980; Rivara et al.; Robbins & Lynn), or to have a sibling who was an unwed parent (Elster & Panzarine; Hendricks, 1980, 1983; Robbins & Lynn). A related finding is that teenage fathers are also more liberal in their attitudes toward abortion (Redmond, 1985). They are more likely than nonfathers, for example, to believe that pregnant teenagers should be allowed to get abortions, to accompany them in going for abortions, and to give emotional support after abortion.

Marriage
and Child Rearing

Studies have consistently shown that before their children are born teenage fathers report intentions to provide financial support and to participate in child care (Barret & Robinson, 1982; Fry & Trifiletti, 1983; Redmond, 1985; Westney et al., 1986). Their knowledge of child development tends to be unrealistic and their expectations for their children reflect impatience and intolerance which frequently result in physical disciplining of children (de Lissovoy, 1973). In comparisons of fathers with nonfathers, however, studies have found that both groups of males have higher expectations of infants than is developmentally appropriate (Rivara, Sweeney, & Henderson, 1986). Fathers and nonfathers in those studies had inadequate knowledge of child development and child health maintenance.

Investigations comparing teenage fathers and adult fathers have reported few differences. Findings indicated that both groups have similar attitudes toward child rearing (Nakashima & Camp, 1984) and, where married, teenage and adult partners of adolescent girls have similar characteristics except in matters of marital conflict (Nakashima & Camp). Older partners of adolescent mothers generally perceive less marital conflict than younger partners. The authors conjectured that teen parents are less likely to compromise and more likely to be immature about the needs of others. A conflicting finding has shown no differences between the perceived quality of marital relationships among teenage fathers and older fathers (Lamb & Elster, 1985).

Psychological
Variables

Because of their youth, the adjustment of adolescent males to fatherhood is a difficult process. Their premature role transition causes stresses and strains that compound tensions already inherent in adolescence. They suffer psychological conflict over the simultaneous roles of adolescent and father (Elster & Panzarine, 1980, 1983; Fry & Trifiletti, 1983; Robinson & Barret, 1985). The role of father involves decisions about the baby and separation from the peer group; domestic problems must be faced by those who live with the mother of their child. Adolescent fathers frequently have difficulty coping with knowledge of the pregnancy and show signs of clinical depression and stress (Elster & Panzarine; Fry & Trifiletti; Vaz, Smolen, & Miller, 1983; Westney et al., 1986). Moreover, they worry about financial responsibilities, education, employment, relationships with their partners, and parenting (Brown, 1983; Elster & Panzarine, 1983; Hendricks, 1980; Hendricks, Howard, & Caesar, 1981; Rivara et al., 1986). Despite these difficulties, research has generally shown that teenage fathers are no different psychologically from adolescent males in general or from adult men who father babies by adolescent females. Studies have indicated that they are similar in intellectual functioning (Nakashima & Camp, 1984; Pauker, 1971), locus of control (McCoy & Tyler, 1985; Robinson, Barret, & Skeen, 1983), personality adjustment (Rivara et al., 1985; Robinson & Barret, 1987), coping style (McCoy & Tyler), social support (Lamb & Elster, 1985), and anxiety and mood (Lamb & Elster, Rivara et al., 1986; Robinson & Barret, 1987).

Consequences of Fatherhood

In contrast to the stereotype, research has revealed that teenage fathers do not normally abandon their female partners. Instead, they demonstrate a desire to participate in childbirth and child rearing and many of them maintain contact with the mother after delivery. Out of the 20 adolescent fathers interviewed by Elster and Panzarine (1983), most were actively involved in the pregnancy. At least 17 attended some of their partner's clinic visits or participated in preparatory classes for labor and delivery. Only three fathers expressed any negative feelings about either fatherhood or the baby. Two-thirds of the 81 teenage fathers in another study stayed with the mother during labor, 25% were in the delivery room, and 88% visited their children in the nursery (Rivara et al., 1986).

A number of studies reported the teenage father's relationship with the mother over various periods of time before and after childbirth. Gabbard and Wolff (1977) reported that 53% of the married teenage fathers in their sample maintained regular and frequent contact and 84% had at least some regular contact throughout the pregnancy. Klerman and Jekel (1973) also found that two-thirds of the fathers they studied contributed at least something to support both mother and child. Vaz and her associates (1983) reported that 81% of the teenage fathers in their sample still dated the mother during pregnancy and after childbirth, 75% helped her by providing money, and 85% helped her in other ways such as transportation and gifts.

At twelve months after childbirth, half of the unwed adolescent parents in another study continued to date each other (Nettleton & Cline, 1975). At fifteen months after the baby's birth, 64% of the teenage fathers continued to contribute financially to the support of the mother and baby (Lorenzi, Klerman, & Jekel, 1977). At 18 months postpartum, most of the 81 teenage fathers in another investigation continued to be involved in the lives of the mother and child (Rivara et al., 1986).

Despite the father's eager involvement, the prognosis for the relationship with his partner, the health of their child, and the educational and economic consequences is bleak. Pregnant teenagers marry only ten percent of the time and when marriage does occur it generally suffers from discord and usually ends in divorce (Card & Wise, 1978; de Lissovoy, 1973; Furstenberg, 1976; Inselberg, 1962; Nye & Lamberts, 1980; Rus-Eft, Sprenger, & Beever, 1979). The divorce rate for parents younger than 18 is three times greater than that for parents who have their first child after age 20, and it is greater for couples with premarital pregnancies than for those who conceive after marriage (Furstenberg; Nye and Lamberts).

Children of teenage parents run the triple risk of being unwanted, born into poverty, and exposed to inadequate parenting. Teenage parents are at higher than average risk for prenatal complications and for having babies who suffer from prematurity, birth defects, mental retardation, and other health problems (Field, Widmayer, Stringer, & Ignatoff, 1980; Phipps-Yonas, 1980; Simkins, 1984). These health problems occur partly because mothers have not reached their full biological maturity and partly because they have poor diets and inadequate prenatal care. Their infants are also at higher risk of being abused (Field et al; Kinard & Klerman, 1980). As a rule, adolescent parents do not possess the emotional and maturational skills necessary for adequate parenting (Capanılo & London, 1981; de Lissovoy, 1973). Risk factors associated with parents who are likely to abuse their children perfectly match the profile of adolescent parents: unplanned births, infants with birth defects or obstetrical problems, and having children to satisfy unmet needs (Zuravin, 1987).

Research has consistently shown that unplanned and premature parenthood preempts the educational, vocational, and social experiences of the adolescent which are essential to prepare him for his adult role. Generally, teenage fathers drop out of school and get poor jobs with low pay (Card & Wise, 1978; Kerckhoff & Parrow, 1979; Rivara et al., 1986; Rus-Eft et al., 1979).

Implications
for Clinicians

In the absence of scientific information on teenage fathers, the professional community has relied on stereotypes that have been debunked by a growing body of research. Research generally has found that teenage fathers are psychologically and intellectually more like than unlike their nonfather peers and older fathers. Teenage fathers need support and guidance rather than the denigration served by past stereotypes. Although the teenage father, as well as the mother, is at risk in teenage pregnancy, both he and his family have been grossly overlooked in service delivery practices. Programs that fail to reach out to young fathers not only ignore their emotional needs, but also overlook a significant support system for the mother and baby. It is important that mental health practitioners examine and, if necessary, overcome sex biases against teenage fathers and try to make sure that these adolescents are included in every aspect of service delivery.

Adolescent pregnancy is a devastating public health problem that harms everyone in its wake: the young mother, the father, and the baby. Teenage fathers face overwhelming odds against success in parenting, marriage, and vocational achievement. Clinicians can play a major role in involving teenage fathers in the lives of their infants and helping these adolescent males cope with the difficult situations in which they find themselves. Outreach programs to young fathers have demonstrated that, once involved, many males are eager to become more competent and caring parents. They need counseling to help them deal with the stresses surrounding the anticipated childbirth and to reconcile the competing role requirements of the teenage years and parenthood. They need vocational counseling so that their good intentions of providing financial support can be realized through education and occupational planning. They need counseling to deal with the stresses of financial responsibilities and problems in their marriages or their relationships with the mother of their child.

Future adolescent pregnancy programs must continue to include the father and have both a preventive and remedial emphasis. More innovative programs are needed whereby social agencies take active measures to reach young fathers. Experts have come to realize that combating teenage pregnancy means using a holistic approach to health care and a variety of measures to meet the multiple needs of this diverse group of young people. Reaching out to teenage fathers has potential advantages for the total family system.

References

Alan Guttmacher Institute. (1982). *Teenage pregnancy: The problem that hasn't gone away.* New York: Author.

Barret, R.L., & Robinson, B.E. (1982). A descriptive study of teenage expectant fathers. *Family Relations, 31,* 349–352.

Brown, S.V. (1983). The commitment and concerns of black adolescent parents. *Social Work Research & Abstracts, 19,* 27–34.

Card, J.J. (1981). Long-term consequences for children of teenage parents. *Demography, 18,* 137–156.

Card, J.J., & Wise, L.L. (1978). Teenage mothers and teenage fathers: The impact of early childbearing on the parents' personal and professional lives. *Family Planning Perspectives, 10,* 199–205.

Caparulo, F., & Lonson, K. (1981). Adolescent fathers: Adolescents first, fathers second. *Issues in Health Care of Women, 3,* 23–33.

de Lissovoy, V. (1973). Child care by adolescent parents. *Children Today, 2,* 22–25.

Earls, F., & Siegel, B. (1980). Precocious fathers. *American Journal of Orthopsychiatry, 50,* 469–480.

Elster, A.B., & Panzarine, S. (1980). Unwed teenage fathers: Emotional and health educational needs. *Journal of Adolescent Health Care, 1,* 116–120.

———. (1983). Teenage fathers: Stresses during gestation and early parenthood. *Clinical Pediatrics, 22,* 700–703.

Field, T., Widmayer, S.M., Stronger, S., & Ignatoff, E. (1980). Teenage, lower-class black mothers and their preterm infants: An intervention and developmental follow-up. *Child Development, 51*, 426–436.

Finkel, M., & Finkel, D. (1975). Sexual and contraceptive knowledge, attitudes, and behavior of male adolescents. *Family Planning Perspectives, 7*, 256–260.

Fry, P.S., & Trifiletti, R.J. (1983). Teenage fathers: An exploration of their developmental needs and anxieties and the implications for clinical-social intervention services. *Journal of Psychiatric Treatment and Evaluation, 5*, 219–227.

Furstenberg, F.F. (1976). *Unplanned parenthood: The social consequences of teenage childbearing.* New York: Free Press.

Futterman, S., & Livermore, J.B. (1947). Putative fathers. *Journal of Social Casework, 28*, 174–178.

Gabbard, G.O., & Wolff, J.F. (1977). The unwed pregnant teenager and her male relationship. *Journal of Reproductive Medicine, 19*, 137–140.

Hendricks, L.E. (1980). Unwed adolescent fathers: Problems they face and their sources of social support. *Adolescence, 15*, 861–869.

Hendricks, L.E. (1983). Suggestions for reaching unmarried black adolescent fathers. *Child Welfare, 62*, 141–146.

Hendricks, L.E., Howard, C.S., & Caesar, P.O. (1981). Helpseeking behavior among select populations of black unmarried adolescent fathers: Implications for human service agencies. *American Journal of Public Health, 71*, 733–735.

Howard, M. (1975). Improving services for young fathers. *Sharing.* Washington, D.C.: Child Welfare League of America.

Inselberg, R.M. (1962). Marital problems and satisfaction in high school marriages. *Marriage and Family Living, 24*, 74–77.

Johnson, L.B., & Staples, R.E. (1979). Family planning and the young minority male: A pilot project. *The Family Coordinator, 28*, 535–543.

Kasanin, J., & Handschin, S. (1941). Psychodynamic factors in illegitimacy. *American Journal of Orthopsychiatry, 11*, 66–84.

Kerckhoff, A.C., & Parrow, A.A. (1979). The effect of early marriage on the educational attainment of young men. *Journal of Marriage and the Family, 41*, 97–107.

Kinard, E.M., & Klerman, L.V. (1980). Teenage parenting and child abuse: Are they related? *American Journal of Orthopsychiatry, 50*, 481–488.

Klerman, L.V., & Jekel, J.F. (1973). *School-age mothers: Problems, programs, and policy.* Hamden, CT: Shoe String Press.

Lamb, M.E., & Elster, A.B. (1985). Adolescent mother-father relationships. *Developmental Psychology, 21*, 768–773.

Lorenzi, M.E., Klerman, L.V., & Jekel, J.F. (1977). School-age parents: How permanent a relationship? *Adolescence, 12*, 13–22.

McCoy, J.E., & Tyler, F.B. (1985). Selected psychosocial characteristics of black unwed adolescent fathers. *Journal of Adolescent Health Care, 6*, 12–16.

Nakashima, I.I., & Camp, B.W. (1984). Fathers of infants born to adolescent mothers. *American Journal of Diseases of Children, 138*, 452–454.

National Center for Health Statistics. (1983). Advance report of final natality statistics, 1981. *Monthly Vital Statistics Report* (DDHS Publication No. PHS 84–1120). Hyattsville, MD: Public Health Services.

Nettleton, C.A., & Cline, D.W. (1975). Dating patterns, sexual relationships and use of contraceptives of 700 unwed mothers during a two-year period following delivery. *Adolescence, 37*, 45–57.

Nye, F.I., & Lamberts, M.B. (1980). *School-age parenthood: Consequences for babies, mothers, fathers, grandparents, and others.* (Cooperative Extension Bulletin 0667). Pullman: Washington State University.

Pauker, J.D. (1971). Fathers of children conceived out of wedlock: Pregnancy, high school, psychological test results. *Developmental Psychology, 4*, 215–218.

Phipps-Yonas, S. (1980). Teenage pregnancy and motherhood: A review of the literature. *American Journal of Orthopsychiatry, 50*, 403–431.

Redmond, M.A. (1985). Attitudes of adolescent males toward adolescent pregnancy and fatherhood. *Family Relations, 34*, 337–342.

Reider, N. (1948). The unmarried father. *American Journal of Orthopsychiatry, 18*, 230–237.

Rivara, F.P. (1981). Teenage pregnancy: The forgotten father. *Developmental Behavioral Pediatrics, 2*, 141–146.

Rivara, F.P., Sweeney, P.J., & Henderson, B.F. (1985). A study of low socio-economic status, black teenage fathers and their nonfather peers. *Pediatrics, 75*, 648–656.

Robbins, M.B., & Lynn, D.B. (1973). The unwed fathers: Generation recidivism and attitudes about intercourse in California youth authority wards. *Journal of Sex Research, 9*, 334–341.

Robinson, B.E. (1987). *Teenage fathers.* Lexington, MA: Lexington Books.

Robinson, B.E., & Barret, R.L. (1985). Teenage fathers. *Psychology Today, 19*, (December) 66–70.

Robinson, B.E., & Barret, R.L. (1987, May). *Myths about adolescent fathers with policy change implications for health care professionals.* Paper presented at a meeting of the Association for the Care of Children's Health, Halifax, Nova Scotia.

Robinson, B.E., & Barret, R.L. (1987). Self-concept and anxiety of adolescent and adult fathers. *Adolescence.*

Robinson, B.E., Barret, R.L., & Skeen, P. (1983). Locus of control of unwed adolescent fathers versus adolescent nonfathers. *Perceptual and Motor Skills, 56*, 397–398.

Rus-Eft, D., Sprenger, M., & Beever, H. (1979). Antecedents of adolescent parenthood and consequences at age 30. *The Family Coordinator, 28*, 173–179.

Simkins, L. (1984). Consequences of teenage pregnancy and motherhood. *Adolescence, 19*, 39–54.

Sonenstein, F.L. (1986). Risking paternity: Sex and contraception among adolescent males. In A.B. Elser & M.E. Lamb (Eds.), *Adolescent fatherhood* (pp. 31–54). Hillsdale, NJ: Lawrence Erlbaum.

Vaz, R., Smolen, P., & Miller, C. (1983). Adolescent pregnancy: Involvement of the male partner. *Journal of Adolescent Health Care, 4,* 246–250.

Westney, O.E., Cole, O.J., & Mumford, T.L. (1986). Adolescent unwed prospective fathers: Readiness for fatherhood and behaviors toward the mother and the expected infant. *Adolescence, 21,* 901–911.

Zuravin, S.J. (1987). Unplanned pregnancies, family planning problems, and child maltreatment. *Family Relations, 36,* 135–139.

Teenage Fathers: Neglected Too Long

· · · · ·

**Robert L. Barret
and Bryan E. Robinson**

R esearch on family life and human development has conspicuously overlooked men in general and fathers in particular (LeMasters, 1974). The beliefs that fathers are unimportant to the development of their offspring was reflected in the famous comment, "Fathers are a biological necessity but a social accident" (Parke, 1981, p. 1), and for a long time we have been led to believe that fathers are clumsy, helpless creatures without the ability or interest to rear their children. An excessively strong emphasis on the mother's role has caused "parenting" to be equated with "mothering" in this society.

Although there has been a dramatic increase in the number of illegitimate births among teenagers, the literature on adolescent parenting blatantly overlooks the role of the father (Chilman, 1979, 1980; and Earls and Siegel, 1980). Most of the articles and books that discuss teenage parents focus exclusively on the mother (Foster and Miller, 1980; and Furstenberg, 1980). A few programs seek to provide services to both teenage fathers and mothers (Howard, 1975; and Pannor and Evans, 1975), but in general agencies that have developed programs for adolescents who have had children reflect a similar neglect. This is also true of empirical research studies.

Unwed Fathers

Social agencies typically do not involve the adolescent father when they provide services to pregnant teenagers or to teenage mothers and their children (Leashore, 1979). For the most part, human service support programs (Earls and Siegel, 1980) and literature written for counselors (Foster and Miller, 1980) have both been centered exclusively around adolescent girls. In fact, Earls and Siegel (1980) argue that the overall decrease in regular contact between unmarried teenage couples who are parents can be attributed to the failure of medical and social service providers to engage the adolescent father actively.

What is generally "known" about the character and emotional needs of unwed adolescent fathers is largely based on society's stereotypes. The teenage father is supposed to be a self-centered and irresponsible male who takes advantage of young women without thinking of the consequences of his behavior. His disappearance shortly after the pregnancy becomes known is seen as proof of his concern, despite the fact that in many cases his girl friend's parents prevent him from becoming more involved (Connolly, 1978). If society seeks these young men out at all, it is usually with a punitive and judgmental intent. Whatever rights they may have or part they are entitled to play in the decision making about their child are generally ignored—except for their financial responsibility (Johnson and Staples, 1979).

Contradicting these stereotypical views is the experience of caseworkers, who have noticed that teenage fathers do express concern about both mother and baby. Workers who contact teenage fathers indicate that these young men are eager to talk about their situation; many of them have few friends with whom they can discuss their troubles, feelings, and fears (Johnson, 1978). Connolly (1978) confirmed the experiences of these workers when he reported the following observations of a social worker in a pioneering program for teenage fathers at the Children's Home Society in California:

> I discovered that I was counseling with the expectation that fathers didn't want to contribute. I wasn't confronted with my own values until I saw some natural fathers who really wanted to get involved, wanted to see their babies, and wanted contact with the adopting couples so that they could clarify why they were [having their children adopted] and prevent distorted information from being passed on. [P. 42]

In keeping with these comments, a study by Pannor, Massarik, and Evans (1971) revealed that most unwed fathers will participate in counseling and are willing to accept responsibility regarding their girl friend's pregnancy. However, if the social agency does not persist in attempts to reach these young men, they usually will not come forward on their own. Most report that they fail to come forward because they feel left out and doubt that the agency is genuinely interested in being helpful. Other research indicates that to unmarried males abortion is "more frustrating, trying, and emotionally costly than public and academic neglect of this subject would suggest" (Shostak, 1979, p. 569). This neglect is magnified by Rothstein's (1978) sobering report of the feelings of a 17 year old at the time that his girl friend was undergoing an abortion:

> I thought I was a much more liberated man and that I'd be able to walk in here, sit down, and say, "Here's an abortion," and that would be it. But now that I'm here, I'm a wreck. I don't think anyone could depend on me in this situation...I'm shaken...I also feel that I was more experienced than my girl friend

and that I should have tried to help more....I really want to know what they will do for her...what I wanted to hear was this big elaborate story of how the doctor is there all the time. I was looking for reassurance.... How about me? Do they have something for me to lay on while I die? [P. 208]

Statements such as these suggest a depth of emotion not traditionally credited to adolescent males.

In 1972, the U.S. Supreme court ruled in *Stanley v. Illinois* that unmarried natural fathers are entitled to equal protection under the law and are also entitled to be involved in custody decisions concerning their child (Pannor and Evans, 1975). This ruling has helped redirect the attention of some social agencies toward the needs of adolescent fathers as well as mothers (Connolly, 1978). For most agencies, however, consideration is limited to perfunctory attempts to contact unwed fathers through notices in newspapers serving the legal community.

Empirical Research

By and large, the research on teenage fathers is not helpful. The data from which conclusions are drawn are found in studies rife with methodological shortcomings, primary among them the use of biased samples that include few young men. The major difficulty is that teenage fathers are hard to locate, a situation markedly different from that typically encountered with teenage mothers. In addition, a number of studies draw conclusions from data collected from adolescent mothers, and these data may not be entirely reliable. Many young women may use their participation in research as an opportunity either to protect the image of the young men by whom they have become pregnant or to ventilate their anger at them.

When data are presented on teenage fathers, there are at least five methodological shortcomings that cloud the empirical investigations. First, most investigations on adolescent parenthood omit the father altogether (see Babikian and Goldman, 1971; Chilman, 1979, 1980; Earls and Seigel, 1980; Foster and Miller, 1980; Furstenberg, 1980; McHenry, Walters, and Johnson, 1979; and Scott, Field, and Robertson, 1980). As indicated earlier, when the literature is examined, extensive investigations can be found regarding teenage mothers (for example, Field et al., 1980; McHenry, Walters, and Johnson, 1979; and Scott, Field, and Robertson, 1980), but a paucity of information exists on teenage fathers, and most of what is available is based on impressionistic data (for example, Howard, 1975; and Pannor and Evans, 1975). This is partly because fewer young unmarried fathers, in contrast to young unmarried mothers, have direct contact with human service organizations, which, through work with adolescent parents, provide researchers with data (Leashore, 1979).

Second, when teenage fathers are included in traditional research on fatherhood, information is often inferred (see Leashore, 1979; and Platts, 1968). For example, in a recent study, researchers used children's names— that is, whether or not children were named after their father—as a clue to the adolescent father's actual and symbolic importance in the kinship system

(Furstenberg and Talvitie, 1980). However, even in their attempts to bring the neglected adolescent father to the forefront, they relied on secondhand reports derived from interviews with teenage mothers—a practice to which they resorted with some misgivings because "most males simply could not be located without an inordinate amount of time and expense" (p. 37). Nevertheless, traditional research on fatherhood in general has revealed the dangers in a reliance on such methodology (LeMasters, 1974).

Third, as suggested earlier, data are confounded because they are assessed indirectly through contact with adolescent mothers, without concern for biased reports (see Earles and Siegel, 1980; and Platts, 1969). A good example of how maternal interviews can conceal or distort the facts was presented by Platts (1968), who reported instances in which adolescent mothers informed caseworkers that their relationship with their child's father had ended, when in actuality they were trying to protect the father from being harassed by the agency. Fourth, the use of retrospective data and post hoc analyses sometimes results in inaccurate assessments of current psychological and cultural changes (see Pauker, 1971; and Card and Wise, 1978). Fifth, unrepresentative sampling procedures have become commonplace (see Finkel and Finkel, 1975). Nevertheless, although empirical investigations are less than informative because of methodological flaws, demographic studies provide a profile of the adolescent father.

Demographics

Using a data base from PROJECT TALENT, a nationwide study to identify the characteristics of talented adolescents, Card and Wise (1978) analyzed responses of a nationwide random sample consisting of 375,000 boys and girls from 1,225 senior and junior high schools. The survey polled the subjects one year, five years, and eleven years after they completed high school. Teenage parents were defined as respondents who became parents before their twentieth birthday. A contrasting sample was made up of some of their classmates who were not parents as of their twentieth birthday.

Generally, both adolescent fathers and mothers obtained substantially less education than their classmates. The younger they were are the time of their child's birth, the more severe the educational setback they endured. The boys and girls who became teenage parents reported having lower income levels and lower academic abilities at age 15 than their classmates; they also had lower educational expectations. As a result of their investigations, Card and Wise concluded that, regardless of background factors, teenage parenthood is a direct cause of "truncated" schooling, a factor that causes teenage fathers to occupy lower prestige blue-collar jobs and to enter the labor force earlier than their unmarried classmates.

In their study, Card and Wise also found young fathers were more likely than young mothers to be single at the conception and birth of their child. The proportion of teenage fathers and mothers who are separated or divorced was higher than that of their classmates at each follow-up period. Five and eleven years after high school, teenage fathers and mothers had been married more often than their classmates. In addition, because teenage parents begin their reproductive careers relatively early, the teenage fathers and mothers studied had more children than their classmates did five years and eleven years after high school.

Many other reports indicate that most adolescent fathers are unmarried at the time their child is conceived (Babikian and Goldman, 1971; Furstenberg, 1976b; and Leashore, 1979). In fact, during the past decade, the percentage of unwed births among total births among adolescents doubled from 20.8 percent in 1965 to 42.9 percent in 1977, and over half of those under 18 who had children were unwed (Furstenberg, Lincoln, and Menken, 1980). Usually, a teenage father and his partner are approximately the same age (Babikian and Goldman, 1971; and Howard, 1975). Data on teenage fathers are often camouflaged within studies of older unmarried fathers; these figures are not entirely suspect because most unmarried fathers are in their late teens and early twenties (Leashore, 1979; and Platts, 1968).

The sexual activity of teenage fathers begins earlier and is more varied than that of teenage mothers. For example, two-thirds of the men in a study by Furstenberg (1976a) were sexually active by age 14. The risk of adolescent fatherhood is greater among black and Hispanic youths than among other groups of young men because of the high incidence of sexual intercourse and lower use of contraceptives among this group (Johnson and Staples, 1979; and Finkel and Finkel, 1975). In general, those who provide social services to young fathers report that these young men are not worldly wise. Their failure to use effective birth control is perhaps an indication that they are as uninformed about sex and sexuality as the women they impregnate (Howard, 1975).

Psychological Factors

There has been speculation that boys in their teens who father children have different psychological needs from their contemporaries who do not become parents. Pannor and Evans (1965) stated the following:

> [These] social workers are convinced that out-of-wedlock pregnancies result from intrapersonal difficulties, which manifest themselves in ineffective or inappropriate interpersonal relationships; that both unmarried parents in general are faced with intrapersonal and interpersonal difficulties; and that the unmarried father enters into the relationship because of his psychic needs, and not by accident. [P. 56]

In addition, Johnson and Staples (1979) suggest that teenage males who are members of minority groups use sexual activity to express their masculinity because more conventional means of doing so are closed to them. However, none of these contentions has been borne out by empirical research. Findings instead generally show that adolescent fathers are psychologically normal (Earls and Siegel, 1980). Pauker (1971) argues that many reports of psychological maladjustment among teenage fathers occur because data are assessed after the unfortunate out-of-wedlock experience,

184

and it is not surprising that depression or emotional conflicts would surface at such a time. To prove his point, Pauker studied scores from the Minnesota Multiphasic Personality Inventory, ACE Psychological Test, and the Cooperative English Test for ninety-four boys who came from Minnesota and had fathered children when they were between the ages of 13 and 19. In addition, ninety-four boys who attended the same school, were of similar age, and were from similar socioeconomic backgrounds but had not fathered children were selected as a control group. Overall, the teenage fathers were psychologically and intellectually more alike than different from the matched control group.

On the other hand, two studies provide evidence that adolescent fathers are psychologically ill prepared for fatherhood, presumably because of their own immaturity. In the first, Rothstein (1978) interviewed thirty-five lower-class teenage males who were between 16 and 24. This sample was randomly selected from the waiting area of Bronx Municipal Hospital's abortion clinic in New York and involved a nearly equal distribution of young men who were married to their partners, engaged to their partners, or neither married nor engaged. Considering that the sample was drawn exclusively from a group of young men who were taking steps to avoid fatherhood via abortion, it is not surprising that the majority of those interviewed (86 percent) were psychologically ambivalent regarding their readiness to assume the fathering role of provider or caretaker. The experience of these young men suggests that those who opt for an abortion as a solution to a pregnancy may realize they are not yet psychologically mature enough to handle the responsibilities of fatherhood.

A second study of forty-eight teenage couples who married during high school also contributes to general knowledge of the psychological maturity found among adolescent parents (DeLissovoy, 1973). The subjects in this study came from rural, working-class families in Central Pennsylvania, and, on the average, the girls were 16½ years old, the boys 17. Both the girls and the boys studied were ill prepared for parenthood. They had unrealistic expectations of child development and a general lack of knowledge and experience concerning children. They were also impatient and intolerant of children and tended toward physical abuse in their child-rearing practices. A later study confirmed that adolescent mothers are generally uninformed about children (Field et al., 1980); however, no additional work on how informed fathers are has been conducted.

Paternal Involvement

Babikian and Goldman (1971) reported that 50 percent of the time teenage fathers abandoned their partner after the pregnancy. Usually the young men distanced themselves by spending much of their time with their families of origin.

However, other sources indicate that a significant number of unmarried fathers in general are interested in and financially support their child

(Leashore, 1979; Sauber, 1966; and Sauber and Corrigan, 1970). This holds true for young unmarried teenage fathers as well (Furstenberg, 1976b). Klerman and Jekel (1973) found that two-thirds of the fathers they studied contributed at least something to support both mother and child. In addition, a study conducted by the Youth Center in Philadelphia concluded that 75 percent of the adolescent fathers in a detention center did not automatically choose to desert or be detached from their girl friend or child (Connolly, 1978).

In a five-year study, Furstenberg (1976a) conducted interviews with adolescent mothers under 18 who registered at the prenatal clinic at Baltimore's Sinai Hospital between 1966 and 1968. The subjects were also interviewed at three additional times: one year after childbirth, again in 1970, and last in 1972, when their child was 5 years old. Interviews were also conducted with as many fathers as could be found. Of the 33 percent located, over half were residing with the young mothers in the study during the period of the interviews.

Most of the marriages that occurred in the sample did not last through the five years of the research. However, it was among the few stable marriages in the group that father-child contact was most intense and father-child relationships the most satisfying. Children of parents who never married were as likely to see their fathers regularly as those whose parents had previously been married. Approximately 25 percent of the fathers visited their child at least once a week, and one-third gave economic support, regardless of whether they had been married to the mother. In general, single fathers tended to be emotionally closer to their children than previously married fathers were. Approximately 63 percent of all the fathers were maintaining contact with their children five years after the children were born, and many (30 percent) living outside the mother's home maintained cordial relationships and visited regularly.

Furstenberg learned from follow-up interviews with the original sample that children of parents who did not marry were frequently named after the father. Furstenberg and Talvitie (1980) described this practice as a deliberate attempt by both parents to strengthen the father-child bond, with the name serving as reminder of the biological tie. Just over 20 percent of the young women in the sample involved their partner in selecting their child's name; most of this group planned to marry. Approximately 50 percent of the male babies born received their father's first name, middle name, or both. In addition, 43 percent of the boys and 46 percent of the girls born were given their father's last name, even when their parents remained unmarried. There was a consistent association between naming patterns and father-child contact. That is, children receiving their father's name were more likely to have regular contact with their father and to receive economic assistance from him. However, Furstenberg and Talvitie stated that "the bestowal of the father's name may be nothing more than an expression of prior sentiment, and acknowledgment of the father's willingness at the time of birth to play an active part in the child's upbringing" (p. 49). Longitudinal studies are needed to clarify the significance of naming patterns.

Recommendations

Caseworkers can do a number of things to improve services for unwed parents of both sexes and further general understanding of teenage fathers. Even though unwed fathers are often reluctant to identify themselves, more and more may come forward as agencies and the helping professions begin to respond to their needs. The following suggestions could help:

1. Empirical studies of unwed fathers should be undertaken to generate data furthering a knowledge of their characteristics.

2. Agencies such as the Children's Home Society, Florence Crittendon Services, and Youth Services Bureau, which routinely have contact with pregnant teenagers, can cooperate with research efforts and can begin to require interviews with fathers as a routine part of their service. It is important that agencies protect their clients from being exploited by researchers. However, in-house studies could be developed that use an outside professional as a consultant.

3. Caseworkers who interact with teenage fathers should carefully monitor their own tendency to characterize these young men in terms of society's stereotypes. Many of these fathers do want to become involved and desire to share the responsibility for their child.

4. Caseworkers should become aware of naming patterns among unwed adolescent parents and their children because such patterns provide clues to the nature of the mother-father relationship.

5. Rather than assume that adolescent males are not interested, agencies should begin to plan programs in sexuality and parenting that involve both young men and young women. Programs in human sexuality can examine the response of both men and women to pregnancy and can emphasize the prospective father's often-intense emotional involvement in a pregnancy.

6. Although many agencies are encountering financial difficulties, caseworkers can collaborate with school counselors to create imaginative programs that serve all school-age youth.

7. Social workers should approach their clients with the intention of recognizing individual reactions to a pregnancy and suggest creative, nontraditional approaches, such as parenting training, vocational training, and life planning, which respond to a broad range of needs. The articulation of specific services that are available may be reassuring to many teenage fathers who fear being punished.

Conclusion

The decade of the seventies has been dubbed "the age of paternal rediscovery" (Lamb, 1979). Recent research has demonstrated that fathers contribute significantly to their child's social, emotional, and intellectual development (Cordell, Parke, and Sawin, 1980; and Parke, 1979). Despite these encouraging trends, in 1978 Connolly lamented that "all eyes are on the unwed mother and her baby, while the other partner stands awkwardly in the background, too often ignored or even forgotten completely" (p. 40). It is to be hoped that during the 1980s the push toward paternal rediscovery will continue by spotlighting the forgotten figure in adolescent parenthood— the teenage father.

Bibliography

Babikian, H.M., and Goldman, A. "A Study of Teenage Pregnancy," *American Journal of Psychiatry*, 128 (1971), pp. 755–760.

Card, J.J., and Wise, L.L. "Teenage Mothers and Teenage Fathers: The Impact of Early Childbearing on the Parents' Personal and Professional Lives," *Family Planning Perspectives*, 10 (1978), pp. 199–205.

Chilman, C. *Adolescent Sexuality in a Changing American Society*. Washington, D.C.: National Institutes of Health, 1979. pp. 79–1426.

———. "Social and Psychological Research Concerning Adolescent Child-bearing: 1970–1980," *Journal of Marriage and the Family*, 42 (1980), pp. 793–805.

Connolly, L. "Boy Fathers," *Human Behavior* (January 1978), pp. 40–43.

Cordell, A.S., Parke, R.D., and Swain, D.B. "Fathers' Views on Fatherhood with Special Reference to Infancy," *Family Relations*, 29 (1980), pp. 331–338.

De Lissovoy, V. "Child Care by Adolescent Parents," *Children Today*, 2 (1973), pp. 22–25.

Earls, F., and Siegel, B. "Precocious Fathers," *American Journal of Orthopsychiatry*, 50 (1980), pp. 469–480.

Field, T., et al. "Teenage Lower-Class Black Mothers and Their Preterm Infants: An Intervention and Developmental Follow-up," *Child Development*, 51 (1980), pp. 426–436.

Finkel, M., and Finkel, D. "Sexual and Contraceptive Knowledge, Attitudes and Behavior of Male Adolescents," *Family Planning Perspectives*, 7 (1975), pp. 256–260.

Foster, C.D., and Miller, G.M. "Adolescent Pregnancy: A Challenge for Counselors," *Personnel and Guidance Journal*, 59 (1980), pp. 236–240.

Furstenberg, F.F. *Unplanned Parenthood: The Social Consequences of Teenage Childbearing*. New York: Free Press, 1976a.

———. "The Social Consequences of Teenage Parenthood," *Family Planning Perspectives*, 8 (1976b), pp. 148–164.

———. "Teenage Parenthood and Family Support," *Dimensions*, 9 (1980), pp. 49–54.

Furstenberg, F.F., Lincoln, R., and Menken, J. (eds.). *Perspectives on Teenage Sexuality, Pregnancy, and Childbearing*. Philadelphia: University of Pennsylvania Press, 1980.

Furstenberg, F.F., and Talvitie, K.G. "Children's Names and Paternal Claims: Bonds Between Unmarried Fathers and Their Children," *Journal of Family Issues*, 1 (1980), pp. 31–57.

Howard, M. "Improving Services for Young Fathers," in *Sharing* (Spring 1975).

Johnson, L.B., and Staples, R.E. "Family Planning and the Young Minority Male: A Pilot Project," *Family Coordinator*, 28 (1979), pp. 535–543.

Johnson, S. "Two Pioneer Programs Help Unwed Teenage Fathers Cope," *New York Times*, March 15, 1978, p. 54.

Klerman, L.V., and Jekel, J.F. *School Age Mothers: Problems, Programs, and Policy*. Hamden, Conn.: Shoe String Press, 1973.

Lamb, M.E. "Paternal Influences and the Father's Role: A Personal Perspective," *American Psychologist*, 34 (1979), pp. 938–943.

Leashore, B.R. "Human Services and the Unmarried Father: The 'Forgotten Half,'" *Family Coordinator*, 28 (1979), pp. 529–534.

LeMasters, M.M. *Parents in Modern America*. Homewood, Ill.: Dorsey Press, 1974.

McHenry, P.C., Walters, L.H., and Johnson, C. "Adolescent Pregnancy: A Review of the Literature," *Family Coordinator*, 28 (1979), pp. 17–28.

Pannor, R., and Evans, B.W. "The Unmarried Father: An Integral Part of Casework Services to the Unmarried Mother, *Child Welfare*, 44 (1965), pp. 15–20.

———. "The Unmarried Father Revisited," *Journal of School Health*, 45 (1975), pp. 286–291.

Pannor, R., Massarik, F., and Evans, B.W. *The Unmarried Father*. New York: Springer Publishing Co., 1971.

Parke, R.D. "Perspectives on Father-Infant Interaction," in J.D. Osofsky, ed., *Handbook of Infant Development*. New York: John Wiley & Sons, 1979.

———. *Fathers*. Cambridge, Mass.: Harvard University Press, 1981.

Pauker, J.D. "Fathers of Children Conceived out of Wedlock: Pregnancy, High School, Psychological Test Results," *Developmental Psychology*, 4 (1971), pp. 215–218.

Platts, H.K. "A Public Adoption Agency's Approach to Natural Fathers, *Child Welfare*, 47 (November 1968), pp. 530–537.

Rothstein, A.A. "Adolescent Males, Fatherhood, and Abortion," *Journal of Youth and Adolescence*, 7 (1978), pp. 203–214.

Sauber, M. "The Role of the Unmarried Father," *Welfare in Review*, 41 (1966), pp. 15–18.

Sauber, M., and Corrigan, E., *The Sixth Year Experience of Unwed Mothers as Parents*. New York: Community Council of Greater New York, 1970.

Scott, K., Field, T., and Robertson, E. (eds.), *Teenage Parents and Their Offspring*. New York: Grune & Stratton, 1980.

Shostak, A.B. "Abortion as Fatherhood Lost: Problems and Reforms," *Family Coordinator*, 28 (1979), pp. 569–574.

An In-School Program for Adolescent Parents: Implications for Social Work Practice and Multi-Disciplinary Teaming

· · · · ·

Paula Allen Meares

T he increasing incidence of pregnancy among teenage girls is an alarming phenomenon of our times.

> Until recently its occurrence was not particularly frequent in the U.S., but rapidly changing attitudes, coupled with the so called "sex revolution" has changed this. No cultural, racial, or socio-economic group has managed to prevent pregnancy among its adolescent women.[1]

During the past ten years the birth rate among teenagers has steadily increased. More than one million teenagers become pregnant each year. Illegitimate births to girls under 20 years swelled from about 48,000 in 1940 to an estimated 239,000 in 1971.[2] The most recent survey (Howard, 1978) estimates that almost one out of ten girls will give birth before she reaches the age of 18. Eighty-five percent of the girls will keep their babies, and almost half of them will be unmarried when they give birth. Other findings suggest that young people are beginning sexual activity at even earlier and earlier ages. While factors related to the increased incidence are merely speculative and findings are often conflicting, a critical strategic institution in ameliorating this phenomenon is the public school. It is imperative that school districts across the country provide these young parents with the appropriate education required to maintain themselves in the mainstream of society and to coordinate these educational efforts with appropriate community social

---

Reprinted and revised with permission from *School Social Work Journal 3* (2), 66–77.

service agencies. The special needs of various groups of children within the public school are currently being addressed on the national level, i.e. PL 94-142 (The Handicapped Children's Act), which includes: due process procedures, nondiscriminatory policies, and the right of all children to receive an appropriate education in the least restrictive environment. These procedures are far-reaching and can appropriately be applied to teenage parents who are excluded.

Needed at the core of this program is an innovative school program for serving pregnant adolescents and the use of multi-disciplinary teaming as an effective mechanism in providing services within the context of the public school. The social work role within the team will be delineated because it is rather unique as it blends some of the traditional tasks and roles with the more recent conceptualizations of role definition identified in the literature (Costin, 1975; Meares, 1977). For example, the role of a social worker in this program would include: providing casework services to pregnant teenagers and follow-up services, coordination of the teams, curriculum development, and policy formulation—how the program fits into the mainstream of the educational system and program monitoring. The roles within the team are interchangeable and shared when appropriate. However, in assigning tasks, consideration is given to the team member's level of expertise and knowledge as it relates to goal attainment.

Traditionally the literature in social work has focused on the importance of teaming and its contribution in rendering effective social services in a variety of settings (Brieland, 1973; Barker & Briggs, 1969). However, the process of developing the "teaming concept," the sharing of professional tasks, is frequently a difficult undertaking. Such factors as: 1) a professional seeking enhancement of his/her professional status; 2) the wish for indispensability leading to increase in professional territoriality; and 3) role specialization to an extreme degree, thus depriving the clients consistent, integrated treatment, operate to hinder the process.[3] There is a considerable lack of scientific information on the dynamics of the process and the facilitative components. It has been stated that "the success of the multi-disciplinary team is dependent on a decreased emphasis on discipline and role, and increased emphasis on orienting themselves to the school and the primary program tasks and goals."[4]

To formulate an effective program it is necessary to examine demographic information, research findings and significant dynamics on a particular target population, some of which substantiates the curriculum of the in-school program and the roles of the various team members. The following is an example of the characteristics of a comprehensive program for serving teenage parents which is also supportive of the in-school program. These specifics can be applied to existing programs in evaluating their comprehensiveness.

Demographic and
Research Findings

Research evidence and descriptive literature provide a variety of explanations as to the increasing incidence of teenage pregnancies. The following statements attempt to highlight some major thinking in the area.

1. "Women who begin child bearing early in their reproductive careers—especially if they give birth as teenagers—subsequently have children more rapidly, have more children and have more unwanted and out-of-wedlock births than women who postpone childbearing...Also, it has been found that there is a direct linear relationship between age of first birth and amount of education. Adolescent childbearers, especially teenage mothers, had much lower educational attainment than their classmates."[5]

2. Recent evidence suggests that those who become parents very young are more likely than others to abuse or neglect their children—data suggests that the strains of early childbearing are intense. "Some data are available on the effects of early parenthood in the later development, as related to parental age at birth, found that childhood mortality at ages 1–4 to be 41 percent above average among children born to adolescent mothers, with a rapid decline as the age of the mother increased. Accidents are an important cause of childhood deaths, and the implication is that teenagers may be too immature to act as responsible parents."[6] "Other studies suggest that children born to adolescent teenagers are more likely to perform poorly on intelligence tests. Also, school failure and behavior problems are prevalent among this population."[7]

3. Young parents are over represented in suicide data. Nine percent of teenage mothers attempt suicide—seven times the national average for teenage girls without children.[8]

4. Historically both psychological and sociological interpretations have been stressed in explaining the basis of out-of-wedlock pregnancies. In the past a number of articles have attributed unwed motherhood to a variety of unconscious psychological needs. Khlentzos and Pagliaro (1965) and Heiman and Levitt (1960) have emphasized the Freudian view that premarital pregnancy is an attempt to compensate for an object loss. Some suggest a character disorder in the acting out of incestuous fantasies as a causal factor (Kasanin & Handchin, 1941). Others maintain that it is a lack or a breakdown in the value system. The sociological perspective maintains that poverty, lack of education, or the equivalent of lower class factors (Lowrie, 1965) are highly related to the phenomenon. Recently, studies have advanced a more balanced interpretation of the cause of illegitimacy: it stresses that on the whole the unwed mother does not differ significantly from her single non-parent counterpart (Gottschalk, 1964; Pope, 1967; and Vincent, 1961).

192

5. "There is an inverse relationship between the quality of prenatal care and the incidence of complications before and after delivery."[9] It is this group which experiences a number of obstetrical and medical problems. They include "premature labor, low birth weight, increased neonatal mortality, anemia, toxemia, prolonged labor."[10] Howard (1978) confirms these findings.

6. There is also a "possible relationship between dropout rates and provisions of in-school programs for pregnant students...generally the lower the dropout rate, the greater the provision of in-school programs for these students."[11] "The younger the pregnant teenager, the more likely she will drop out of school. Among teenage mothers under the age of 15, four in every ten never complete eighth grade. Many girls who continue in school during pregnancy drop out after delivery because of problems in arranging regular and adequate child care."[12] The Commissioner of the United States Office of Education in 1972 stated: "Every girl in the United States has a right to and need for education that will help her prepare herself for a career, for family life, and for citizenship. To be married or pregnant is not sufficient cause to deprive her of an education and the opportunity to become a contributing member of society."[13] Title IX of the Education Amendments of 1972 (effective July 12, 1975) prohibits schools which receive federal funds from excluding any student on the basis of pregnancy or a pregnancy-related condition. Even so, the extent to which young women stay in school during pregnancy or are able to return after a birth varies widely.

7. Role-confusion is also another dynamic component in the problem configuration and description of this group. "Girls who become pregnant in their teens experience simultaneously two major developmental crises: they have not yet fulfilled their female adolescent maturational functions and imposed on this is the crisis of pregnancy. Some girls also marry prior to or after the pregnancy occurs, adding a third crisis...and they are often still students attempting to reach educational goals and are in the process of making vocational choices and establishing life goals."[14] The multitude of roles and psychological demands placed upon these teenage parents at a critical phase of their own development must be addressed when planning in-school community based programs in providing direct services.

The In-School Program

A comprehensive program for teenage parents should incorporate the following characteristics: be consumer oriented, preventive, comprehensive, accessible, and coordinated. An explanation of each component is provided as follows: "1) A consumer oriented system is a program based upon a thorough knowledge of the needs of the target population to be served...; 2) A preventive system is one that anticipates most of the problems encountered by the group...Three levels of preventive services should be considered: a) primary refers to services designed to prevent the occurrence; b) secondary refers to services designed to facilitate the most optimal course of action to deal with confirmed pregnancies; and c) tertiary preventive services are designed to reduce the extent of impact of social, medical, legal and educational problems associated with parenthood; 3) A comprehensive system is one that includes the full range of services needed by the (target population) parent; 4) An accessible system is one that has minimal constraints, i.e. conveniently located and; 5) A coordinated system is one that has formal linkages established among service providers."[15] It has been claimed that young women who have received comprehensive service programs have healthier pregnancies and babies, lower repeat pregnancy rates, higher educational attainment, less welfare dependency and a stronger concept of the responsibilities of parenthood (Cox, 1978). The in-school program presented contains a coordinated comprehensive effort among an interdisciplinary team within the context of the school and meets the criteria previously identified. It is accessible because the program exists within the school building with local service agencies providing the community based services. Thus, opportunities to identify, serve and provide follow-up services exist on two levels: school and community. A brief description of the program, its goals, objectives and content will confirm the fact that the program was developed, and based upon needs of this consumer group, addresses recent research findings, and is comprehensive in content. Most importantly the focus is on prevention and includes the three levels discussed previously.

The class is called the Home and Family Education.[16] It is open to both male and female students. However, those who generally enroll are pregnant adolescent females. The class is flexible; girls are admitted as soon as they are identified, and scheduling has taken place with consultation from their academic counselor. If a student's schedule conflicts in terms of time, then schedule changes are made to accommodate the course. However, if there is a full schedule of required courses needed to meet graduation requirements, then the student is seen individually by various team members and is invited to participate in selected sessions which are critical to her stage of the pregnancy. This is done with approval from the regular classroom instructor. The social worker who coordinates the program has the responsibility of interviewing each student who is referred and collecting significant data to be shared with the team.

The primary focus of the program is on prenatal and postnatal education. Academic credit is given, provided that each student satisfactorily completes all assignments, exams and requirements of the team. An explanation of the program's components is provided:

1. *Prenatal* — student enters in lieu of physical education. The curriculum includes: nutrition, Lamaze instruction, signs of labor and delivery, health care, fetal development and related complications.

2. *Postnatal*—students have the option of enrolling for one semester when they return to school after their postpartum medical examination. This phase was added after a critical analysis of the needs of this particular target population. Students encountered a number of problems when returning to school, i.e.—child care arrangements and response to academic pressures and parenting pressures. Consequently, the option of continuing enrollment with a change of focus—on the mother-child dyad, child development, selection of the child care facilities, care of infant, parenting skills, career choices and long-term planning—was suggested and later implemented.

The course is not mandatory but highly recommended, and students are encouraged to remain in school for as long as it is physically and emotionally possible. The goals and objectives of the program are as follows:

1. To provide emotional and psychological support to the teenage parent during the critical phase of her development. Examples of this process include: providing casework and group work services, educational counseling, referrals to social service agencies (public health and public aid, adoption agencies, Planned Parenthood, health service clinics), and providing a peer supportive milieu.

2. To provide these critical services specific to successful functioning, i.e., homebound instruction before and after delivery, follow-up services to assist in child care arrangements and living arrangements if needed, career counseling and planning, and the identification of financial resources.

3. To provide each girl with an unsegregated, least restrictive learning experience. The aim is to promote their social and educational growth during the entire pre and postnatal stages. A concerted effort is made to foster and maintain the teenage parents' identity with the public school and those significant others (referring to team members).

4. To provide comprehensive and coordinated follow-up services, including local social service agencies. The primary focus is to provide information on medical care for both baby and mother, to assist in value clarification and life choices, to provide emotional support related to developing adequate parenting skills, to provide a peer support group in order that issues related to role confusion and conflict can appropriately be ventilated and identified, and to prevent and reduce potential child abuse.

5. To provide in-school classroom instruction on fetal development, nutrition, child care, delivery, Lamaze, postpartum care of mother and child, child development activities which encourage cognitive and affective stimulation of the infant, and the identification and discussion of "life-supporting" social service agencies specific to this target population.

Multi-disciplinary Teaming

"Multi-disciplinary practice requires ability to practice one's own profession and ability to link into the work of others. This requires knowledge and skill that differentiates one's work from that of others within...several frames of reference. Clients gain from the advantages of inter-dependent practice in that various needs are met, continuity of service is likely, and practitioners are open to several approaches...The term multi-disciplinary practice denotes professional activity by two or more practitioners belonging to different professions, directed at a common client system."[17] There are several attitudes within the team which must be present if successful intervention is to be obtained:

1. "Thorough commitment to the profession's values and ethics, and belief in the usefulness of one's own profession.
2. Belief in a holistic approach to client problems.
3. Recognition of the interdependency of practice.
4. Recognition of the expertise of colleagues and others."[18]

The Home and Family Education Course is taught by a team of five, each planning and teaching units in their areas of expertise. The team includes a social worker, school nurse, public health nurse, nutritionist and a community resource coordinator. The team has regular conferences and staffings. These meetings focus on 1) new referrals to the program, 2) teaching assignments, 3) status of those girls who are currently enrolled, 4) referrals and follow-up services which need to be initiated, 5) delegation of tasks to team members, 6) and the current status of the program (problems, issues, as they relate to the needs of the target population) and curriculum changes. As stated earlier, a commitment to the profession of helping, a belief in the holistic approach to client problems, and recognition of the interdependency and expertise of other colleagues is evident. Each team member brings to the group unique knowledge which is shared in the best interest of the client and the willingness to delegate tasks in order to render comprehensive services.

The author will briefly discuss the respective team member roles to clarify the process described above, although it is impossible to elaborate on every detail within the context of the paper.

1. The social worker is the coordinator, team leader, program developer, and is responsible to the Assistant Superintendent of Special Education and the building principal. The social worker leads discussions on the emotional demands of parenting, interpersonal and family relationships, values clarification, communication skills, assertiveness training, and developing long-term goals.
2. The school nurse teaches a child development unit which includes: normal growth and development with emphasis on reasonable expec-

tations for the infant, care of the sick child, preventive health care, and infant feeding.

3. The public health nurse is a qualified Lamaze instructor and teaches the unit on body psychology, anatomy, labor, delivery, and birth control. The public health nurse also makes home visits, contacts each student during the homebound phase and monitors the progress of the mother and child to identify potential problems.

4. The food service director for the school district teaches a unit on nutrition. This unit includes information on nutrition during pregnancy and after, consumerism, food preparation, budgeting, and the use of WIC (a food supplement for women, infants, and children provided by a federal program).

5. The fifth team member is a Title I nurse who coordinates field trips to hospitals, Planned Parenthood Clinics, WIC, and local day care centers that accept infants of school-age mothers. Community social services which are appropriate are discussed and representatives from various agencies are invited to speak to the students.

Each team member is responsible for grading the student on her respective unit. Grades are a combined decision of the team.

Social services representatives periodically are invited to share their agency's procedures and services with the team members. Referrals are made by the various team members to such agencies as the Mental Health Center, Department of Children and Family Services, Planned Parenthood, public aid, WIC and Illinois Children's Home and Aid Society after discussion within the team. Thus, any member of the team can refer a student; referral is not limited to the social worker, who traditionally performs such tasks. Home visits are made by the school nurse, public health nurse and social worker depending upon the level of involvement and the established working relationship with the teenage parent. Generally each team member develops some rapport with the student, thus offering each young parent a multi-disciplinary "support system" and access to a number of intervention strategies. The self-determination of each student is valued and students are encouraged to work with any team member on personal problems and academic assignments. The team functions with a dual perspective—the education of the teenage mother and the future implications of her unique situation as it relates to the rights of the child.

Since the team does not operate in isolation, it is having an impact on other parts of the high school curriculum. For example, the team recommended that the health education requirement focus more on reproduction and adolescent sexuality, that it be presented at an earlier stage than the junior level and that a full-time staff person be hired. This recommendation was implemented with some modification due to budget constraints. Currently, some members of the team are providing consultation to the Home Economics Department in developing a course on parenting skills for high school students. This course will be co-educational and open to the entire student body. The content of the course is being developed by the social worker, home economics teachers, nurses, consultation from the Illinois Office of Education, public health nurses, etc. The concern emerged from observing the problems that young teenage parents who are enrolled in the Home and Family Education Course frequently experience and the potential of child abuse among the group.

In summary this in-school program for teenage parents combines several significant components in delivering social work services in the schools. It addresses a critical phenomenon of our times—the increasing incidence of school-age parents; it recognizes the effectiveness and facilitative qualities of multidisciplinary teaming; it encourages and provides an example of innovative leadership-oriented social work practice in the public schools; and it illustrates the impact one program can have on other parts of the school curriculum which is preventive in nature.

Footnotes

1. Zackler, Jack, et al. (ed.) *The Teenage Pregnant Girl,* Charles C. Thomas Publisher, Springfield, Illinois, 1975, p. 83.

2. Ibid., p. 3.

3. Falck, Hans S. "Interdisciplinary Education and Implications for Social Work Practice," *Journal of Education for Social Work,* Spring, 1977, Vol. 13, No. 2, p. 36.

4. *Multi-Disciplinary Teams Serving the "Total School": A Formula for Improved and Broadened Special Services In Rockford Public Schools.* Prepared for distribution at the PPS Consortium Conference, Oak Brook Hyatt House, March 23, 1974, p. 1.

5. Trussell, James, and Menken, Jane. "Early Childbearing and Subsequent Fertility," *Family Planning Perspectives.* Vol. 10, No. 4, July–August, 1978, p. 209.

6. Baldwin, Wendy H. "Adolescent Pregnancy and Childbearing—Growing Concerns for Americans," *Population Bulletin.* Vol. 31, No. 2, Population Reference Bureau, Inc., Washington, D.C., 1976. p. 25.

7. Ibid., p. 25.

8. Roland, J.E. *Knowledge and Attitudes of Administrators, Board Members, and Teachers Regarding the Education of Pregnant Students in Illinois.* (Doctoral Thesis, University of Illinois), 1973.

9. Zackler, p. 107.

10. Ibid., p. 88. Also see Howard, M. "How Can Classroom Teachers Help?" *Today's Education,* February–March, 1978. Vol. 67, pp. 62–66.

11. Bakalis, Michael. *Incidence of Pregnancy Among Students in Illinois Public Secondary Schools: A Report of Related Educational Provisions and Policies.* Office of Public Instruction—Research Section, 1972, p. 8.

12. Downs, Cathy. *School-Age Parents,* (Unpublished paper). University of Illinois-Champaign, November 1, 1978, p. 6.

13. Howard, M., and Eddinger, L. *School-Age Parents*, National Alliance Concerned with School-Age Parents, Syracuse, N.Y., 1973, p. 29.

14. Weatherford, Shouse J. "Psychological and Emotional Problems of Pregnancy in Adolescence," in Zackler et. al. (eds.), *The Teenage Pregnant Girl*, Charles C. Thomas Publisher, Springfield, Illinois, p. 161.

15. Gullerud, Ernest. *Organizing a Comprehensive Service System for Unmarried Parent(s): Characteristics of a Model System*—Unpublished paper—Prepared for the DCFS Task Force Services on Unmarried Mothers, 1977, p. 2–4.

16. Also see Wilson, Janice. "An Innovative Project to Serve School-Age Parents," *Illinois Teacher*, March–April, 1978.

17. Falsh, p. 33.

18. Ibid., p. 36.

Bibliography

Bakalis, Michael. *Incidence of Pregnancy Among Students in Illinois Public Secondary Schools: A Report of Related Educational Provisions and Policies.* Office of Public Instruction, Research Section, 1972, p.8.

Baldwin, Wendy H. "Adolescent Pregnancy and Childbearing—Growing Concerns for Americans," *Population Bulletin*, Vol. 31, No. 2, Population Reference Bureau, Inc., Washington, D.C., 1976, p. 25.

Barker and Briggs, T. *Using Teams to Deliver Social Service.* Syracuse University, September 1969.

Brieland, Donald, Briggs, T., and Leuenberger, P. *The Team Model of Social Work Practic.* Syracuse University, School of Social Work, July 1973.

Costin, Lela. "School Social Work Practice: A New Model." *Social Work*, Vol. 20, March 1975, pp. 135–139.

Cox, B. *Should School Systems Provide A Special Program for Pregnant Students and Young Parent?* Unpublished paper, Bradley University, 1978.

Downs, K. *School-Age Parents*, Unpublished paper, University of Illinois-Champaign, November 1, 1978, p. 6.

Falck, Hans S. "Interdisciplinary Education and Implications for Social Work Practice," *Journal of Education For Social Work*, Spring, 1977, Vol. 13, No. 2, pp. 30–36.

Gottschalk, Louis A., Titchener, James, Picker, H., and Stewart, S. "Psychological Factors Associated with Pregnancy in Adolescent Girls: A Preliminary Report," *Journal of Nervous and Mental Disease*, Vol. 138, No. 6, 1964, pp. 524–534.

Gullerud, Ernest. *Organizing a Comprehensive Service System For Unmarried Parent(s): Characteristics of a Model System.* Unpublished paper—prepared for the DCFS Task Force Services on Unmarried Mothers, 1977, pp. 2–3.

Goula, Ketayun. *In-School Program: Pregnant Girls, Wed/Unwed Mothers.* Unpublished paper, University of Illinois, 1972.

Heiman, Marcel, and Levitt, Esther G. "The Role of Separation and Depression in Out-of-Wedlock Pregnancy," *American Journal of Orthopsychiatry*, January, Vol. 30, 1966, pp. 166–174.

Howard, M. "How Can Classroom Teachers Help?" *Today's Education*, February–March, 1978, Vol. 67, pp. 62–66.

Kasanin, J., and Handehin, S. "Psychodynamic Factors of Illegitimacy," *American Journal of Orthopsychiatry*, 1974, Vol. 11, pp. 66–85. Also see Gould, K., Grant Proposal—Services for Teenage Mothers, Unpublished, 1972.

Khlentzos, Michael T., and Palgiaro. "Observations from Psychotherapy with Unwed Mothers," *American Journal of Orthopsychiatry*, Vol. 35, 1965.

Lowrie, Samuel H. "Early Marriage: Premarital Pregnancy and Associated Factors," *Journal of Marriage and Family*, Vol. 27, No. 1, 1965, pp. 49–56.

Meares, Paula. "An Analysis of Tasks in School Social Work," *Social Work*, Vol. 22, No. 3, May, 1977, pp. 196–201.

Multi-Disciplinary Teams Serving the "Total School," A Formula For Improved and Broadened Special Services in Rockford Public Schools. Prepared for distribution at the PPS Consortium Conference, Oak Brook Hyatt House, March 23, 1974, p. 1.

Roland, J.E. *Knowledge and Attitudes of Administrators, Board Members, and Teachers Regarding the Education of Pregnant Students in Illinois*. Doctoral Thesis, University of Illinois, 1973.

Trussell, James, and Menken, Jane. "Early Child Bearing and Subsequent Fertility," *Family Planning Perspectives*, Vol. 10, No. 4, July–August, 1978, p. 209.

Pope, Hallowell. "Unwed Mothers and their Sex Partners," *Journal of Marriage and Family*, Vol. 29, No. 3, 1967, pp. 555–567.

Vincent, Clark E. *Unmarried Mothers. New York: Free Press Glencoe, 1961*.

Weatherford, Shouse J. "Psychological and Emotional Problems of Pregnancy in Adolescence," in Zackler et al. (Eds.), *The Teenage Pregnant Girl*, Charles C. Thomas Publisher, Springfield, Illinois, p. 161.

Wilson, Janice. "An Innovative Project to Serve School-Age Parents," *Illinois Teacher*, March–April, 1978.

Zackler, Jack, et al. (Eds.). *The Teenage Pregnant Girl*. Charles C. Thomas, Publisher, Springfield, Illinois, 1975, pp. 3–107.

Pregnancy Prevention:
A Private Agency's Program
in Public Schools

. . . . .

Mary Booth Doty
and Myramae King

I t is time for social work to deal preventively with the epidemic of teenage pregnancy. For years social workers have been aware of the rapidly increasing rate of teen pregnancy. They are familiar with the figures: over 1.1 million teenagers 15–19 years and thirty thousand in the 10–14 category become pregnant every year.[1] They know firsthand the negative social, emotional, and financial consequences many of these early pregnancies bring to families. School social workers are particularly aware of the educational toll that results when 70 percent of the teenagers who have babies drop out and never finish high school.[2]

For years social workers have responded by developing programs for girls who were parents or pregnant, but few social work programs serve both boys and girls and focus on preventing pregnancy. Too often a teenager is offered information or counseling about sexual concerns only after a problem has developed—a pregnancy scare, a pregnancy, or a case of venereal disease.

The need for a prevention program is clear not only from the statistics, but also from the social milieu teenagers grow up in today. The media present sexually provocative and confusing material. Peer pressure to engage in sexual relations is increasing, as is acceptance of teenage parenthood. Widespread support for using birth control is not present among teens.[3] Talking about sex with a partner early in a sexual relationship is not the norm, nor is thinking through the consequences of sexual activity. The normal sexual concerns of teens are often overlooked or denied by adults. A teenager has to look to friends or to himself or herself to resolve uncertainties about sexuality and sexual relationships.[4]

Many social workers have the skill and sensitivity to carry out comprehensive programs of sex education and counseling. What social workers need are a determination to develop and fund programs and a commitment to provide ongoing preventive service. This commitment could be grounded in the research done by Schinke in Seattle and by the direct social service program developed by Inwood House in New York City. Both these school-based programs for preventing teenage pregnancy used group training for boys and girls. Led by social workers, the group sessions focused on human sexuality; reproduction; techniques of contraception (including abstinence); and skills in interpersonal relationships and decision making.

The students in the Seattle study had "fewer instances of intercourse without contraception, more birth control use, and greater commitment to delaying pregnancy" than the students in the control group.[5] Inwood House, which has prevention programs in six public senior high schools and two public junior high schools in New York City, coded the contraceptive pattern of 368 teenage girls identified as sexually active. During one year, participants in the program used contraceptives in 55 percent of their instances of intercourse.[6] This contraceptive rate compared to a rate of 26 percent among New York City teenagers and 34 percent nationwide.[7] The number of reported pregnancies at one school in the Inwood House program declined by 39 percent after eighteen months of services.[8] Over a four-year period, prior to the time this article was written in 1982, Inwood House reached 18,147 teenage girls and boys through a combination of classroom teaching, group work, and casework.

The remainder of this article describes the Inwood House program. The authors hope that other private agencies will initiate pregnancy prevention programs in public schools and that school social workers in public school systems will expand their services to develop preventive programs.

The Inwood House Program

Inwood House is a human service agency that has served young women and their children since 1830. Since 1971 almost all its clients have been pregnant teenagers and teenage mothers. Inwood House provides maternity residence care, joint foster care for young mothers and their babies, long-term residential care for girls who have been pregnant, and transitional services after discharge.

Throughout its history, Inwood House has adapted its programs to meet changing social needs. Known in the schools as Teen Choice, the Community Outreach Program was conceived and developed in this tradition. In cooperation with the New York City Board of Education's Bureau of Education and Vocational Guidance, the program places part-time social workers and social work graduate students in selected public schools to offer information, counseling, and referral on human sexuality, birth control methods, venereal disease, pregnancy, and parenting. The model includes individual counseling, group counseling, classroom teaching, school-site drop-in centers, and close working relationships with neighborhood clinics.

Boys Included. A key component in the Inwood House program is working with boys. In addition to the seven female social workers who worked with boys in coed groups and individual counseling, three male workers participated in the program. The boys were excellent attenders and active participants in the groups. They were eager for information and counseling referrals. The misinformation, ignorance, and mythology that abound in boys' views of sex contribute to the stereotypic macho, conquest-oriented male attitude. At the same time, males have a great influence over the decisions of females to have or not have sexual intercourse and to use or not use birth control. It is thus essential to include boys in a pregnancy prevention program. After participating in the program, a ninth-grade boy said:

> I learned that before having sex you should think about it. Or you should walk around prepared. And if you have sex and you want to have a baby you should have a good job.

Another described the effect of the program this way:

> Well, I really got to start thinking about sex more. Not just have sex and leave them, but to have a good relationship and have good communication.

Public and Private Cooperation. The combined efforts of a private agency and public schools have led to a strong, viable program that neither the agency nor the schools could have developed separately. It took careful planning by both Inwood House and the Board of Education to start the program. This was followed by constant coordination and evaluation as the program grew and became successful.

To establish a program of pregnancy prevention in public schools, a private agency needs to accomplish the following steps:

1. Gain enough support from the agency's board of directors to allocate staff time for fund raising and exploratory work.

2. Approach the local school board to discuss the problem of teenage pregnancy and to propose a cooperative program of prevention.

3. Hire a social worker with expertise in the areas of adolescence and human sexuality.

4. Cooperate with a board of education staff person in interpreting the program to school principals and in identifying principals who will agree to have the program in their schools.

5. Meet with the officials and the general membership of the PTA to seek their support.

6. Secure rooms in the school and install a telephone.

7. Speak with school administrators and faculty to interpret the program and identify sympathetic staff.

8. Meet with student government representatives to get student input and support.

9. Visit community agencies that deal with youths and establish connections that will facilitate referrals.

10. Publicize the program to students through articles in the school newspaper, announcements in the weekly school calendar, posters in hallways and bathrooms, and presentations in classrooms.

11. Build educational resources for staff, including charts on reproductive anatomy, materials on birth control methods, and pamphlets that can be made available to students.

12. Provide ongoing staff development and support.

13. Raise additional money to expand the program.

Advantage of Cooperation. A cooperative program like Teen Choice has mutual benefits to the schools, the agency; and the students in at least three ways:

Welcome Outside Help. The schools are given a social service program free of charge at a time when reduced school budgets have cut back counseling programs. School guidance and social work staffs are overworked and usually welcome outside help, especially in dealing with the extremely sensitive area of sexual behavior.

Confidentiality. Social workers from a private agency can operate on the agency guidelines of confidentiality, not the school guidelines, which give priority to parent rights over student rights. The school and the agency agreed that students attending the Teen Choice program in high schools are seen without the notification or permission of the parent. Students in the junior high program obtain permission to participate by giving their parents a "negative consent" form (which states that if the parents do not return the form they are giving their consent). Agency social workers do not inform school personnel about who attends the program or what problems are discussed. Teachers and administrators are told only if the referrals they made have been followed up by an interview. Confidentiality is a cornerstone of the program. Most students who attend individual counseling are self-referred or referred by friends. This attests to the trust the program has generated among students.

Accessibility. The advantage of having agency personnel in the school is invaluable to the success of the program. Teenagers are more likely to seek help in an environment that is familiar and comfortable than to go to an unknown site for counseling help. The students come to know there is a resource in the school from which they can seek confidential help. This enables them to seek help earlier, as in the following example, whether for prenatal care, pregnancy testing, family planning, or saying no.

> Joan, 16, requested counseling in October after a second group session. She first had sex a month earlier. Neither she nor her partner used protection, and she was concerned she might be pregnant. She could not discuss sexuality with

either her mother or her older sisters. Joan was helped to make an appointment for a pregnancy test, which was negative. She decided to use the pill.

In follow-up counseling in Teen Choice, Joan revealed she had not started the pill because she was reconsidering her decision to be sexually active. Joan continued in frequent counseling until the end of the school year. She also phoned twice over the summer for counseling around pressure boys put on her to have sex and in both instances decided not to.

During the next school year, Joan was seen many times. Counseling supported her decision to delay further sexual involvement and helped her sort out her relationships with her mother and siblings.

The case example that follows demonstrates that the accessibility of help is particularly important for students who are not sexually active but who are confused by sexual desire or sexual pressure.

The first person to respond to this year's ad was a 15-year-old girl who was having difficulty saying no to her 19-year-old boyfriend. He was pressuring her to have sex with him, and she felt strongly about the importance of being a virgin. She talked at length about her tendency to dress and make up herself to look much older than she was and about her repeated involvements with older guys. She also spoke about her academic achievements, her intention of going to college, and her new interest in dating guys who were classmates.

Students can come for group or individual counseling during school hours. The program can be designed in such a way that students get credit for group participation and can be officially excused from class for individual counseling. Adolescents are notorious for missing appointments, but Teen Choice's accessibility to students, visibility in the school, and support from school personnel make it more likely that students will come to appointments with program staff and come regularly. Over 30 percent in individual counseling come for more than five sessions.

Importance of a
Value Base

A pregnancy prevention program should be grounded in a value base. Students need not agree with values, but they should be clearly stated so students can make decisions against a known standard. The Teen Choice program takes a stand on issues without being judgmental of individuals who choose different values. The value base includes the following:

Being a teen parent is not a good idea; it brings with it social, emotional, educational, financial, and medical problems.

No one should be pressured into a sexual act against his or her will or against his or her principles.

The double standard for males and females, which still exists in our society, is not to be condoned.

Postponement of sexual intercourse should be encouraged until after high school or until marriage.

If a couple decides to have sexual intercourse, there should be no sex without birth control.

The practical importance of these values is apparent in Pamela's case history:

> Pamela, age 14, heard about Teen Choice from a friend who had been in a group. She had sex once, was not enthusiastic about it, and had abstained for two months despite her boyfriend's continued pressure. Although she felt sexual activity was inevitable, she didn't want a baby and came for birth control information.
>
> Strong advice was given against having sex at such a young age. She was given information on birth control, cautioned not to have sex again without protection, and advised to talk with her boyfriend about what it would mean to have a baby at this time in their lives when they were 18 and 14 years old.
>
> Pamela returned in one week after talking with her boyfriend. She learned that he definitely wanted a baby. His cousin and his best friend had babies, and he thought he should have one too. Subsequently, Pamela decided to break up the relationship.

Inwood House has learned that taking a stand on values does not stop students from coming to the Teen Choice program. In four years, over five thousand students have signed up for groups and individual counseling. Almost all groups are reluctant to end. The most common suggestions by students to improve the program is to "have more sessions." At the end of the term, participants are asked for written, anonymous responses to the question, "What kinds of things have you learned that have helped you get along better in your everyday life?" These are common responses:

> I learned protection is important if you're not ready for a baby.
>
> You shouldn't do it if you don't want to.
>
> I learned how to say no to a boy who is pressuring me to have sex.
>
> You shouldn't have sex just because everybody's doing it.
>
> The group helped me express my feelings and not feel that I'm the only one who wants to wait a while before having sex.
>
> I learned how to talk straight to my boyfriend about not wanting to get pregnant.

If a pregnancy occurs, a pregnancy prevention program should be ready to offer accurate information about options. Early prenatal care is important. Termination should be obtained only at a reputable medical facility.

Getting Started

School social workers can play an innovative role in starting pregnancy prevention services. They need not wait for an outside agency to come into the school. They can start by running support groups for ninth graders. These newcomers to high school are often overwhelmed by a variety of pressures in a new school. One demand is pressure to become socially accepted and to maintain a certain image of masculinity or femininity. Ninth graders are stimulated and confused by older teens. They usually don't have the basic information or emotional maturity they need to make responsible decisions.

They need support in establishing their identities and deciding on their social and sexual behaviors.

Preventive groups organized by school social workers can help these students cope with the transition from junior to senior high. These social workers are already an integral part of the school, and they can develop programs more quickly than private agency workers, as long as they take careful steps to gain school administrators', parents', and students' support on the issue of pregnancy prevention.

Notes and References

1. *Teenage Pregnancy: The Problem That Hasn't Gone Away* (New York: Alan Guttmacher Institute, 1981), pp. 4 and 20.

2. Sol Gordon and Irving R. Dickman, *Schools and Parents—Partners in Sex Education*, Public Affairs Pamphlet No. 581 (New York: Public Affairs Committee, May 1980), p. 2.

3. Susan Ross, *The Youth Values Project* (Washington, D.C.: Population Institute of New York: State Communities Aid Association, 1978), pp. 24–45.

4. In a true/false questionnaire given at the beginning of group sessions, a surprising 67 percent marked true for the statement "more than 90 percent of teenagers are having sex." Although the number of sexually active teenagers is rising sharply, some sources report a rate closer to 50 or 75 percent. See *Teenage Pregnancy: The Problem That Hasn't Gone Away*; and Ross, *the Youth Values Project*.

5. Steven Paul Schinke, "School-Based Model for Preventing Teenage Pregnancy," *Social Work in Education*, 4 (January 1982), p. 39.

6. *Community Outreach Project, Summary Report: Fall 1981– Spring 1982* (New York: Inwood House, 1982), p. 2 (Photocopied).

7. Ross, *The Youth Values Project*, p. iii; and *Teenage Pregnancy: The Problem That Hasn't Gone Away*, p. 11.

8. *Report on Pregnant Students Served at Brandeis High School by Inwood House Teen Choice Program in 1980-81 School Year* and *Report on Pregnant Students Served at Brandeis High School by Inwood House Teen Choice Program in 1981–82 School Year* (New York; Inwood House, 1981 and 1982 respectively).

Primary Prevention of Adolescent Pregnancy

. . . . .

Steven Paul Schinke,
Betty J. Blythe, Lewayne D. Gilchrist,
and Gloria Adele Burt

P regnancy in adolescence is accompanied by health, emotional, and socioeconomic problems. Pregnant teenagers, adolescent parents, and children of young mothers face discouraging futures and require professional attention (Chilman, 1979; Schinke, 1978, 1980, in press-e). Nearly all the difficulties these clients encounter could be obviated by delaying pregnancy and childbearing until later years. Professional social workers and kindred practitioners need strategies to help young people avoid unplanned pregnancy.

This paper details experiential and research backing for a primary prevention group work strategy aimed at adolescents. Adumbrated are the magnitude and untoward sequelae of adolescent pregnancy, childbearing, and parenthood. Next given are the background and rationale that sponsor a cognitive-behavioral approach to social group work prevention. Delineation of primary prevention concepts and operations is followed by results from two field research studies. Lastly discussed are advantages of the approach,

Reprinted by permission from Schinke, S.P., Blythe, B.J., Gilchrist, L.D., and Burt, G.A., Primary prevention of adolescent pregnancy, *Social Work with Groups*, Vol. 4, No 1/2. Copyright 1981 by The Haworth Press, Inc., 12 W. 32 St., New York, NY 10001.

The authors thank Anna Bolstad, Leona Eggert, Joan Hiltner, Lois Holt, and Andrew Renggli. Funding was by grants HD 11095 and HD 02274 from the National Institute of Child Health and Human Development (National Institutes of Health) and by Maternal and Child Health Training Project 913 from the Bureau of Community Health Services (Health Services Administration) awarded to the University of Washington Child Development and Mental Retardation Center and administered through the United States Public Health Service, Department of Health and Human Services.

conclusions allowed by empirical findings, and future directions for a cognitive-behavioral group context to primary prevention with young people.

Magnitude and Untoward Sequelae

Each year in the United States over 1.3 million 13- to 19-year-olds get pregnant (Tietze, 1978). With the number of births to young people growing at an annual rate of 16%, adolescents are responsible for one of every five deliveries (National Center for Health Statistics, 1979). Most pregnancies are unintended and unwanted (National Center for Health Statistics, 1978); however, less than 7% of teenaged mothers give up their babies for adoption or for substitute care (Zelnik & Kantner, 1978b). The one-third of adolescents who interrupt their pregnancies account for 31% of reported abortions (Tietze, 1978). In 1977, abortions to U.S. teenagers totalled 413,420 (Forest, Sullivan, & Tietze, 1979). Increasing by 41,000 per annum, 1980 abortions for the age cohort exceed one-half million (National Center for Health Statistics, 1980). Earlier menarche (Bongaards, 1980) and fertility (Anastasiow, Everett, O'Shaughnessy, Eggleston, & Eklund, 1978) combined with youth's precocious sexual activity (Zelnik & Kantner, 1977) foretell continued prevalence of adolescent pregnancy.

Many negative sequelae support remediation of this unhappy phenomenon. Pregnant teenagers, compared to adult women, have higher rates of anemia, preeclampsia, labor complications, and mortality (Evrard & Gold, 1978). Intercourse and pregnancy in adolescence are linked with cervical cancer (Marano, 1977) and uterine complications that necessitate hysterectomy (Koepsell, Weiss, Thompson, & Martin, 1980). Babies born to adolescents have high mortality and morbidity. The latter embody low birthweight, congenital malformations, and developmental disabilities of mental retardation, blindness, epilepsy, deafness, and cerebral palsy (Hunt, 1976). Social and psychological research denotes behavior disorders, school problems, and low intellectual acumen among offspring of adolescents (Baldwin, 1980; Belmont, Stein, & Zybert, 1978).

Teenage parents experience social, legal, psychological, educational, and economic struggles. Their marital problems and divorce rates are greater than those of couples marrying later (Furstenberg, 1976). Early childbearing yields large terminal families (Card & Wise, 1978) marked by rapid fertility, short birth intervals (Bumpass, Rindfuss, & Janosik, 1978), and unwanted children (Trussell & Menken, 1978). Contrasted with youngsters of older parents, adolescents' children spend more of their lives in one-parent homes and themselves are at high risk for teenage childbearing (Baldwin & Cain, 1980). Immature parenthood sets the stage for child abuse and neglect (American Humane Association, 1978; Herrenkohl & Herrenkohl, 1979). Young parents' educational setbacks are frequent and irreparable. Teenagers list pregnancy as the most common reason for dropping out of high school (The Alan Guttmacher Institute, 1976), and they seldom recapture their lost years of education (Moore & Waite, 1977). Early parenting is followed by unemployment (Bureau of Labor Statistics, 1980), reduced income (Hofferth & Moore, 1979), and dependence on public welfare (Clapp & Raab, 1978). Young mothers are twice as likely to fall below poverty lines than women first having babies beyond the teen years (Moore, 1978). Suicide attempts are pervasive among women pregnant as adolescents (Gabrielson, Klerman, Currie, Tyler, & Jekel, 1970).

A Cognitive-Behavioral Strategy for Primary Prevention

BACKGROUND AND RATIONALE

A viable strategy for the primary prevention of teenage pregnancy starts by identifying the failures of extant social and health services. Scores of family planning programs provide sex education, free birth control, and medical services for already pregnant youths and teenage mothers and their babies (Furstenberg, Masnick, & Ricketts, 1972.) Sponsored by hospitals and public health centers, medically oriented programs are not affecting the problem (Jekel, Harrison, Bancroft, Tyler and Klerman, 1975). Social and health programs often fail to reach young people (Urban and Rural Systems Associates, 1975). Marring these services is a futile search for a pathology of adolescent pregnancy. Worse yet, social and health programs systematically overlook educational, cognitive, and interpersonal factors skewing youths' ability to understand and regulate contraception (Dembo & Lundell, 1979). Exclusion of social work group methods also flaws adolescent pregnancy prevention. Adequate family planning for young people redresses these lacunae.

Contrary to the notion that only deviant youngsters get pregnant (Hertz, 1977; Shafer, Pettigrew, Wolkind, & Zajicek, 1978), the present prevention strategy is applicable to every teenager. The tautology of sexual activity leading to pregnancy is borne out by findings "that teenagers are placed at contraceptive risk not by any pathology, personal, moral or otherwise, but by a unique convergence of factors that are 'normal' to the lives of many adolescents" (Cvetkovich & Grote, in press, p. 2). Survey research on the normalcy of this risk concludes that two-thirds of American women and three-fourths of American men have sexual intercourse by age 19 (Zelnik & Kantner, 1980; Zelnik, Kim & Kantner, 1979). Youths' poor planning is shown by the 70% who concur "I feel I shouldn't have intercourse at all, so I wouldn't plan ahead to do it or use birth control" (Goldsmith, Gabrielson, & Gabrielson, 1972). Another poll found 71% of nonvirgin teenagers agreeing, "If a girl uses birth control, it makes it seem as if she were planning to have sex" (Sorensen, 1973). One in ten first sexual encounters is planned (Sorensen, 1973); about a third involve birth control (Zelnik & Kantner, 1978a). Cvetkovich, Grote, Bjorseth, and Sarkissian (1975) sum up the dilemma: "Adolescents are being required to make a decision about contraceptive use at a time when they are sexually undifferentiated and perhaps unprepared for such analytical thinking" (p. 266).

210

Primary prevention to assist adolescents in thinking analytically about their sexual behavior must stress problem solving and decision making. Problem-solving deficiencies are witnessed by adolescents' reluctance to see themselves vulnerable to personal and social exigencies—e.g., pregnancy risk (Zelnik & Kantner, 1979). Frequently, they cannot say in advance how to resolve a problem (Little & Kendall, 1979). Their inability to anticipate environmental reactions to solutions further impedes youths' analytical thinking and decision making (Schinke, in press-a, in press-d).

To implement decisions in social situations, youths need interpersonal communication skills. Behind this assumption is the link between unplanned pregnancy and communication deficits (Campbell & Barnlund, 1977). Other data depict adolescent women engaging in sex because they cannot say "no," want to please their partners, or see intercourse as expected (Cvetkovich & Grote, Note 1). Correspondingly, young men do not discuss birth control with their sexual partners (Francome, 1980). Interpersonal influences on sexual behavior are obvious in the relationship of teenagers' inadequate contraception to their susceptibility to social pressure (Mindick, Oskamp, & Berger, Note 2). The developmental, nondeviant nature of pregnancy risk in adolescence points to primary prevention of problem-solving, decision-making, and interpersonal communication. Small groups are ideal for delivering cognitive-behavioral primary prevention.

CONCEPTS AND OPERATIONS

The above rationale is strengthened by the importance of small groups in our field, as iterated by this journal's inaugural editorial: "There is no profession that places greater value on the individual in his social context than does the profession of social work. For most people the social context becomes manageable and definable through the small group" ("Editorial," 1978, p. 3). Buttressing the emphasis is social work with groups of children (McCarnes & Smith, 1979; Schinke, in press-b), adolescents (Blythe, Gilchrist, & Schinke, in press; Schinke, Gilchrist, Smith, & Wong, 1978), adults (Galinsky, Schopler, Safier, & Gambrill, 1978; Schinke, Gilchrist, Smith, & Wong, 1979), and families (Bergofsky, Forgash, & Glassel, 1979; Wayne, 1979) within and outside of agency milieus (Schinke, Blythe, Gilchrist, & Smith, in press; Schinke & Rose, 1976; Schinke, Smith, Gilchrist, & Wong, 1978).

Group cognitive-behavioral prevention that lets young people sidestep unplanned pregnancy builds on this foundation and on the authors' earlier theory (Schinke, Blythe, & Gilchrist, in press; Schinke, Gilchrist, & Blythe, 1980). Preventive social group work for the demands of adolescence weights equally cognitions and behavior. As we said elsewhere, the "cognitive-behavioral approach to prevention is based on the premise that many adolescents get pregnant not because they lack relevant information, but because they lack cognitive and behavioral skills necessary to use information" (Schinke, Gilchrist, & Small, 1979, p. 84).

Cognitive-behavioral prevention is operationaled in the field by professional social workers. Female-male teams of social worker leaders guide mixed-sex groups of eight to twelve teenagers through fourteen 1-hour meetings. Leaders use audio and visual media, guest speakers, and Socratic exchanges to equip youths with facts about human reproduction and contraception (Schinke, in press-e; Tepper & Barnard, 1977). Cognitive problem solving follows Goldfried and Goldfried's (1980) schematic to assist youths in recognizing problems, deriving a variety of solutions to problems, and anticipating outcomes when solutions are exercised. Once they arrive at reasoned solutions about dating, sexual activity, and birth control, young group members practice and orchestrate decision implementation. Nonverbal and verbal communication is taught relative to problems and decisions. Broaching the topic of sex while on a date so requires getting the partner's attention, making eye contact, and stating the desire to discuss and resolve issues. A young man alone with his partner might look at her and say: "Marilynne, we've got to talk. We just can't keep going all the way without some kind of birth control. Neither of us wants you to get pregnant. I don't want to have sex again unless it's safe."

Communication skills to grapple with sexual topics are acquired via behavioral group methods (Feldman & Wodarski, 1975; Rose, 1977, 1980; Schinke, in press-b). Leaders demonstrate requisite physical gestures, body posture, facial expressions, affect, and verbal content. After youths model the skills for each other, they break into dyads and triads for role-play practice. Role play focuses and engages group members, facilitates vicarious learning, and allows them to rehearse applications of new knowledge and comportment. Throughout subgroup rehearsals leaders and youths provide feedback, reinforcement, and coaching to individual protagonists: "That's good, you're making eye contact. But don't mumble when you say words like 'going all the way' and 'birth control.' Keep it up, you're doing better!"

Group members planfully transfer rehearsed behavior to the natural environment (Wodarski, 1980). Written agreements detail problem situations, youths' desired responses, and ways to verify whether interactions came off as planned. One young man wanted to get hold of reliable birth control. He and his partner settled on condoms and spermicidal foam and decided he would pick them up within the week. Mission accomplished, he called in a report and brought his purchases to the next group. Every youthful group member ultimately realizes parallel achievements in the extragroup environment. Critical to this and any social change effort, the maintenance and generalization of learning are engineered by opportunities to identify problems, acquire adaptive skills, and successfully try them out (Schinke & Rose, 1976; Schinke & Wong, 1978).

RESULTS

Cognitive-behavioral group work to prevent unplanned pregnancy has been evaluated in two controlled studies. Study 1 was done with 30 primiparous teenage women enrolled in an inner-city vocational program. Study 2 took in 53 nulliparous young women and young men attending public school. With research designs and multimodal assessment these studies compared cohorts of adolescents who got cognitive-behavioral group training to youths in test-only control groups. Displayed in Table 1, at postintervention

TABLE 1

Percentage of correct responses on postintervention tests of adolescents' contraceptive knowledge, problem solving, and interpersonal communication

	Study 1		Study 2	
	Cognitive-behavioral groups ($n = 18$)	Control groups ($n = 22$)	Cognitive-behavioral groups ($n = 26$)	Control groups ($n = 27$)
Contraceptive knowledge	92%	63%	88%	54%
Problem solving	86	47	90	56
Interpersonal communication	82	52	89	48

youths in the former groups, more than those in the latter groups, had enhanced contraceptive knowledge, better problem solving, and greater interpersonal communication skills.

Follow-up data characterized longitudinal results of the primary prevention strategy. Six, nine, and twelve months after groups ended, trained teenagers were avoiding unwanted pregnancy. Table 2 juxtaposes youths randomly assigned to both kinds of groups in the two studies. Balanced

TABLE 2

Percentage of adolescents reporting pregnancy prevention activities and attitudes at six-, nine-, and twelve-month follow-up

	Study 1		Study 2	
	Cognitive-behavioral groups ($n = 18$)	Control groups ($n = 22$)	Cognitive-behavioral groups ($n = 26$)	Control groups ($n = 27$)
Six-month follow-up				
Incidences of unprotected intercourse	5%	23%	7%	31%
Habitual use of birth control	81	52	72	44
Positive attitudes toward family planning	96	78	88	72
Nine-month follow-up				
Incidences of unprotected intercourse	8	26	11	42
Habitual use of birth control	77	49	91	50
Positive attitudes toward family planning	93	76	93	84
Twelve-Month follow-up				
Incidences of unprotected intercourse	6	30	11	41
Habitual use of birth control	83	53	89	47
Positive attitudes toward family planning	95	80	97	91

against control groups, cognitive-behavioral prevention groups had fewer incidences of unprotected intercourse, greater habitual use of birth control, and more positive attitudes toward family planning.

Comments from adolescents, parents, and teachers manifested the subjective worth of group work prevention. Youths' anonymous comments on end-of-session questionnaires endorsed group process and content. Illustrative were, "This is good stuff!" "I like role playing." "Seeing other kids like me have problems is good." "Let's keep doing like we have to do on dates. I really can use it!" Participant feedback was mirrored in comments from parents. The mother of one young woman wrote, "I'm delighted with the results of the groups J— attends. She talks with me and her sister about things we never talked about before." Follow-up with teachers uncovered similar praise. The collective faculty from a participating school penned: "Thanks to you, our students are now able to communicate their concerns on a variety of subjects—not only sex, but lots of other important issues as well. Please accept our appreciation."

Discussion

Small group, cognitive-behavioral prevention of adolescent pregnancy has several advantages. Without question, the negative consequences of teenage pregnancy are best skirted by primary prevention (Gilchrist, Schinke, & Blythe, 1979). The group context enables professionals to reach significant numbers of young people. Treating sexual issues and pregnancy risk as normal in adolescence, social workers can introduce information and pertinent skills to all teenagers (Schinke, in press-a). Particular teenagers are not singled out as deviant or specially needing services (Schinke, in press-c). The group format and skills-acquisition methods offer teenagers chances to discuss heretofore taboo topics, find out from each other what is normative, and gradually learn how to deal with peers, family members, teachers, and a congeries of people who affect them (Schinke & Gilchrist, 1977).

As well as being logical, efficient, and nonjudgmental, cognitive-behavioral prevention is effective. Field evaluations with teenage parents and groups of young women and men who had not experienced pregnancy evidenced positive payoffs. Contrasted with young people in untrained control groups, adolescents in primary prevention groups gained knowledge, cognitive skills, and communication acumen. The longevity and impact of cognitive-behavioral group prevention was confirmed as trained youths reported improved attitudes toward family planning, greater regular contraception, and less unsafe sex at six-, nine-, and twelve-month follow-up. Consumer satisfaction from adolescents, parents, and teachers painted prevention groups as wise investments of time and resources. The heavy financial burdens of teenage childbearing and parenthood limn the cost effectiveness of primary prevention (Cox, Keith, Otten & Raymond, 1980).

Future endeavors must corroborate the prevention strategy's efficiency and efficacy. Of major benefit will be studies that use the present data to refine cognitive-behavioral prevention. Since two-fifths of adolescents who sexually debut at age 15 or younger never use contraception (Zabin, Kantner, & Zelnik, 1979), primary prevention ought to begin very early. Social workers committed to adolescent clients could expand group content to preventing cognate personal and social struggles—alcohol and drug abuse, delinquency, marital and family conflicts, parenting difficulties, and necessities of independent living, money management, and career achievement (Schinke, in press-d; Schinke & Olsen, in press). Practitioners employing cognitive-behavioral prevention with young people could ply factorial research designs to test variant group work methods. Such could isolate the relative effects of same-sexed groups vs. both-sexed ones, large vs. small groups, and whether groups profit from indigenous and peer leaders. In sum, perhaps these modest and auspicious experiences, data, and suggestions will urge social work colleagues to carry forth cognitive-behavioral group strategies for the primary prevention of adolescents' problems.

Reference Notes

1. Cvetkovich, G., & Grote, B. *Psychosocial development and the social problem of teenage illegitimacy.* Paper presented at the Conference on Determinants of Adolescent Pregnancy and Childbearing, Elkridge, Maryland, May 1976.

2. Mindick, B., Oskamp, S., & Berger, D.E. *Prediction of adolescent contraceptive practice.* Paper presented at the meeting of the American Psychological Association, Toronto, Canada, August 1978.

References

American Humane Association. *National analysis of official child neglect and abuse reporting: An executive summary.* Englewood, CO: Author, 1978.

Anastasiow, N.J., Everett, M., O'Shaughnessy, T.E., Eggleston, P. J., & Eklund, S.J. Improving teenage attitudes toward children, child handicaps, and hospital settings: A child development curriculum for potential parents. *American Journal of Orthopsychiatry*, 1978, 48, 663–672.

Baldwin, W.H. Adolescent pregnancy and childbearing—Growing concerns for Americans. *Population Bulletin*, 1980, 31(2), 1–37.

Baldwin, W., & Cain, V.S. The children of teenage parents. *Family Planning Perspectives*, 1980, 12, 34–43.

Belmont, L., Stein, Z., & Zybert, P. Child spacing and birth order: Effect on intellectual ability in two-child families. *Science*, 1978, 202, 995–996.

Bergofsky, R.E., Forgash, C.S., & Glassel, A.F. Establishing therapeutic groups with the families of spina bifida children in a hospital setting. *Social Work in Groups*, 1979, 2, 45–54.

Blythe, B.J., Gilchrist, L.D., & Schinke, S.P. Pregnancy-prevention groups for adolescents. *Social Work*, in press.

Bongaards, J. Does malnutrition affect fecundity? A summary of evidence. *Science*, 1980, 208, 564–569.

Bumpass, L.L., Rindfuss, R.R., & Janosik, R.B. Age and marital status at first birth and the pace of subsequent fertility. *Demography*, 1978, 15, 75–86.

Bureau of Labor Statistics, U.S. Department of Labor. *Employment and earnings: February 1980.* Washington, DC: U.S. Government Printing Office, 1980.

Card, J.J., & Wise, L.L. Teenage mothers and teenage fathers: The impact of early childbearing on the parents' personal and professional lives. *Family Planning Perspectives*, 1978, 10, 199–205.

Chilman, C.S. *Adolescent sexuality in a changing American society: Social and psychological perspectives.* Washington, DC: U.S. Government Printing Office, 1979.

Campbell, B.K., & Barnlund, D.C. Communication patterns and problems of pregnancy. *American Journal of Orthopsychiatry*, 1977, 47, 134–139.

Clapp, D.F., & Raab, R.S. Follow-up of unmarried adolescent mothers. *Social Work*, 1978, 23, 149–153.

Cox, S., Keith, J.G., Otten, G.L., & Raymond, F.B., III. Cost-effectiveness of primary and secondary prevention. *Health and Social Work*, 1980, 5, 56–60.

Cvetkovich, G., & Grote, B. Psychosocial maturity and teenage contraceptive use: An investigation of decision-making and communication skills. *Population and Environment*, in press.

Cvetkovich, G., Grote, B., Bjorseth, A., & Sarkissian, J. On the psychology of adolescents' use of contraceptives. *Journal of Sex Research* 1975, 11, 256–270.

Dembo, M.H., & Lundell, B. Factors affecting adolescent contraception practices: Implications of sex education. *Adolescence*, 1979, 14, 657–664.

Editorial, *Social Work with Groups*, 1978, 1, 3–5.

Evrard, J.R., & Gold, E.M. A one-year study of teenage pregnancy at Women and Infants Hospital of Rhode Island. *Journal of Reproductive Medicine*, 1978, 21, 95–101.

Feldman, R.A., & Wodarski, J.S. *Contemporary approaches to group treatment.* San Francisco: Jossey-Bass, 1975.

Forrest, J.D., Sullivan, E., & Tietze, C. Abortion in the United States, 1977–1978. *Family Planning Perspectives*, 1979, 11, 329–341.

Francome, C. Abortion policy in Britain and the United States. *Social Work.* 1980, 25, 5–9.

Furstenberg, F.F., Jr. *Unplanned parenthood: The social consequences of teenage childbearing.* New York: Free Press, 1976.

Furstenberg, F.F., Jr., Masnick, G., & Ricketts, S. How can family planning programs delay repeat teenage pregnancies? *Family Planning Perspectives*, 1972, 4, 54–60.

Gabrielson, I.W., Klerman, L.V., Currie, J.B., Tyler, N.C., & Jekel, J.F. Suicide attempts in a population pregnant at [sic] teenagers. *American Journal of Public Health*, 1970, 60, 2289–2301.

Galinsky, M.J., Schopler, J.H., Safier, E.J., & Gambrill, E.D. Assertion training for public welfare clients. *Social Work with Groups*, 1978, 1, 365–379.

Gilchrist, L.D., Schinke, S.P., & Blythe, B.J. Primary prevention services for children and youth. *Children and Youth Services Review*, 1979, 1, 379–391.

Goldfried, M.R., & Goldfried, A.P. Cognitive change methods. In F.H. Kanfer & A.P. Goldstein (Eds.), *Helping people change* (2nd ed.). New York: Pergamon, 1980.

Goldsmith, S., Gabrielson, M., & Gabrielson, I. Teenagers, sex and contraception. *Family Planning Perspectives*, 1972, 4, 32–38.

The Alan Guttmacher Institute. *Eleven million teenagers: What can be done about the epidemic of adolescent pregnancies in the United States.* New York: Planned Parenthood Federation of America, 1976.

Herrenkohl, E.C., & Herrenkohl, R.C. A comparison of abused children and their nonabused siblings. *Journal of American Academy of Child Psychiatry*, 1979, 18, 260–269.

Hertz, D.G. Psychosocial implications of adolescent pregnancy: Patterns of family interaction in adolescent mothers-to-be. *Psychosomatics*, 1977, 18, 13–16.

Hofferth, S.C., & Moore, K.A. Early childbearing and later economic well-being. *American Sociological Review*, 1979, 44, 784–815.

Hunt, W.B., Jr. Adolescent fertility: Risk and consequences. *Population Reports*, 1976, J, 157–176.

Jekel, J.F., Harrison, J.T., Bancroft, D.R.E., Tyler, N.C., & Klerman, L.V. A comparison of the health index and subsequent babies born to school-age mothers. *American Journal of Public Health*, 1975, 65, 370–374.

Koepsell, T.D., Weiss, N.S., Thompson, D.J., & Martin, D.P. Prevalence of prior hysterectomy in the Seattle-Tacoma area. *American Journal of Public Health*, 1980, 70, 40–47.

Little, V.L., & Kendall, P.C. Cognitive-behavioral interventions with delinquents; Problem solving, role-taking, and self-control. In P.C. Kendall & S.D. Hollon (Eds.), *Cognitive-behavioral interventions*. New York: Academic Press. 1979.

Marano, H. Can certain semen seed cervix Ca? *Hospital Tribune*, September 19, 1977, 11(5), 1:14

McCarnes, K., & Smith, L.L. Evaluating a children's group treatment program. *Social Work with Groups*, 1971, 2, 343–354.

Moore, K.A. Teenage childbirth and welfare dependency. *Family Planning Perspectives*, 1978, 10, 233–235.

Moore, K.A., & Waite, L.J. Early childbearing and educational attainment. *Family Planning Perspectives*, 1977, 9, 220–225.

National Center for Health Statistics, United States Public Health Services, DHEW. Wanted and unwanted childbearing in the United States, 1968, 1969, and 1972 National Natality Surveys. *Vital and Health Statistics*, 1978, Series 21, No. 32.

National Center for Health Statistics, United States Public Health Service, DHEW. Advance Report: Final natality statistics, 1977. *Monthly Vital Statistics Report*, 1979, 27(11), 1–27.

National Center for Health Statistics, United States Public Health Service, DHEW. *Health, United States, 1979.* Washington, DC: U.S. Government Printing Office, 1980.

Rose, S.D. *Group therapy: A behavioral approach.* Englewood Cliffs, NJ: Prentice-Hall, 1977.

Rose, S.D. *A casebook in group therapy: A behavioral-cognitive approach.* Englewood Cliffs, NJ: Prentice-Hall, 1980.

Schinke, S.P. Teenage pregnancy: The need for multiple casework services. *Social Casework,* 1978, 59, 406–410.

Schinke, S.P. Research on adolescent health: Social work implications. In W.T. Hall & C.Y. Young (Eds.), *Health and social needs of the adolescent: Professional responsibilities.* Pittsburgh: University of Pittsburgh Graduate School of Public Health, 1979.

Schinke, S.P. A school-based model for teenage pregnancy prevention. *Social Work in Education,* in press. (a)

Schinke, S.P. (Ed.). *Behavioral methods in social work: Helping children, adults, and families in community settings.* Hawthorne, NY: Aldine, in press. (b)

Schinke, S.P. Ethics. In R.M. Grinnell, Jr. (Ed.), *Social work research and evaluation.* Itasca, IL: F. E. Peacock, in press. (c)

Schinke, S.P. Interpersonal-skills training with adolescents. In M. Hersen, R. M. Eisler, & P. M. Miller (Eds.). *Progress in behavior modification* (Vol. 11). New York: Academic Press, in press. (d)

Schinke, S.P. Sexual counseling with adolescents. In C. S. Chilman, *Social and psychological aspects of adolescent sexuality.* New York: Wiley, in press. (e)

Schinke, S.P., Blythe, B.J., & Gilchrist, L.D. Cognitive-behavioral prevention of adolescent pregnancy. *Journal of Counseling Psychology,* in press.

Schinke, S.P., Blythe, B.J., Gilchrist, L.D., & Smith, T.S. Developing intake interviewing. *Social Work Research and Abstracts,* in press.

Schinke, S.P., & Gilchrist, L.D. Adolescent pregnancy: An interpersonal skill training approach to prevention. *Social Work in Health Care,* 1977, 3, 159–167.

Schinke, S.P., Gilchrist, L.D., & Blythe, B.J. Role of communication in the prevention of teenage pregnancy. *Health and Social Work,* 1980, 5(3), 54–59.

Schinke, S.P., Gilchrist, L.D., & Small, R.W. Preventing unwanted adolescent pregnancy: A cognitive-behavioral approach. *American Journal of Orthopsychiatry,* 1979, 49, 81–88.

Schinke, S.P., Gilchrist, L.D., Smith, T.E., & Wong, S.E. Improving teenage mothers' ability to compete for jobs. *Social Work Research and Abstracts,* 1978, 14(3), 25–29.

Schinke, S.P., Gilchrist, L.D., Smith, T.E., & Wong, S.E. Group interpersonal skills training in a natural setting: An experimental study. *Behavior Research and Therapy,* 1979, 17, 149–154.

Schinke, S.P., & Olson, D.G. Home-based remediation of subacute sclerosing panencephalitis. *Educational Treatment of Children,* in press.

Schinke, S.P., & Rose, S.D. Interpersonal skill training in groups. *Journal of Counseling Psychology,* 1976, 23, 442–448.

Schinke, S.P., Smith, T.E., Gilchrist, L.D., & Wong, S.E. Interviewing skills training: An empirical evaluation. *Journal of Social Service Research*, 1978, 1, 391–401.

Schinke, S.P., & Wong, S.E. Teaching child care workers: A behavioral approach. *Child Care Quarterly*, 1978, 7, 45–61.

Schafer, D., Pettigrew, A., Wolkind, S., & Zajicek, E. Psychiatric aspects of pregnancy in schoolgirls: A review. *Psychological Medicine*, 1978, 8, 119–130.

Sorensen, R. *Adolescent sexuality in contemporary America.* New York: World, 1973.

Tepper, S.S., & Barnard, G. *Choices.* Denver: Rocky Mountain Planned Parenthood, 1977.

Tietze, C. Teenage pregnancies: Looking ahead to 1984. *Family Planning Perspectives*, 1978, 10, 205–207.

Trussell, J., & Menken, J. Early childbearing and subsequent fertility. *Family Planning Perspectives*, 1978, 10, 209–218.

Urban and Rural Systems Associates. *Improving family planning services for teenagers.* Washington, DC: Office of the Assistant Secretary for Planning and Evaluation, DHEW, 1976.

Wayne, J.L. A group work model to reach isolated mothers: Preventing child abuse. *Social Work with Groups*, 1979, 1, 7–18.

Wodarski, J.S. Procedures for the maintenance and generalization of achieved behavioral change. *Journal of Sociology and Social Welfare*, 1980, 7, 298–311.

Zabin, L.S., Kantner, J.F., & Zelnik, M. The risk of adolescent pregnancy in the first months of intercourse. *Family Planning Perspectives*, 1979, 11, 215–222.

Zelnik, M., & Kantner, J.F. Sexual and contraceptive experience of young unmarried women in the United States, 1976 and 1971. *Family Planning Perspectives*, 1977, 9, 55–71.

Zelnik, M., & Kantner, J.F. Contraceptive patterns and premarital pregnancy among women aged 15–19 in 1976. *Family Planning Perspectives*, 1978, 10, 135–142. (a)

Zelnik, M., & Kantner, J.F. First pregnancies to women aged 15–19. 1976 and 1971. *Family Planning Perspectives*, 1978, 10, 11–20. (b)

Zelnik, M., & Kantner, J.F. Reasons for nonuse of contraception by sexually active women aged 15–19. *Family Planning Perspectives*, 1979, 11, 289–296.

Zelnick, M., & Kantner, J.F. Sexual activity, contraceptive use and pregnancy among metropolitan-area teenagers: 1976–1979. *Family Planning Perspectives*, 1980, 12, 230–237.

Zelnick, M., Kim, Y.J., & Kantner, J.F. Probabilities of intercourse and conception among U.S. teenage women, 1971 and 1976. *Family Planning Perspectives*, 1979, 11, 177–183.

Conclusion

· · · · ·

Lynn Videka-Sherman

I n this reader, four themes stand out as pertinent to understanding teen parenthood. These are:

   using a developmental perspective to understand teen pregnancy and its impact,

   the role of values in understanding and providing services to teen parents,

   the risks and needs of teen parenthood, and

   approaches to providing services to teens.

In this concluding chapter, we will consider each of these themes and develop their implications for providing sensitive and effective case management services to unwed parents.

A Developmental Perspective

We have come a long way from the view that teen pregnancy is a result of unconscious psychological determinants. We no longer believe that teen pregnancy is necessarily a product of the teen's psychic needs. Our view has become more pragmatic, focusing on the behaviors which lead to teen pregnancy and on the effects of teen pregnancy and parenthood on the lives of teens and their children. Most important is the realization that teen parents are still teens themselves and therefore have their own needs.

Adolescent development tasks include those that Freeman discusses:

   identity consolidation,

   successful separation from family-of-origin,

   peer relationships,

   heterosexual relationships, and

   work-role launching.

220

As Freeman and de Anda and Becerra point out, the juxtaposition of the "adult" parenting role with that of "teen" creates dilemmas for teens and complicates their mastery of these developmental tasks. The pregnancy and resulting child create a new role, that of parent, for teens who choose to keep their babies. This new role is frequently in conflict with the role of teen and can create identity conflicts. New demands are placed on the teen, leaving less time and energy for establishing and maintaining peer relationships and preparing for a career by attending to schooling or other vocational planning. Rather than leading to independence, parenting usually increases teens' dependence on their families of origin or on community support. Furstenburg and Crawford point out that family support is crucial if the teen mother is to stay in school and achieve a stable economic status.

This developmental perspective provides a useful framework for case managers to assess the needs of teen parents. The challenge for the people who are important to the teen parent, including case managers, is to provide assistance that allows the teen parent to meet her obligations as a parent, but to be a teen as well.

The Importance of Values

Personal and cultural values permeate the help and assistance available to teen parents. Values congruence between the case manager and the client is essential to providing effective services to teen parents and their families. Values imbue the status and experience of being a teen-aged parent with meaning. The teen, the baby's father, the teen's parents, and the case manager are all working in the context of the dominant societal values which Butts indicates are in conflict. While provocative sexual stimuli permeate the life-space of most teens through mass media, the overt societal message is that teens should not be sexually active, or at least not show evidence of their sexual activity through pregnancy. Another article cited in the Annotated Bibliography (Buccholz and Gol, 1986) illustrates how our society's pejorative view of teen parenthood colors our perceptions of and expectations for teen parents. These authors expand the view of teen parenthood by focusing on opportunities and positive status changes afforded by parenthood.

Cultural and family values of the teen may further complicate the values picture. Butts describes how procreative sexuality and the role of a parent are more highly valued by some blacks than by mainstream white society. Martinez describes the reverence with which the role of parenthood is held in most Hispanic cultures. He also notes, though, that many Hispanic cultures view out-of-wedlock pregnancies as shameful. Cultural reference group and family values systems are sometimes in conflict with the values of the dominant culture. It is important for the case manager to understand the values of the client, her family, and their cultural reference group. The case manager must decide whether a values conflict is operating and, if so, how to address it in order to provide services for the teen parent. Effective services cannot be provided if they are not congruent with the value system of the client and her family. Potential clients do not become engaged in the intervention process unless service goals are congruent with their values. This is a precondition to forming an effective contract with the teen client and her family.

The final piece in the values picture is the values of case managers. It is important for case managers to identify how they feel about teenage sexuality and whether their values are congruent with those of the teen parents and their families. In the case where there is a discrepancy or conflict in values, case managers must first of all manage their own feelings about the differences in values. It is then the case managers' task to find some "common ground" between themselves and the clients so that contracts for services can be mutually agreed upon. When there is conflict between the values of the teen parents and their parents, an important role for case managers is to help negotiate this conflict so that the teen parents can be best served. It is important to remember that the teen mother very much needs the help of her own parents and the baby's father if she is to adapt optimally to becoming a parent.

The Needs
of Teen Parents

For decades, teenage parenting has been defined as a social problem because of the many other problems associated with this status. These include poor educational outcomes for teen parents and their children, the increased risk that children of teen parents will be maltreated or otherwise developmentally disadvantaged, and a lifetime of poverty. The more recent research reflected in the essays by Furstenburg and Crawford, Barrett and Robinson, Robinson, Zuravin, Bolton and associates, and Kinard and Klerman indicates that teen parenthood does not unequivocally doom the parent and her offspring to a lifetime of difficulties. There are several factors that mitigate this relationship. These findings are of the utmost importance to case managers because they directly suggest resources that "make the difference" in successful outcomes for teen parents. These mitigating factors include:

the concrete assistance and emotional support of the teen's own family,

the instrumental and emotional support that can be provided by the teen father,

other life stresses which influence quality of parenting, and

education for teen parents which plays a central role in equipping them to avoid the most damaging life stresses of unemployment, large numbers of children, and poverty.

FAMILIES AS A RESOURCE

There are several implications of these findings for case managers. Case managers should see family support as the teen's biggest potential resource, far surpassing the importance of professional services. Case managers must be careful not to restrict their view of resources to agency-based services when developing a service plan. Whenever possible, case managers should look first to the client and her own informal social network (family and friends) in providing resources to meet her needs. The teen's family should be involved extensively in planning and carrying out service plans with the teen. Conflicts between the teens and their families should be negotiated by case managers so that the families can act as resources for the teen parents. Families may need extra supports themselves so that they can provide support to their teens. Case managers should be aware that those teens who do not have family support available to them for whatever the reason are particularly vulnerable to the ill effects of teen parenting. They need access to high quality child care, educational and vocational training, and emotional support for themselves to cope with the multiple demands placed on them as teen parents.

THE ROLE FOR TEEN FATHERS

Fathers of the children of teen mothers, many but not all of them teens themselves, have long had an ambiguous role in providing help to teen mothers. Two essays (Robinson and Barrett and Robinson) show that two-thirds to three-quarters remain involved with the teen mother and their offspring after the child is born, although the prospects for a long-term relationship between teen parents is dim. Teen fathers provide instrumental supports to the teen mother in the form of money, gifts, and transportation. They also provide emotional support. However, they have been largely ignored by agencies serving teen mothers and are often scorned by the teen's own family.

Teen fathers also need help with their own educations and job preparations. Because they have little understanding of child development or the parenting role, they have unrealistic expectations for the children and parenthood. Bank Street College has developed an effective program to serve the needs of teen fathers. They focus on teen fathers' opinions of their most pressing needs—education and vocational training. This program also provides education on child development and parenting. Even if services especially designed for teen fathers are not available locally, case managers should see teen fathers as a resource for teen mothers if the teen mother desires the relationship to continue. In order to be maximally supportive to the teen mother, teen fathers need training in parenting skills and infant development.

Reducing Life Stresses for Teen Parents

Most broadly stated, the most important function of services to teen parents is to prevent or reduce stresses. Thus, teen parents can function optimally in their dual roles as adolescents and parents. The single most important service that reduces the likelihood of future life stresses is education. Enabling the teen to stay in school is crucial to preventing negative sequelae leading to poverty. Staying in school is often difficult to achieve. Time management and planning are necessary in order to enable the teen to fulfill both parenting and school role requirements. Child care that is accessible and trusted is prerequisite to the teen's returning to or remaining in school. Quality day care has also been shown to enhance children's development. This is an important service, since children of teen parents are considered at risk for developmental delays. Of utmost importance is clear and explicit agreement between the teen mother and others she relies on to provide child care (her own parents, the teen father, extended family, and neighbors) concerning who is responsible for what aspects of child care and when.

When the teen parent is not motivated to return to traditional school, the problem is more complex. Careful assessment is necessary in order to learn about the teen's educational and vocational history and goals. Academic and career options may not be obvious to the teen who has a history of academic difficulty and few role models for vocational success. It is important for the case manager to make sure that the teen parent is aware of the vocational and educational options available to her.

A number of essays in this reader also outline services that enable teens to deal with stresses in their lives and to assume an active, in-control orientation toward their lives. These programs are exemplified in the essays by Meares, Schinke and associates, Schinke and Brindis and associates, and Doty and King. The programs vary in many respects, but contain a common core of service philosophy and components. They are all geared to reducing stresses in the teen parents' lives. Their common components include:

> access to health care,
>
> parental skills training,
>
> life skills training, including decision-making and problem-solving skills training, along with communication and assertiveness skill training, and
>
> assistance in providing for instrumental needs for the teen and her child, including money, shelter, clothing, food, and furniture.

HEALTH CARE

Health care includes prenatal care, post-partum and family planning care, well-baby care, and basic health knowledge so that the mother carries out good health practices during her pregnancy and knows what to look for in terms of common childhood illnesses such as infant diarrhea and middle ear infections. It is an important role of the case manager to make sure that the teen parent obtains health care and health knowledge. Brindis and associates found that most case managers lacked health education training. If there are few health education resources available to the teen mother, it is important for the case manager to have basic knowledge about reproductive health and child health so that she can be a resource to the teen mother. This information can be obtained from a health text written for the lay public, such as the Columbia University Physician's Guide to Health Care, or from consultation with health care professionals. Case managers should develop these working relationships in the community broker role.

PARENTING SKILLS

Several studies have documented deficient parenting skills and resulting inappropriate expectations regarding parenting and child behavior and development. This skill deficit may lead to child maltreatment, whether intentional or unintentional. One of the most important preventive services that case managers can provide to teen parents is an opportunity to develop appropriate parenting skills. These skills protect children and provide parents with resources to meet the demands of parenting.

LIFE SKILLS

Life skills training is important because it gives a clear message to teen parents that they can make decisions and gain control over their lives. Life skills empower teen parents and give them an opportunity to take an active, in-charge stance toward their lives. This attitude can affect many decisions, including whether and when to have another child, planning to reach educational and vocational goals, and managing interpersonal relationships. Finally, none of the above can be accomplished if the teen parent's basic needs of food, shelter, clothing, and security cannot be met.

Final Thoughts on the Case Manager's Role

This reader provides several perspectives on programs and intervention for teen parents. We will conclude with a summary of the central features of the role of case manager for teen parents.

Case management involves the dual role of counselor and broker. While counseling is not the sole role of the case manager, counseling proves indispensable in helping clients to actually obtain help from formal and informal sources. It is the case manager's responsibility to know what services are available to the teen and her family. This involves establishing good working relationships with other service providers in the community and with important members of the client's social network.

Effective case management uses short-term, goal-oriented approaches to service. Contracts are necessary in order to confirm the commitment of all parties to work toward explicit service goals. The contracting process will usually reveal values incongruence or different views of the problem by clients and case managers.

Case managers must consider informal (family and friends) as well as formal (agency) resources in meeting clients' needs. Serious consideration of informal sources of help usually leads the case manager to work with family members and, in some cases, friends of the teen parent.

Finally, case managers should constantly be aware of the enormous potential of their preventive role in working with teen parents. Recent research, some of which is included in this reader, has indicated that life stresses make the difference between good and poor outcomes for teen parents and their children. Much of the case manager's work impacts directly on the life stresses experienced by the teen parent. The important long-term benefits of avoiding stresses such as lack of education and of finding resources such as child care to reduce the stress of parenting while being a student constitute an important contribution that case managers make to the lives of their teen parent clients.

Annotated Bibliography

. . . . .

Overview

Teenage pregnancy is a great national concern. About one million teenagers become pregnant each year. Approximately half of these pregnancies are aborted or miscarried, while the other half are carried to term. Scholars estimate that 85 to 90 percent of all teenagers decide to keep their children rather than relinquish them for adoption. The reasons for teenage pregnancy are myriad. The interconnecting links of adolescent development, human sexuality, cultural norms, family dynamics, and socioeconomic issues influence the outcome of teenage pregnancy. How can we understand the complex problems of pregnancy, adolescence, family needs, educational-vocational issues, parenting skills, economic independence, and cultural norms and be helpful to our clients?

This annotated bibliography's purpose is to give the reader a capsule version of the salient articles about adolescent pregnancy. Each article was selected on the merits of its information and general relevance.

Bolton, F.G. (1980). *The Pregnant Adolescent* (Vol. 100). Beverly Hills, Calif.: Sage Publications.

This book is a reader which reviews all the various aspects of teenage pregnancy and parenting. The author summarizes a number of other researchers' main viewpoints.

Buchholz, & E.S., Gol, B. (1986). More than playing house: A developmental perspective on the strengths in teenage motherhood. *American Journal of Orthopsychiatry, 56*(3), 347–359.

The authors review a number of studies in the medical, psychological, sociological, and family literatures. Their intent is to inform the reader about the potential strengths that can be developed during a teenage pregnancy and childbearing. Their viewpoint is stimulating, especially since the literature usually focuses upon the negative effects. Reading the article will help practitioners and case managers bolster their own spirits when faced with a difficult case and case load. The article can help one to focus upon a balanced picture in helping pregnant teenagers.

Chilman, C.A. (1983). *Adolescent sexuality in a changing American society* (2nd. ed.). New York: John Wiley and Sons.

The first ten chapters provide the reader with a basic knowledge of adolescent sexuality, dating, birth control, abortion, teen childbearing, adolescent parenthood, teenage marriage, and a biopsychosocial viewpoint of adolescent development. The material is a synthesis of Dr. Chilman's work with the National Institute of Health, Education, and Welfare. Chapters 11 through 16 include specific articles on service and intervention strategies with teenagers. Topics include contraception, human sexuality education, and public policy. The use of case illustrations is very helpful to the reader.

Freeman, E.M. (1987). Interaction of pregnancy, loss, and developmental issues in adolescents. *Social Casework, 68*, 38–46.

The author explores the losses and needs of an adolescent pregnant parent. By integrating the tasks of adolescent development and the grief work processes, the article integrates a crisis intervention perspective with teenage development. The article's point of view helps the reader to recognize that adolescents may be experiencing pain that they are unable or unwilling to acknowledge or verbalize.

Furstenberg, F.F. (1976). *Unplanned parenthood.* New York: The Free Press.

————. (1976). The social consequences of teenage parenthood. *Family Planning Perspective, 8*, 148–164

Frank Furstenberg is a renowned sociologist who has studied the social implications of teenage childbearing. His book is a longitudinal study of the effects of adolescent parenthood on the lives of young women. The book is readable, and the journal article summarizes his thoughts and findings. Both works emphasize the significant support a teenager must have in order to finish her education and have vocational opportunity. The works demonstrate that providing aid at the beginning of the pregnancy process through the early child-bearing years may break the cycle of a "culture of poverty" for the individual and society. Both works maintain that the pregnancy is not consciously or deliberately sought out in the large majority of client situations. Those youngsters having children were found to have financial problems, school disruption, marital instability, and family planning difficulties.

McGoldrick, M., & Carter, E.A. (Eds). (1980). *Family life cycle: A framework for family therapy.* New York: Gardener Press.

This book presents an overview of the family life cycle perspective. The chapters which discuss adolescence and single parenting are summations of the tasks of families with teenagers or of single parents. Review of the chapters may help the reader to think through and add some knowledge about family transitions and development.

Phipps-Yonas, S. (1980). Teenage pregnancy and motherhood: A review of the literature, *American Journal of Orthopsychiatry, 50*(3), 402–431

Plionis, B.M. (1975). Adolescent pregnancy—Review of the literature. *Social Work,* 20, 302–327.

Although the articles present materials written from the early to late 1970s, the concepts presented have not drastically changed. The messages offered in the article are that teenage pregnancy is a complex issue involving multiple causes. The intervention process must be broad-based. Plionis and Phipps-Yonas review the human development, medical, psychological, sociological, and social policy literature in order to inspire the reader to have a broad and deep viewpoint concerning the problem.

Zelnick, M., Kantner, J.F., & Ford, K. (1981). *Sex and pregnancy in adolescence* (Vol. 133). Beverly Hills, Calif.: Sage Publications.

Zelnick and Kantner have collaborated on a book after many years of independent research that produced many journal articles. This book incorporates the work of Kathleen Ford. The authors address the myriad complexities of teenage sexuality and childbearing. The authors integrate their findings about contraception and premarital pregnancy with informative material on family background, the costs to society and the teenager, and the social consequences of pregnancy.

Adolescent Fathers

Literature about the teenage father's role in decisions about sexual relations, dating, contraception, child rearing, and adoption is very stereotyped. Authors, researchers, and service program providers often describe adolescent fathers as apathetic, irresponsible, immature, and unreliable. However, there is evidence that with support, teenage fathers can provide their children with emotional and sometimes financial assistance.

Barret, R.L., & Robinson, B.E. (1982). Teenage fathers: Neglected too long. *Social Work,* 6, 484–488.

This article reviews the literature on teenage fatherhood. Although little has been written on the subject, the authors state that social services can help male adolescents cope with their responsibilities as parents. The article provides the practitioner with useful information on dealing with teenage fathers.

———. (1982). A descriptive study of teenage expectant fathers. *Family Relations, 31,* 349–352

The authors report results of a questionnaire they gave to 114 fathers-to-be in the 16 to 20 age range. The sample return rate was 26%, or 30 returns out of 114 distributed questionnaires. The majority of respondents were black males whose average age was 19. The authors state that, based on this small sample, the subjects had positive relationships with the mother and her family. Male respondents also met some parenting obligations. The article's most noteworthy point is that teenage parents can support each other during a turbulent period.

Butts, J.D. (1981). Adolescent sexuality and teenage pregnancy from a black perspective. In Ooms (Ed.), *Teenage Pregnancy in a Family Context* (pp. 307–325). Philadelphia: Temple University Press.

The author reviews the historical, social, medical, and public policy implications of black teenage pregnancy within the context of a mostly white society. The public policy of separating pregnant teenagers from their families is myopic, and, in early independence, it promotes poverty. The author also states that teenaged parents have a perception of a dim future. She proposes several areas of intervention.

Elster, A.B., & Lamb, M.E. (1986). Adolescent fathers: The understudied side of adolescent pregnancy. In J.B. Lancaster and B.A. Hamburg (Eds.), *School-Age Pregnancy and Parenthood* (p. 177–190). New York: Aldine De Gruyter.

The article addresses a main issue: the needs of teenage fathers and promotion of father-child interaction and bonding. Teenage fathers' developmental needs conflict when adolescence and parenting combine. Reasons to include the father in his companion's pregnancy are to aid in the pregnancy-obstetrics process and to help with decisions regarding his relationship to the mother and baby. The authors states that enhancing a teenage father's relationship with the mother and baby can be a source of support and communication and aid in defining the relationship. A caseworker, too, can better understand a young man's emotional, vocational, educational, and parental needs and desires. An expanded version of these issues and service delivery to teenage fathers is also in M.E. Lamb and A.B. Elster (Eds.), *Adolescent fatherhood.* (Hillsdale, New Jersey: L. Erlbaum Assoc., 1986.)

Robinson, B.E., & Barret, R.L. (1985). Teenage fathers, *Psychology Today, 19,* 66–70.

The authors have written a succinct overview of teenage fathers. Teenage fathers want emotional bonding with their babies, and they have a need to be involved in the pregnancy, birthing process, and decision making for the baby. Negative attitudes of the mother's family toward the father, a male's guilt and responsibility about precocious sexuality, and the conflict of interest between needing independence and having responsibility of a baby must be worked on during the pregnancy.

Shapiro, J.L. (1987). The expectant father. *Psychology Today, 21,* 36–42.

The author briefly outlines numerous concerns men have about pregnancy. Although the research dealt with married men, the author's findings, adjusted for an adolescent context, can be applied to intervention with unwed men. Topics include men's perspectives on gestation, reproduction, labor, delivery, and obstetrics care; uncertainty about increased financial and emotional responsibility; feelings of loss when the mother's attention is diverted by children; and fear of being replaced by a rival. The article makes the important point that men need to accept their fears, concerns, and feelings and to have them accepted by significant others. Discussing their needs and worries can help deepen their relationships with their mates and children.

Westncy, O.E., Cole, O.J., & Munford, T.L. (1986). Adolescent unwed prospective fathers: Readiness for fatherhood and behavior towards the mother and the expected infant. *Adolescence, 21*(84), 901–911.

This article reports on a survey of 28 unmarried teenage fathers. The data suggests that a number of teenage fathers-to-be are unprepared for the responsibility of parenthood. Although a number of young men reported that they contribute financially to their children's support, many said they are unwilling or unable to be emotionally supportive to their female companion. The data suggest that males may be unable to be responsible; the article proposes outreach to adolescent fathers, based on the authors' findings.

Contraception

This section reviews articles that discuss birth control and teenagers. Included are the family's role in discussing human sexuality with children, the role of the school in providing access to information on human sexuality, the complex biological and cognitive processes at work during puberty and adolescence, and the ethical-moral societal dilemmas of giving teen-agers the dual message, "Do your own thing' sexually but don't get caught."

Chilman, C. (1983). *Adolescent sexuality in a changing American society*, (3rd. ed.). New York: John Wiley and Sons.

This book provides well-founded, interesting, and readable information on the complexities of adolescent sexuality in modern American society. Chapters 1 to 8 cover the interlocking biological, family, social, and psychological interactions among adolescent development, sexuality, and conception. The book takes a humanistic approach toward adolescents and their families. Both research and social-work practice issues are included. In Chapters 12 to 14 the book's focus is on education, counseling, and birth control measures.

Dryfoos, J. (1985). School-based health clinics: A new approach to preventing adolescent pregnancy? *Family Planning Perspectives, 17*(2), 70–75.

Family planning clinics that serve junior and senior high schools are the topic of this article. The author explains that cooperation between employees of these clinics (nurses, aides, social workers) and school officials, principals, teachers, and the community is important in maintaining the health service, as well as gaining approval and support.

Furstenberg, F., Herceg-Baron, R., Shea, J., & Webb, D. (1986). Family communication and contraceptive use among sexually active adolescents. In J.B. Lancaster and B.A. Hamburg (Eds.), *School-Age Pregnancy and Parenthood* (pp. 219–243). New York: Aldine DeGruyter.

The authors review the literature and investigate the premise that family planning programs must involve parents in decisions about birth control information and contraceptive distribution. However, the authors contend that mandated involvement and reporting is a programmatic nightmare. They state that improved family communication does not always improve teenage contraceptive use. A flexible programmatic approach must be taken to involve parents in the process. Providing parents and teenagers with accurate information will also help adolescents become responsible adults.

Furstenberg, F. (1971). Birth control experience among pregnant adolescents: The process of unplanned parenthood, *Family Planning Perspectives, 19,* 192–203.

The author, in this early study, cautiously suggests that unplanned pregnancy is a result of a family conspiracy of silence about sexual behavior and values. Parents and children are reluctant to openly discuss sexuality and the precautions that need to be taken in order to avoid becoming pregnant. Furstenberg states that teenage pregnancy is usually unanticipated. He adds that in families where the mother and child have a positive relationship, she can be helped to openly discuss dating and sex with her child.

Johnson, R.L. (1986). Preventing adolescent pregnancy: Meeting the comprehensive range of needs. *Journal of Community Health, 11*(1), 35–40.

The author provides a very good argument that a teenager's biopsychosocial developmental stages must be taken into account in making decisions about birth control measures. The author describes three distinct teenage developmental periods in adolescence (early, mid and late) and outlines human sexuality and family planning for each phase.

Schinke, S.P., Blythe, B.J., & Gilchrist, L.D. (1981). Primary prevention of adolescent pregnancy. *Social Work With Groups, 4*(1,2), 121–134.

This article provides a practical guide for social workers' intervention with teenagers who are at high risk of becoming pregnant. A cognitive behavioral group approach is discussed that incorporates facts about human sexuality, decision making, and dating skills. This approach can help social workers apply an intervention strategy that can be useful for parenting and pregnant teens.

———. (1981). Cognitive behavioral prevention of adolescent pregnancy. *Journal of Counseling Psychology, 5,* 451–454.

This article maintains that teenagers' failures in contraception use are associated with cognitive and behavioral styles. The authors demonstrated through an experimental group design that teenagers can be taught effective contraception, problem solving, communication, and decision-making about sexual behavior. High school sophomores who were taught how to make decisions were practicing effective family planning and solving dating problems.

Schinke, S.P., Gilchrist, L.D., & Small, R.W. (1979). Preventing unwanted adolescent pregnancy: A cognitive-behavioral approach. *American Journal of Orthopsychiatry, 49*(1), 81– 88.

This journal article outlines a cognitive behavioral approach to educate teenagers about choices in sexuality. The article's theme is that teenagers lack information about human sexuality and family planning. The authors say appropriate choices are made in dating behaviors and sexuality only when a teen possesses the following: *1)* adequate information on contraception and reproduction, *2)* adequate perception, memory, and comprehension about birth control and human sexuality, *3)* the ability to think through personal choices, and *4)* the ability to act on appropriate information and to perceive consequences.

Cultural Issues
(See also Family Support)

Pregnancy cannot always be viewed as an interruption in career, vocation, or education or as social malady. Career aspirations may not be the norm in some working class families and depressed communities. In some cases, child bearing may be an attempt at growing up, an available means of becoming economically independent, a means of self-expression toward adult roles, and/or a means to strengthen family bonds. Each family situation may be different and need not be interpreted from a middle-class values framework.

Becerra, R.M., & de Anda, D. (1904). Pregnancy and motherhood among Mexican American adolescents. *Health and Social Work, 9*(2), 106–123.

This study compared three groups of 13- to 20-year olds participating in a supplemental food program for mothers and children in Los Angeles, California: one white, one English- speaking Mexican American, and one Spanish-speaking Mexican- American. The groups differed on birth control, reproduction, and teenage pregnancy according to ethnic values and acculturation levels rather than age levels. The authors conclude that birth control and pre- and post-natal interventions must take into account the level of acculturation into society in order to be effective.

de Anda, D., & Becerra, R. (1984). Support networks for adolescent mothers. *Social Casework, 65*, 172–181.

The authors contrasted Hispanic-speaking Mexican-Americans, English-speaking Mexican-Americans, and white teenage mothers for sources of support within their social network. They found that there was considerable potential and actual support in their subjects' interpersonal networks. The primary assets in the interpersonal environment for the English-speaking Mexican-Americans and the white adolescents were the young women's mothers. The girls' mothers were helpful emotionally and practically after the birth of the child. The non-English speaking Mexican-Americans were emotionally close to their mothers, but their families of origin lived at a great distance. Boyfriends, husbands, and siblings were also found to be helpful; the least help-ful were the young women's natural fathers. Any intervention plan needs to incorporate the positive strengths within the teenager's social system. The au-thors postulate that building upon the positive areas will reduce conflicts and enhance mother-infant adjustment.

Gabriel, A., & McAnarney, E.R. (1983). Parenthood in two subcultures: White middle-class couples and black low-income adolescents in Rochester, New York, *Adolescence, 71,* 679–694.

The authors chose to study two groups in Rochester, N.Y.: black low-income teenagers and white middle-class couples. In the white group, teenage preg-nancy was seen as detrimental to achieving future goals; the black teenage girls saw motherhood and its responsibilities as a pathway to adulthood. The black adolescent teenagers said that they did not see marriage, completion of schooling, or economic independence as phases that must be completed before parenthood. Black teenagers did not view motherhood negatively, but thought it would help them achieve maturity and acceptance as adults. The blacks' viewpoint was found to be based on their perception that they lacked alternative adult roles; white couples, in contrast, saw other future opportuni-ties and possibilities.

Goodwin, N.J. (Ed.). (1986). Black adolescent pregnancy: Prevention and man-agement. *Journal of Community Health, 11,* 5–74.

This journal report is a special edition that covers a number of issues related to pregnant black adolescents. The journal reviews a number of points: pre-vention, obstetrical care, education needs, dealing with the adolescent male, and the politics of pregnancy. All articles are related to the black experience in New York State. Each article contains a practical and a general overview of trends in black adolescent pregnancy. This special edition is worth the effort of being read in its entirety.

Held, L. (1981). Self-esteem and social network of the young pregnant teenager. *Adolescence, 64,* 905–912.

Although some investigators in the field have argued that teenage pregnancy results in low self-esteem, this author's findings yield a contrasting opinion. In comparing black, white, and Mexican-Americans through the Coopersmith Self Esteem Inventory Personality Test, the author found that the black teenag-ers scored highest among the three groups. The author found that parenthood may be viewed as a source of self-esteem rather than a drain on identity and achievement. The author notes that the discrepancies in testing scores may be based on the values of the teenagers' subcultures.

Martinez, A.L. (1981). The impact of adolescent pregnancy on Hispanic adoles-cents and their families. T. Ooms (Ed.). *Teenage Pregnancy in a Family Context* (pp. 326–345). Philadelphia: Temple University Press.

The author outlines the significant cultural family issues within Spanish-speaking minorities. Hispanic teenagers are seen as being caught between two cultures: traditional Spanish values and typical American here-and-now attitudes. Hispanic culture is dependent upon intergenerational living, as opposed to white society, which is centered on a nuclear family. Role models, family norms, and the meaning of family are much different in Hispanic than in white society. Therefore, findings from white adolescents' pregnancy experiences cannot be directly applied to Hispanics. Educational, career, and economic opportunities, cultural behaviors, and the impact of the Roman Catholic Church on contraception, to name a few issues, must be thought through before applying an intervention strategy to the pregnant Hispanic pregnant adolescent. This is a very comprehensive and succinct article.

Adoption

Approximately 85 percent of babies born to teenage mothers are kept by their mothers rather than given up for adoption. Birth control, abortion, and married couples who postpone having children have also restricted the number of healthy infants available for adoption. Psychological reasons have been cited for mothers to keep a child. In addition, cultural factors play a part in a decision to raise a child. Why decide to release a child for adoption when the baby could languish in a foster home indefinitely? Why surrender a child when it is a part of a family and cultural heritage? Why surrender a child when the baby is a part of you?

Barth, R.P. (1987). Adolescent mothers' beliefs about open adoption. *Social Case-work, 68,* 323–331.

This article explores reasons why women choose adoption versus rearing a child and reviews literature on the topic. One common thread is the expectation that adolescents who choose adoption will wonder about their child in the future. This uncertainty over the child's well-being suggests that open adoption—where the biologic mother is allowed to have ongoing contact with the child—may appeal to young mothers. Surrendering may be influenced by the youthful here-and-now, rather than future orientation. The author also concludes that many maternity-health programs infrequently discuss the open adoption option.

Churchill, S.R., Carlson, B., & Nybell, L. (Eds.). (1979). *No child is unadoptable* (Vol. 8). Beverly Hills, CA: Sage Human Services Guides.

This book offers the reader a number of journal articles on adoption, foster care, children with special needs, and program innovations. Especially relevant are chapters that discuss the needs of adoptable black children. Chapters 3 and 17 cover ways agencies can reach out to the black community to help promote minority adoptions. The book also discusses the needs of older children who are being adopted and the needs of single persons who adopt.

Grow, L. (1979). Today's unmarried mothers: The choices have changed. *Child Welfare, 58,* 363–371.

This article reviews earlier research and explores the reasons why adolescents keep their children. Young women who keep their children are younger, receive emotional support from their family, and have maintained contact with the baby's father. The influence of having been raised in a one-parent home in the midst of current changing views on alternative family life and marriage was seen as another reason unmarried mothers might want to keep their babies.

Leynes, C. (1980). Keep or adopt: A study of factors influencing pregnant adolescents' plans for their babies. *Child Psychiatry and Human Development, 11*(2), 105–112.

This study examines why young women decide to keep or relinquish a baby for adoption. The research reflected the notions that psychological stability and maturity were the two main factors adolescent childbearers considered in deciding to relinquish a child. Socioeconomic status and fathers' attitudes were also influential in the decision. Young women who had unrewarding relationships with their parents and saw children as filling a void tended to keep their babies. Adolescents who give their babies up for an adoption undergo a psychological upheaval and a deep grieving process. The feelings of sadness, guilt, and anger continue to influence the mother for some time. The author found that supporting the mother's decision to surrender is very helpful in the resolution of that grieving process.

Musick, J.S., Handler, A., & Waddill, K.D. (1984). Teens and adoption: A pregnancy resolution alternative? *Children Today, 13*(6), 24–29.

This article reviews reasons adolescent mothers do not place their children for adoption. The authors found that adolescents have erroneous beliefs about adoption and that agencies may tend to support their keeping a child rather than exploring the adoption alternative. The Ounce of Prevention Fund helps service providers and adolescents understand adoption as an alternative to raising a child.

Resnick, M.D. (1984). Studying adolescent mothers' decision making about adoption and parenting. *Social Work, 29*(1), 5–10.

The author reviews the literature on reasons adolescents choose to keep or place a child for adoption. He found that past studies have resulted in the perception that unwed pregnant adolescents and mothers are socially deviant or emotionally maladjusted. He criticizes these studies as outdated. The author strongly suggests that young adolescents are not focused on the future and so do not realize the consequences and implications of their decisions. He also suggests that developmental and sociocultural issues should be included in studies dealing with attitudes toward adoption.

Sisto, G.W. (1985). Therapeutic foster homes for teenage mothers and their babies. *Child Welfare, 64*(2), 157–163.

This article discusses a child welfare program that provides foster homes for unwed teenage mothers and their infants. Mothers are provided with emotional support, child care, education, guidance in self-sufficiency, and infant-care help. The program also evaluates the risk of child abuse and neglect and provides follow-up day care help for the baby once the mother and infant have left the foster home.

Education

Completion of high school is a key indicator of future economic and vocational rewards. Too often, a pregnant teen faces difficult choices: completion of school or rearing a child. There are school programs that enable a teenager to complete her education and parent. A key to supporting teenage parents is to help school districts provide innovative programs that enable teenage parents to complete high school and vocational training.

Campbell, F.A., Breitmayer, B.J., & Ramez, C.T. (1986). Disadvantaged single teenage mothers and their children: Consequences of free educational day care. Special issue: The single-parent family. *Family Relations, 35*(1), 63–68.

The authors discuss the outcome of their four and one-half year longitudinal study, in which single teenage mothers were divided into two groups: fourteen mothers and their children received free day care help, and fifteen mothers and their children were placed in a control group. Children in the free day care setting were found to be intellectually ahead of those receiving no day care. Also, the mothers who received day care help were found to be more likely to complete high school, obtain vocational training after graduation, and support themselves financially. The public policy implications of the results of the study are also discussed.

Doty, M.B. (1985). Pregnancy prevention: A private agency's program in public schools. *Social Work in Education, 7*(2), 90–99.

The City School District of New York and a social work agency collaborated on a coeducational teenage program aimed at pregnancy prevention. The article describes these cooperative efforts: teens received information on human sexuality, reproduction, and family planning from social work graduate students and part-time social workers in individual, group, and psycho-educational programs. Networking among the school district and community health resources improved the quality of intervention. The article provides information on how to help nonprofit social work agencies operate within a public school setting.

Flood, M.F., Greenspan, S., & Mundorf, N.K. (1985). School- based services for pregnant and parenting adolescents. *Special Services in the Schools, 2*(1), 27–44.

A literature review of school-based programs is the central focus of this article. The authors describe five services which they view as necessary in school-based programs: case management/counseling, school-based day care, family planning information/dissemination of contraception, values clarification, and parenting skills. They provide information on how pupil-services personnel can carry out the plan and how school districts can implement the programs.

Klein, L. (1975). Models of comprehensive services: Regular school-based. *Journal of School Health, 5,* 271–273.

Although the article is nearly 15 years old, the points made in it are noteworthy. The author describes the administrative excuses that are made to justify asking pregnant students to leave school. Through a school program example, the author reviews a number of reasons to keep pregnant students in school and the means to ensure that they complete school.

McAfee, M.L., & Geesey, M.R. (1984). Meeting the needs of the teenage pregnant student: An in-school program that works. *Journal of School Health, 9,* 350–352.

This paper reports on a York, Pa. school program, "Changing Roles," which was designed to keep pregnant teens in school. The school district found that its truancy and drop-out rates have been significantly reduced. Pregnant girls receive traditional schooling as well as medical and parenting education. This intensive program provides the teen with the necessary support to continue her education.

Meares, P. (1979). An in-school program for adolescent parents: Implications for social work practice and multi-disciplinary teaming. *School Social Work Journal, 3*(2), 66–77.

The author describes an interdisciplinary school personnel approach to help teenagers cope with the dual role of parent and pupil. Classes are taught by a multidisciplinary team that meets periodically to assess educational goals and parenting achievement. The article indicates that if a school district provides appropriate programming, teenage parents can achieve both as students and as parents.

Family Support
(See also Cultural Issues)

During a pregnancy, support is needed to help a woman cope with the profound biological, psychological, and social changes that take place. An adolescent who is pregnant or a parent usually needs some assistance. Ordinarily, families undergoing any transition experience profound changes. How can families be helpful and also be helped? Does pregnancy exacerbate underlying family strain, create strain, or both?

Bernstein, R. (1965). Are we still stereotyping the unmarried mother? In H. Parad (Ed.), *Crisis Intervention: Selected Readings* (pp. 100–110). New York: Family Service Association of America.

During the 1960s, Rose Bernstein wrote several articles on teenage pregnancy. This article reviews her clinical knowledge about adolescent pregnancy. Salient points about a family-service worker's judgmental attitude, making plans for a baby, feelings during pregnancy, and single causality are reviewed. Her article also points out the need for family and individual assessment of strength and weaknesses and for exploring the meaning of the pregnancy to family members before launching into a treatment process.

Colletta, N.D., Hadler, S., & Gregg, C.H. (1981). Early motherhood, *Adolescence, 16,* 499–512.

The authors' study measured coping responses of teenage mothers. Their findings showed that adolescents cope by asking significant others for support. Task-oriented problems (e.g., child-rearing advice, housework, baby sitting, etc.) were frequently solved with a family member's help. Most teenagers saw the usefulness of having a family network to help cope with life's problems. Another major finding was that, when faced with interpersonal problems within the support system, the teenagers avoided the conflict.

Crawford, A.G., & Furstenberg, F.F. (1978). Family support: Helping teenage mothers to cope. *Family Planning Perspectives, 10,* 322–333.

This article reviews research findings on support received by teenage mothers from their families. Most young mothers' support is supplied by their nuclear families. Free room, board, and child care, for example, are provided more often to teenage mothers who stay at home than to those who live on their own. The authors also question public welfare policies that run counter to or undermine the natural support system. Another valid point they make is that young mothers lack the skills and experience to be sole caretakers; mothers depend on others for help, reassurance, and guidance. As a result, understanding the total family situation can aid the case management process.

Furstenberg, F.F. (1980). Burden and benefits: The impact of early childbearing on the family. *Journal of Social Issues, 36,* 64–87.

This report suggests that adolescent mothers rely heavily on their families for support. Many adolescent mothers spend a period of time with their nuclear families. The author found that young mothers who remained single and received help from their families were buffered from the negative consequences of giving birth and raising children; child care aid, for example, helped young mothers to complete their education or vocational training. Mothers and sisters of unwed mothers were found to be significantly helpful.

Hill, R. (1965). Generic features of families under stress. In H. Parad (Ed.) *Crisis intervention: Selected readings* (pp. 32–52). New York: Family Service Association of America.

This article reviews crisis intervention theory and its application to adolescent pregnancy. The author presents a clearly written overview of family decompensation and recovery after a stress situation. The points made in the article about family alliances, interpersonal relationships, and family norms and values are helpful in assessing families experiencing adolescent pregnancy.

Landy, S., Schubert, J., Cleland, J.F., & Clark, J.F. (1983). Teenage pregnancy: Family Syndrome? *Adolescence, 18,* 679– 694.

This article is based on a short-term study of teenage mothers and their families. The authors conclude that a pattern of neglect and hostility pre-existed in families of teenage mothers. As a result, their research data suggests, there is a pre-existing association with psychological motivation and teenage pregnancy.

Miller, A.G. (1974). The relationship between family interaction and sexual behavior in adolescents. *Journal of Community Psychology, 2*(3), 285–288.

This article briefly reports on clinical research in which family members were asked about their pregnant teenage relatives. The author concludes that clinical literature that describes an absent father, domineering mother, and a dependent, pregnant adolescent is confirmed by the research.

Ooms, T. (Ed.) (1981). *Teenage pregnancy in a family context.* Philadelphia: Temple University Press.

This book is an overview of teenage pregnancy in a family context. The preface, introduction, and Chapter I clearly state the book's objective: to underscore the family dimension of teenage pregnancy. In the appendix, the editor proposes a family public-policy intervention process to measure a program's direction. The book also contains salient articles that focus on culture, birth control and contraception, teenage parenting, education, and other areas relating to adolescent pregnancy. Very worthwhile reading.

Health

Health professionals are concerned about the serious medical problems of very young mothers and their babies. There is evidence that the maternal and infant mortality rates are higher for teenage mothers than for women conceiving in their twenties. Also, the increased risks lead to a disproportionate number of complicated deliveries, birth defects, and low birth weights. There are questions, however, about whether or not health risks are a function of age only or of a combination of age, low socioeconomic status, and access to consistent support and health care services.

American Academy of Pediatrics statement on teenage pregnancy. (1979). *Pediatrics, 63,* 795–797.

This article briefly reviews the serious medical problems for young mothers and their babies. The paper clearly outlines the dangers of maternal and infant mortality for adolescents.

Baldwin, W., & Cain, U.S. (1980). The children of teenage parents. *Family Planning Perspectives, 12,* 34–43;

James, W. (1972). Newer approaches in the management of the pregnant unmarried adolescent. *Journal of the American Medical Association, 64,* 483–487.

240

A common theme in the literature is that teen mothers have increased obstetrical and gynecological risks. These two articles, however, demonstrate that these complications can be minimized. Dangerous medical outcomes for a mother and her baby can be lessened with teenagers who are involved in prenatal intervention programs and who receive health and nutritional care. Their infants also develop within the normal range.

Canada, M.J. (1986). Adolescent pregnancy: Networking and the interdisciplinary approach. *Journal of Community Health, 11*(1), 58–62.

This article clearly demonstrates the need for case management and service networking among various service providers who engage teenage parents. The article discusses the effort at networking in Brooklyn, N.Y. The author demonstrates that effective, positive client impact through case management improves service delivery, family support and communication, parenting skills development, medical care, and financial support for teens.

Horon, I.L., Strobino, D.M., & MacDonald, H.M. (1983). Birth weights among infants born to adolescent and young adult women. *American Journal of Obstetrics and Gynecology, 146*(4), 444–449.

Infants of adolescent mothers were compared to infants born to women in their twenties. When tests of significance were used to compare the birth weights of infants born to teens and infants born to young adults, there were similar birth-weight gains. Maternal age may not be the best predictor of low birth weight. The best predictors may be prenatal care and socioeconomic status.

Mackinson, C. (1985). The health consequences of teenage infertility. *Family Planning Perspectives, 17*(3), 132–139.

This article reviews and compares health findings from five western countries—the U.S.A., Canada, Great Britain, France, and Sweden. The article points out that chronological age is not a significant factor in predicting infant and adolescent mother health risks. The author's findings lend credence to the point of view that prenatal health risks are much more related to socioeconomic factors. Also, the American policy of withholding human sexuality information has not led to reduced teenage pregnancies; in contrast, other countries that have disseminated relevant material have experienced better awareness of sexual responsibility on the part of teenagers. Finally, the costs of teenage pregnancy are viewed as hurting young people who have poor employment potential, inadequate education, and lowest access to adequate services.

Olds, D. L. (1984). Case studies of factors interfering with nurse home-visitors' promotion of positive care-giving methods in high-risk families. *Early Child Development and Care, 16*(1,2), 149–165.

This article describes the difficulty of involving nursing professionals with teenage mothers, their babies, and their families. The article points out that the twin objectives of providing adolescent mothers with post-natal care and child health information may be resisted due to underlying psychological and social factors that frustrate the nurses' efforts. The article shows that the nurses' efforts, however, did reduce the risks of social, psychological, and medical maladies.

Poverty and Case Management

Poverty has been viewed as a causative factor of teenage pregnancy. Dependence upon public welfare increases when teens must drop out of school, have little incentive for a future vocation, and provide care for a child without family/community help. Case management expertise can help lessen the long-term need for public welfare support. Case managers can refer teen parents to the resource that will ensure that they receive appropriate help.

Brindis, C., Barth, R.P., & Loomis, A.B. (1987). Continuous counseling: Case management with teenage parents. *Social Casework*, March, 164–172.

The three authors review the role of a case manager in a comprehensive inter-agency delivery system for adolescent parents. The role of the case manager is to ensure high quality services as well as identify the development of new services.

Burden, D.S., & Klerman, L.U. (1984). Teenage parenthood: Factors that lessen economic dependence. *Social Work, 29,* 11–16.

The authors argue that women's role in society is the reason underlying teen mothers' high rates of impoverishment. The article reviews the continuing rise in the number of teens on the welfare roles and the consequences to society. The authors' recommendations go beyond pregnancy prevention and job training to a restructuring of the underlying causes of welfare dependence.

Cartoof, V.G. (1978). Postpartum services for adolescent mothers. *Child Welfare, 10,* 660–666.

This article focuses on the home case-management program offered by the Florence Crittendon Hastings House in Boston. Successful caseworker ser-vices include outreach to the home; focus on assessment of educational, vocational, family planning, and parenting needs; exploration of community resources; referral and networking to agencies; and, most importantly, accom-paniment of the client to the resource.

Gibbs, J.T. (1984). Black adolescents and youth: An endangered species. *American Journal of Orthopsychiatry, 54*(1), 6–21.

Maintaining that current problems are much worse than those of 20 years ago, the author amply describes the interrelated issues of unemployment, delinquen-cy, substance abuse, poverty, teen pregnancy, and mental health risks to black youths. Preventive approaches coordinated and collaborated with social service agencies and community groups are offered as the means to address problems at a local level. A federal policy for children and families is also discussed.

Moore, K.A. (1983). *Teenage parents and teens at risk of pregnancy: Federal welfare, social services, and related programs to serve adolescents.* Flint, Mich.: Mott (C.S.) Foundation.

The potential for teenage mothers' dependency on welfare is very high, and this paper outlines the federal, state, and local public policy strategies that are needed for adolescents. The focus is on the multitude of services that are needed.

Quint, J.C., & Riccio, J.A. (1985). *The challenge of serving pregnant and parenting teens. Lessons from project redirection.* New York: Ford Foundation, Office of Youth Programs (DOL).

This report describes the efforts to link teens to community agencies. Volunteers were used and community networks were formed to help teen parents become self-sufficient. This project was located in four urban locations (New York, Boston, Phoenix, and Riverside, Calif.). Results of the project indicate that brokering and networking with existing community resources are necessary, that services should be delivered to teens on an open-ended basis (i.e., the longer help is offered, the better the outcome), and that young mothers need a variety of intensive services.

Schinke, S.P. (1978). Teenage pregnancy: The need for multiple casework services. *Social Casework, 7,* 406–410.

The social problems related to teenage pregnancy and childbearing are described in this article, as are the casework efforts needed to lessen the impact on society and the adolescent parent. A single-cause perspective on teenage pregnancy breeds inadequate services delivery. The author describes a multiple casework approach to helping adolescents. Casework services that aim at primary prevention, early intervention, and postpartum services prove to be very helpful.

Prevention of Child Abuse

A number of reports, articles, and books have cited the association of teenage pregnancy and child maltreatment. Recent information, however, has pinpointed socioeconomic issues underlie child abuse and neglect. Child abuse and neglect is a complex problem. In the interim of the debate and social policy implications, teenage parents need support services in order to enhance their parent-child relationships.

Barrish, H.H., & Barrish, I.J. (1985). *Managing parental anger.* Shawnee Mission, Kans.: Overland Press, Inc.

This book, written for parents, provides "down-to-earth" practical principles about parenting. The information follows the principles of behavioral and reality theories. Methods of successful parenting and disciplining without anger are explained in the book.

Bolton, F.G., Laner, R.H., & Kane, S.P. (1980). Child maltreatment risk among adolescent mothers: A study of reported cases. *American Journal of Orthopsychiatry, 3,* 489–504.

The authors provide evidence of a relationship between child maltreatment and the age of the mother. Adolescent pregnancy, the researchers found, was associated with abuse and neglect. Their sample was drawn from Maricopa County in the State of Arizona.

Earp, J.L., & Orz, M.G. (1980). The influence of early parenting on child maltreatment. *Child Abuse and Neglect, 4,* 237–245.

Through a review of the literature and an examination of 50 child-abuse case records, the authors were able to identify antecedents to abuse. They found that family disruption, psychological disturbance, and alienation from the community were precursors to child maltreatment.

Gelles, R.J. (1986). School-age parents and child abuse. In J.B. Lancaster and B.A. Hamburg (Eds.), *School-Age Pregnancy and Parenthood* (pp. 347–360). New York: Aldine DeGruyter.

The article questions linking teenage childbearing and increased risk for child maltreatment. The author's findings suggest that this link is ambiguous. The research is contradictory, and there may be a link between social class and poverty.

Kinard, E.M., & Klerman, L.U. (1980). Teenage parenting and child abuse: Are they related? *American Journal of Orthopsychiatry, 50*(3), 481–488.

This article reviews the association between child abuse and adolescent parenting. The authors' findings suggest that impoverishment and lower socio-economic status are the underlying problems rather than parental age. Disturbed family life may also be a factor in child maltreatment. The authors suggest that sex education, contraception, parenting skills training, and child development education are needed to support a positive parent-child relationship.

Kinard, E.M., & Reinherz, H. (1984). Behavioral and emotional functioning in children of adolescent mothers. *American Journal of Orthopsychiatry, 4,* 578–594.

The authors' research compared children of mothers in three age groups, 15 to 17, 18 to 19, and 20 to 24 years. All participants were first-time parents. The study found that the children of adolescents were at no greater risk for behavioral and emotional problems. The critical factor was not maternal age, but maternal education. Adequate education may improve a parent's ability to sustain a family, seek out support, and provide for better child rearing practices. Low levels of education may be associated with a lack of knowledge about child development, low tolerance of children's problems, and mothers' unrealistic expectations of their children. In summary, appropriate schooling may provide an incentive to a positive environment through the offering of instruction in child development and parenting skills.

Miller, S.H. (1983). *Children as parents.* New York: Child Welfare League of America.

This booklet explores the parenting skills and pregnancy needs of mothers 12 to 15 years old. Specific recommendations include an understanding of the medical and developmental issues of early teenage childbearing (low birth-weight or premature birth), a need for long-term educational and social services support to acquire independence, and the need to enhance extended family (including the baby's father) support of mother and baby.

Zitner, R., & Miller, H.S. (1980). *Our Youngest Mothers.* New York: Child Welfare League of America.

The authors review services given to approximately 185 mothers from the south and midwest by the Florence Crittendon Homes. They found mothers who had early intervention had more use of and success with support services. Young women formed a support network from family and friends, and fathers of the babies played a supportive role. There is a need for ongoing help with education, vocational training, and child care.